good enough is the new perfect

Finding Happiness and Success in Modern Motherhood

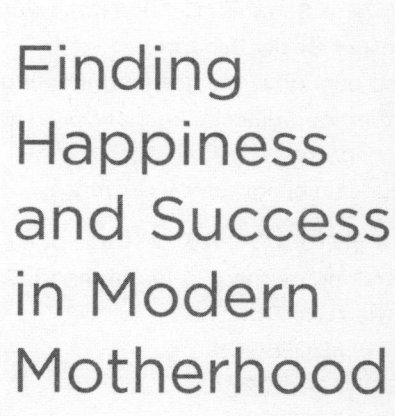

Becky Beaupre Gillespie &
Hollee Schwartz Temple

good enough is the new perfect

ISBN-13: 978-0-373-89237-2

© 2011 by Becky Beaupre Gillespie and Hollee Schwartz Temple

Library of Congress Cataloging-in-Publication Data
Gillespie, Becky Beaupre.
Good enough is the new perfect : finding happiness and success in modern motherhood / Becky Beaupre Gillespie and Hollee Schwartz Temple.
     p. cm.
Includes bibliographical references.
ISBN 978-0-373-89237-2 (trade pbk.)
1. Working mothers. 2. Motherhood. 3. Work and family. I. Temple, Hollee Schwartz. II. Title.
HQ759.48.G56 2011
306.874'3—dc22
2010032860

www.eHarlequin.com

Printed in U.S.A.

For Beth & Katie,
You are the reasons I sought balance
and for Pete,
You are why I was able to find it
—BBG

* * *

For John, Gideon & Henry
Always near my heart
—HST

CONTENTS

INTRODUCTION

This is not a book about settling. Or mediocrity. Or about anything other than getting *exactly* what we want as mothers, professionals and women. (Not everything we *sort of* want, but the things we want the most.)

This *is* a book about refusing to live by other people's rules. It's about taking control and accepting that we're not going to Have It All just by working a little harder.

But it's also about choosing to work hard—not because it's the "next logical step" or someone else's dream—but because we love what we do. It's about reaching stunning heights of success by pursuing our passions at work and at home.

We wanted to point this out right up front because we're full-disclosure women, and we know a few people take issue with our title. Including a couple of the women featured in the book. Including one of Hollee's good friends, who suggested that we might as well call the book *Sucky Is the New Awesome*.

We can live with that. Because, in our minds, good enough is not about aiming lower or doing less or slacking off. It's about knowing that what's good enough for one woman isn't necessarily what's good enough for another. And that if we're living up to our own standards, there isn't anything more to want.

Some people call this perfect. We call it the New Perfect.

* * *

Before we go further, though, allow us to introduce ourselves. Becky is a journalist (married to a lawyer) and Hollee is a lawyer (married to a journalist)—and like all the women we interviewed, we're also mothers who have struggled to blend family and ambition. Becky was a newspaper reporter when the first of her two daughters was born; she was working in a job she loved, surrounded by people she respected. When the first of Hollee's two sons came along, she was a lawyer at a prestigious firm, a job she'd earned after years of hard work and academic achievement.

And, yet, we each left our jobs within seven months of returning from maternity leave.

The difficult decisions we've made as mothers, and the things that happened afterward, inspired us to write this book. And the people we met while writing it—well, they inspired us in countless other ways.

Good Enough Is the New Perfect is based on journalistic research we conducted over two years, beginning in 2008. It draws on exclusive data—our survey of 905 working mothers born between 1965 and 1980 and representing almost every state in the nation—as well as in-depth interviews with more than 100 working mothers. Some of these women were subjects of multiple interviews conducted regularly over one or two years; their generous gifts of time gave us deep insight into the wide range of factors that shape women's choices today. We also have drawn from expert research into issues ranging from marriage to feminism to business; some of the experts we consulted shared hours of time to help us better understand our findings.

Our key findings, by the way, surprised us. Our research revealed two types of working mothers: the Never Enoughs, who felt a constant need to be "the best," and the Good Enoughs, who said that being "the best" wasn't important, as long as they were good enough and happy at work and at home. What caught our attention wasn't that these two groups existed—it was how differently they fared in their attempts to balance work and family.

We want to be clear on one point right away. We intentionally chose to examine only a slice of the maternal population—mothers who had the privilege of education and a certain amount of choice regarding work, including the ability to temporarily scale back hours, switch jobs or take time off. Almost all the women we interviewed—though diverse in race, geography, profession and family background—were college-educated and relatively secure financially. (Which isn't to say that they didn't feel money pressures; many did. But most weren't worried about putting food on the table at night.) Almost all of our survey respondents had attended college, and nearly half worked in jobs that required an advanced degree. We're very much aware that other groups face work/life issues, and that many women do not have much (or any) choice with respect to their work—but that's not the focus of this book.[1]

We also decided not to concentrate on women who defined themselves as at-home mothers; we believe there's a new Mommy War (chapter 3), and it's not about working versus staying home. That being said, several of the mothers we feature (including Becky) stayed home for significant stretches, and in chapter 10, we discuss career makeovers and transformations for moms who have spent time outside the paid workforce.

The final point we'd like to address, since it will undoubtedly be made, is that both of us—and all the women we interviewed—know that we are luckier than most. These women spoke very honestly about their happiness and challenges and guilt. They talked about settling for jobs that didn't quite fit because they didn't think other opportunities existed—and because they worried that expressing this would make them seem "ungrateful." Women told us over and over again that they felt alone. And we think a good deal of this loneliness stems from our reluctance to talk honestly with each other about the parts of our lives that don't work, the stuff that pushes us to the brink—and the things we'd like to change. Some of us stay mum because we don't know how or where to bring this up (work/life has been seen as a private issue until very recently).

But, also, a lot of us don't want to seem *whiny*.

In fact, we have witnessed a certain amount of vitriol aimed at women who do open up about the struggle to find the right fit between work and home. We've seen women harshly criticized for admitting that they feel overwhelmed by their choices or that they are unhappy because their choices aren't working. Sometimes these condemnations have come from other women facing similar struggles—women who have needed empathy themselves. We have even seen it on our own blog, where critics have lashed out against women who have walked away from their big-money, high-prestige jobs because they weren't the right fit. ("Boo hoo, poor you and your six-figure salary," wrote one particularly angry person.)

But we invested our hearts in this project because we don't want to perpetuate a *new* Problem That Has No Name: This issue deserves a place in the national conversation. Mothers shouldn't be afraid to discuss what so many told us was "the most pressing issue" in their lives. Fitting family and career into the same life is really hard, despite what we may have believed growing up. And these challenges are also exceptionally common, despite how alone we may have felt.

It's okay to say these things out loud.

Because we feel so strongly about this, we decided (against our journalistic instincts) to include our own stories, to share our very private feelings about our experiences as wives and mothers.

At the start of each chapter, we've offered some bullet-point "tips"—some insights shared by the women we've interviewed or gleaned from our research. These are points of guidance . . . but the real work is up to each of us. What really makes you feel alive? What stirs your passion and makes you eager to get up each morning? What does success mean to you?

For modern moms, there is no clear-cut path, no one right way. This book shares stories of women who have forged their own paths professionally and personally—as employees, employers, wives and mothers. It is our hope that you will come away from this book understanding the myriad options out there for working mothers; but we also hope that you come away with a strong understanding of how you, too, can find greater happiness and success by creating your own New Perfect.

The stories of the women of *Good Enough Is the New Perfect* filled us with optimism and inspiration. Most of all, that's what we hope you will find here.

—*Becky and Hollee*
April 2011

I QUIT

- You can do *anything*—this doesn't mean you have to do *everything*.

- Your sacrifices should reflect *your* priorities.

- Delegate. Say *no*.

- Sometimes, you have to move on.

- Knowing when to move on means knowing yourself; the answer is different for each of us.

Becky was brooding at her desk in the *Chicago Sun-Times* newsroom. She knew the avocados at home weren't organic, and to make matters worse Pete was probably feeding their eighteen-month-old daughter instant mashed potatoes for dinner. Again.

Fantastic.

Becky glared at the phone on her desk, willing it to ring. It was Saturday, February 1, 2003. The space shuttle *Columbia* had crashed that morning, and Becky was supposed to be interviewing Jim Lovell because, well, he was a famous *Apollo 13* astronaut and he lived near Chicago.

But Lovell hadn't called back, and Becky couldn't stop thinking about the avocados. This was new: She used to obsess over news and now she was fixated on a vegetable. Or were avocados a fruit? And why was she still listening to those übermoms from Gymboree, with their whole-wheat pasta and home-made baby food and in utero Spanish lessons?

Becky's gaze returned to the phone. *Please,* she thought, *call back so I can go home.* Thoughts of the dead astronauts crept into her mind, and Becky guiltily pushed them away. One member of the shuttle crew, Laurel Clark, had been a mother—a thought that had gnawed at Becky all day. Motherhood had done this to her; it had made certain tragic stories just too hard to bear.

Motherhood had done other things to Becky, too. She could no longer com-pletely lose herself in her work. And she didn't feel like an integral part of the newsroom anymore; she'd taken more than a year off and now only worked two days a week. She knew she was supposed to be grateful for the opportunity to be both a reporter and a nearly full-time mom—hadn't she *asked* to do this? Why was she making it so hard?—but, the truth was, she felt cheated at home *and* at work. She rarely had time for the long, data-heavy stories that had defined her newspaper career, and most of the time she left the newsroom feeling as if she'd failed to accomplish much. Instead, she ached for her daughter and felt wounded when she missed something new. Three months before, Elizabeth had taken her first steps while Becky was filling in for an assistant city editor.

Becky sighed. Had Pete started dinner? Was he doing the Hungry Jack thing again? Could pesticides leak through the skin of an avocado?

Relax, she told herself. *All you need to do is work a little harder. You are stronger than this.*

But she wasn't. An hour later, on the ride home, she decided to quit her job.

* * *

Hollee's "I Quit" moment happened about two years later, as she was hunched over the arm of the baby-blue glider in her younger son's nursery. She'd been up almost all night, vomiting in the bathroom after a migraine had awoken her from a restless sleep. Her thirty-five-year-old husband, John, was in a hospital bed a mile away; earlier that day, his heart had begun racing more than 200 beats per minute, so quickly that the ambulance drivers worried that it would stop altogether. John, her strength, the six-foot-two strapping picture of perfect health, who could stay up all night driving or writing or sanding floors, who hadn't visited a doctor since he needed a physical to run cross-country in college. There were panicked phone calls, IVs and a frantic team of emergency room doctors. Hollee couldn't get the words *life-threatening* out of her head.

But it was now approaching sunrise and her six-month-old was starting to stir; he'd soon want to curl up in the glider to nurse. Hollee had breast-fed her older son, Gideon, for eleven months, and she was hoping to get her gold star from the American Academy of Pediatrics for reaching the recommended full year of breast-feeding with Henry. This time around, she had a new job with flexible hours, so she didn't have to lock her law office door to stealthily pump breast milk. Now she could just zip home from her law school teaching job in about four minutes, scoop Henry from the babysitter's arms and head to the glider, nursing until the chubby-cheeked baby was gurgling and full. With Henry, she had planned to do it perfectly.

But that night, life intervened. And though she didn't know it then, John's health crisis was going to get much worse. Hollee sat in the glider, exhausted and afraid, and got ready to unbutton her nightgown—and then lurched over the padded arm, wailing so uncontrollably that she worried that she'd wake three-year-old Gideon, who'd gone to bed wondering why Daddy wasn't there to kiss him good-night.

I just can't do this, Hollee thought. She tiptoed downstairs, unsealed the Enfamil formula can she had stashed on a high shelf and mixed Henry a bottle. The "breast is best" moms in her Tuesday morning playgroup disapproved of formula. But Hollee's life—the life that had once felt almost too good to be true—was careening out of control, and now wasn't the time for perfect.

Henry happily sucked down the *verboten* substance. Hollee would never breast-feed her baby again.

* * *

It wasn't supposed to be like this.

Not for us, the generation of girls who grew up dancing around the living room in Wonder Woman Underoos, waiting to inherit those limitless possibilities we'd been promised by our Baby Boomer parents. We were all girl power and go-get-'em back then, tapping along with the drumbeat that had followed us since birth: You can be anything. You can do anything.

We were *supposed* to Have It All—the full deck of maternal experiences, soaring careers, happy families.

And so, dutifully, we tried: We earned the degrees, landed the dream jobs, had the babies. But on the way to the promised land, something happened. Perfection became an addiction, motherhood a competitive sport. We raced to make partner at work while playing Mozart to our pregnant bellies. We joined playgroups as soon as our C-sections had healed and filled our shelves with advice books on sleep schedules and potty training. We carried our Black-Berries to the zoo, enrolled our toddlers in Itsy Bitsy Yoga and fed them the right mix of brain-building omega-3s. We did everything *right*.

But, soon, life became a snowballing sprint from wakeup until bedtime— with lots of worry in between. We began taking shortcuts, silently lambasting ourselves for each perceived failure. At night, after we picked up the baby from day care and picked up dinner from the drive-through and tried to pick up the mess of toys and Cheerios that blanketed every floor in the house, we collapsed in our beds and sometimes cried. Exactly how we wound up here, roiling in this perfect storm of compulsive perfection, is a story for the next chapter; what's important now is what happened next.

In the midst of this meltdown, some of us lifted our heads, took a deep breath and did the very thing we'd been taught *never* to do:

We quit.

Hopped off the paths we had always planned and moved the finish line within reach. Some of us quit jobs. Others quit believing that the words "You can do *anything*" meant "You can do *everything*." It wasn't easy. Some of our choices drew criticism, and that was the downside of taking control. We had to think hard about what we really wanted, take action—and then accept responsibility for the outcome.

We practiced saying "no." We learned to separate other people's ideas of greatness from our own. Some of us even learned to live with less income for a while. These were our choices, but we second-guessed them, especially when a friend announced that her children had given up refined sugar and television and were now learning to speak Mandarin Chinese. Or when our former colleagues were promoted and we felt jealous and left behind. We weren't always sure we were doing the right thing. And with good reason: The right thing was different for each of us—and rarely was it as simple as whether to work full-time or part-time or not at all.

Was this shift in expectations a cop-out—or was it courageous? Had we just traded our professional and personal success for midday ice cream cones on the front porch? Or jeopardized our children's futures because we'd ditched the Supermom cape?

Imagine our surprise when we discovered that just the opposite was true, that lowering our expectations for some things (and raising them for others) could lead us to stunning new heights. That we could pursue our professional passions and revel in motherhood without going crazy. That the key to success was, quite simply, to redefine it.

Quitting, as it turns out, was the best thing we could have done. It taught us what the words *good enough* really mean.

GOOD ENOUGHS AND NEVER ENOUGHS

When we began interviewing women in the summer of 2008 for a book on working motherhood, we were surprised to discover that most fell into two categories: those who were relatively at peace with their sacrifices and those who felt stuck. The mothers in the latter group were beset by guilt, frustration and a constant feeling that they were somehow failing to measure up. They wanted their lives to change, but many didn't know where to begin. All the women interviewed, more than sixty at that point, were smart and well-educated. Financial constraints didn't seem to account for the difference. So why was one group wrestling with their choices more than the other?

We set out in search of answers. Both of us—we had become friends years before, when Becky was Hollee's first editor at the *Daily Northwestern*—were intrigued not just as journalists but as mothers, too. Becky was still struggling to build a rewarding work life that gave her enough time with her two young daughters, Elizabeth and Katie; and Hollee was weaving time with her sons, Gideon and Henry, around her job as a law professor.

So, in May 2009, we sought the help of a research specialist and conducted a national survey of more than 900 working moms born between 1965 and 1980. We asked about the women's sacrifices, successes and priorities, the things that made it harder and easier for them to juggle everything, and the mothers' approaches to making it all work.

The women in the survey represented every racial group, nearly every state in the nation and a wide range of professions: a rabbi from California, a college professor from Hawaii, an electrical engineer from Georgia, a banker from Texas, an advertising executive from New York.

The majority fit snugly into two distinct groups of similar size. The first group of moms could be characterized as Never Enoughs, high achievers who reported "a strong need to be the best at everything." And the other mothers—many of whom, incidentally, were also high achievers—could be called Good Enoughs; they said that being the best was not important, as long as they felt "good enough and happy, both at work and at home."

Predictably, the Never Enoughs made a bit more money (roughly 18 percent more), but was it enough to compensate for their concessions, which often included dizzying to-do lists and heaps of guilt? In their relentless pursuit of perfection, several mothers we encountered admitted to less-than-healthy behaviors and attitudes. One said she interviewed more than thirty nannies; another interviewed ten babysitters for a sixty-minute job. One mother confessed that she still fixates, daily, on the only pediatrician appointment that she's ever missed—and it was two years ago. Several admitted to creating spreadsheets of their children's feedings and diaper changes; one (seriously) vowed to keep her child safe from— drumroll, please—white bread.

The Good Enoughs, on the other hand, were more satisfied at work and at home—yet they had given up astonishingly little professional ground to achieve this state of contentment. Good Enoughs who remained in the same careers after having kids were *just as likely* as their Never Enough counterparts to advance. They also felt better about their ability to connect with spouses, to find time to spend with friends and family, and to devote time to their personal needs (perhaps because they were also more likely to have cut back their hours since having kids). The Good Enoughs were less likely to say they had sacrificed too much and far less likely to feel stymied by pressure to be the best—all measures of success that arguably outweigh the extra $13,000 per year earned by the Never Enoughs.

The survey also overwhelmingly confirmed what we had begun to believe after nearly a year of research: Unrelenting perfectionism is a liability—and overcoming it is the key to leading a well-rounded and satisfying life. Perfectionism emerged in the survey as the single greatest roadblock to juggling work and family; the "constant need to be the best at everything" far outweighed all other factors, including financial pressures that forced mothers to work more than desired, difficulties delegating responsibility, inflexible employers, inability to afford extra help with cooking and cleaning and husbands who didn't contribute enough at home.[1]

In other words: After all these years of railing against inflexible work policies, unfair division of household labor and societal pressures— admittedly very real challenges—we're realizing that our biggest obstacle is ... *ourselves.*

But Good Enoughs seem uniquely able to overcome this hurdle: In the survey, only about half of the Good Enoughs agreed that their perfectionism had impeded their ability to juggle work and family—compared with more than 90 percent of Never Enoughs.

Consider these findings:

- Never Enoughs were more likely than Good Enoughs to say they sacrificed *too much* either at work or home—and less likely to say that their sacrifices reflected their priorities.

- The Good Enoughs who stayed in the same profession after having kids were just as likely as their Never Enough counterparts to have advanced to more prestigious or demanding positions.

- Despite this, the Good Enoughs were much more likely to have cut back their hours since having kids.

- And the Good Enoughs felt better about their marriages, too: Never Enoughs were twice as likely to describe their ability to connect with their spouses as "not very good" or "a disaster." Never Enoughs also were more likely than Good Enoughs to rate themselves as "not very good" or "disasters" when it came to taking time for themselves or finding time to spend with family and friends. (Neither group clustered around the "superstar" answers for these topics, but the Good Enoughs had a more positive outlook overall. When it came to connecting with spouses, for instance, they were nearly twice as likely as the Never Enoughs to describe themselves as—no surprise—good enough.)

- Finally, the Never Enoughs were nearly *six times more likely*—42 percent compared with 7 percent of Good Enoughs—to describe their approach to juggling work and family as this: "I try to be a superstar at work AND at home, even if it kills me."

Anecdotally, the case for the New Perfect is just as compelling. When we closely examined the mothers who were most satisfied with their performance at work and at home, we found that these women shared several traits. They had created their own definitions of success, learned to delegate and say "no" when necessary—and had made room for imperfection. Some had found their *greatest* success (sometimes even earning more money) when they relaxed certain standards and reevaluated their priorities. In most cases, the women interviewed still had extremely high expectations for themselves. It is possible that a few of them would have reported a "strong need to be the best at everything" in the survey. (As with many data sets, the numbers do a great job uncovering trends, but don't explain every individual choice or reason for choosing a survey answer.) In interviews, we encountered women who described themselves as perfectionists—including a few who took issue with the words *good enough*—but still had more in common with the Good Enoughs in the survey than their more frustrated peers. What set these women apart was their definition of *the best:* They all had learned to expect the best from themselves *without needing to be the best at every moment.*

The most successful women made conscious sacrifices; they weren't trying to do everything because they firmly understood that they couldn't. This essential capitulation allowed them to concentrate on the things that mattered most. They were able to identify their priorities, allocate their time effectively—and move on when things didn't go as planned.

They included mothers like Jen Canter, a child abuse pediatrician and the mother of two sets of twins who launched her own toy company while continuing her medical career *and* studying for a new board certification. And Kimberly Oster Holstein, the CEO of a multimillion-dollar company, who finds time to meditate, help lead her daughter's Girl Scout troop, and revel in everyday activities like taking the kids to school. They were women like Nikki Adcock Williams, an attorney who worked on the Enron bankruptcy before scaling back so she could spend more time with her preschoolers. And Jennifer Pate, a former Hollywood casting director who created a popular, award-winning online talk show about contemporary moms.

These women don't possess superhuman powers. Quite the opposite.

They understand one simple fact: Perfect doesn't exist.

Jennifer Pate, 43
Co-Executive Producer and Cohost of *Jen and Barb: Mom Life*
Los Angeles, California
Mother of Cooper and Lilah

Nobody is perfect all the time. [On my show], I let it all hang out. I definitely embrace who I am. It doesn't mean I don't aspire to really wonderful things. But I don't beat myself up. It's liberating if you let go of that—it's amazing how much happier you are.

PERFECTION JUNKIES

So, what gives?

Why is perfectionism still such a big issue if it has become increasingly apparent that good enough is, well, *good enough?* Why are so many women still hell-bent on being the best at everything?

For starters, the movement toward the New Perfect is particularly challenging for the "shoot for the stars" women of our generation; most of the mothers who eventually embraced this concept confessed to perfectionist pasts. And, anecdotally, we found that the moms who had successfully transitioned tended to be further along in motherhood.

Second, Never Enough is a hard habit to kick. And, to be fair, it did serve many of us pretty well for a while, and aspects of our perfectionism still serve us well. Our hard-driving nature helped us earn those degrees and land those high-powered jobs. It fueled our fight. Even at the height of our misery, some of us balked at the idea of slowing down because we didn't truly believe we could find success any other way. To let go would entail a complete shift in mind-set—and a stomach-churning leap of faith.

To make matters worse (and, yes, this does make it worse), we have unprecedented advantages even beyond our gender's expanded professional opportunities. We have technology that gives us the freedom to leave the office and still do our jobs, easy access to mind-boggling amounts of information, husbands who contribute more at home than any previous generation of men, and increasing flexibility at work. But many of these advantages have flip sides that we don't always acknowledge: Technology tethers us to work and creates barriers to meaningful communication; information can overload us. Shifting gender roles mean we have new territory to navigate in our marriages. And flexible work policies, if not properly executed, can leave us feeling as though we *should* have the tools to "balance" our lives—even when we don't. Some of us have wondered whether the availability of part-time positions compels us, as "good mothers," to take the mommy track even if that isn't what we really want.

Now add one more hurdle: The idealization of *work/life balance*. What do these words even mean? Trying to devote equal amounts of time to both career and family sometimes isn't much easier than trying to do it all. (And, besides, isn't work a part of life?) Never Enoughs seem to struggle with this concept the most because, for many, *balance* (and the inability to reach anything even close to it) feels like yet another failure, just one more reason to wish there were more hours in the day.

Many of the mothers interviewed for this book described being torn between long-planned career goals and wanting to be great moms, a proposition that is particularly confounding now that the standards of maternal success have been elevated to such dizzying levels.

How many of our Baby Boomer mothers seriously contemplated whether we had the right mix of organic vegetables on our plates when they were shooing us into the neighborhood with peanut-butter-and-Fluff sandwiches? Hollee and her older brother, Matt, spent many perilous snow days navigating their makeshift sleds down a Pittsburgh cliffside—without helmets or any parental supervision. And a generation before that, the sort of hyperparenting that's become so commonplace wasn't even on the radar screen. Becky's grandmother Betty Luker Haverfield would never have worried whether the toys in her daughter's nursery were designed for infant brain development; she never even read a book about pregnancy. And as Becky's mom remembers it, vegetables usually came from a can, and when they didn't, they were so overcooked that no vitamin content could possibly have survived.

These previous generations might not have gotten the nutrition piece just right, but they didn't get everything wrong, either. In fact, experts have argued that "good enough" is much better than "perfect" when it comes to raising children. British pediatrician and psychoanalyst Donald Winnicott was the first to laud the "good enough" approach to parenting, arguing that a mother who gradually allows her child to separate, problem-solve and even experience discomfort bestows greater gifts than the outwardly "perfect" mother, who stifles independence by fixing every problem immediately.[2] Parenting expert Ellen Galinsky, author of *Mind in the Making: The Seven Essential Life Skills Every Child Needs,* told Hollee that when parents model perfection, they teach their children an awful lesson: Mistakes are unacceptable.

"We grow and change in motherhood," Ellen said. "It's very scary to feel like you're going to make a mistake with your child, like you're not doing the best thing. But we all need a little perspective. You start off really wanting to be perfect, and some people can get a little crazy doing 'the best they can.' But then you move toward good enough."

Nonetheless, many of today's moms have been sucked into the perfection maelstrom, feeling as if they need to coordinate and supervise their kids' all-important activity schedules—while staying up-to-date on every trend *and* keeping pace at the office and at home. In fact, in 2000, employed mothers spent the same amount of time interacting with their children as at-home moms did in 1975.[3] The frustration, and sheer exhaustion, that inevitably followed this high-speed lifestyle was palpable in the heartfelt comments of the women who participated in our New Perfect survey.

Wrote four Never Enoughs:

I wish I could do it all and am frustrated by the sacrifices, but it is what it is. I regularly quote Bon Jovi: "I'll sleep when I'm dead."

I'm not entirely happy with my sacrifices, but also unwilling to live with less career or parenting time. What I really need is a thirty-hour day.

I'm trying to accept the fact that if it doesn't get done today, it's not the end of the world; I can pick back up with it tomorrow. I've not devoted enough time to myself or my husband. I have had to eliminate exercise from my daily routine because there's just not enough time.

Life stopped being about me a long time ago.

The specific stumbling blocks for the Never Enoughs—the factors that make it hardest for them to stop striving for perfect—are areas where the majority of Good Enoughs excel:

- Never Enoughs have a harder time delegating responsibility (even to their own husbands)—more than half cited this as a challenge compared with less than one-third of Good Enoughs. They also have a harder time saying "no."

- Never Enoughs are also more likely to say they feel "obligated [to work] because I worked so hard to get to where I am."

- Never Enoughs were also far less likely to say that they had realistic expectations for themselves.

But still, the Good Enoughs had to *learn* to let go—at home and at work—and after so many years in relentless pursuit of perfection, that didn't come easily.

Wrote three Good Enoughs:

It took me a long time to accept that I could not meet my own standards. I decided that my standards had to change or my sanity and my marriage would be sacrificed.

I've learned to approach life very differently. I do less "wanting" of things to be different . . . and am more focused on being grateful for the time with our children, which goes so quickly.

I gave up a little at home and a little at work to make it all work. There are days that I have regrets on both sides and days where I would KILL for more "me time," but when I sit down and think about it, I am comfortable with the decisions I have made thus far.

The traits highlighted in this book don't, of course, apply to every working mother, and plenty of Good Enoughs have bad days, bouts of regret and exhaustion—and even periods where they fit the Never Enough mold. (Becky was often in "perfectionist" mode while writing this book and had to work hard to keep that confined to her home office.) The women who appear in this book aren't easy to categorize; they are at different stages on their journey to "balance"—and they have defined success in many different ways.

Some particularly prescient women embraced the New Perfect from the beginning; they had an advanced take on the philosophy, knowing just when to pull out all the stops and when to let it go and relax. But most of us have found our way here by navigating a path riddled with angst and indecision. And though the journey has included an examination of our approaches to mothering, marriage and numerous other areas that will be addressed in later chapters, many of us started in the same place:

Figuring out what to do about work.

FINDING THE COURAGE TO LEAP

Even when she was a kindergartner back at Markham Elementary School in the Pittsburgh suburbs, Libby Windsor got the message that she was "supposed" to shoot for a high-flying career. She remembers being five and marveling at the half-time shows at the Pittsburgh Panthers football games she attended with her parents—and deciding that when she grew up, she would become a Pitt Golden Girl twirler, adorned with a kicky skirt, sparkly baton and shiny hair bow.

"What about a doctor or the president?" her parents suggested.

Libby got the message. She zipped through her elementary school years expecting to be "the best" in every class. She usually succeeded. Her one slip, when she was eleven and didn't get the highest grade in a prealgebra class, made her "feel like a complete failure."

So Libby became more determined to conquer everything she tried: She aced her comprehensive exams in art history at Kenyon College (her professor said she was "the best" art history student to ever walk the leafy campus); graduated magna cum laude from Boston University Law School; nabbed a sought-after federal clerkship after law school; and began working her way up the partnership ladder at one of the country's most elite law firms.

But now, perhaps for the first time in her adult life, Libby is facing a problem that she can't easily outsmart: how to balance her boundless ambition with her competing desires to be a good wife to her husband, Ben, and a good mother to her sons, William and Andrew.

Elizabeth "Libby" Windsor, 34
Employment Litigator for an International Law Firm
Mt. Lebanon, Pennsylvania
Mother of William and Andrew

I've always felt a lot of pressure to be the best version of myself in every capacity. My parents invested so much in me, and not just from a financial perspective, so I could never imagine just walking away from my work.

But when I graduated from law school and got a federal clerkship and realized that it would be possible for me to have this really successful, lucrative career, I felt terrified about what it would be like to have kids in this field. I even flubbed an interview with a big Boston firm because I spent the whole time drilling the interviewer about how she balanced her life.

I never wanted to be a stay-at-home mom. When I was on maternity leave with Will, I felt a little lost when I traveled with the baby and people didn't bother to ask me about my career. So I didn't have a lot of guilt about going back to work full-time after Will was born. In fact, I felt relief when I went back, and I wasn't a total wreck and realized the world wasn't ending. I sometimes felt sadness when I would hear him singing in the background when I called to check in with the nanny, but it wasn't guilt.

But after Andrew was born, everything changed. When I went back to work, Will was a complete mess. The second I walked in the door—before I could even put my purse down—he would just cling to me with this anxiety. I could not even pick up the baby without him losing it; it was like my own baby was becoming a stranger to me. Will started waking up in the middle of the night and insisted on sleeping literally on top of me. I felt shocked that this was happening; I was on such a good track with work. But in my heart, I knew I had to do something.

The angst Libby described is a defining trait of today's working moms—and one that hits a crescendo on the path from Never Enough to Good Enough. As the most educated and financially successful women in American history, our careers are more than afterthoughts. In the past several years, we've taken almost half the seats in entering law school and medical school classes, and we're earning almost 40 percent of the MBAs. The degrees have opened doors to unprecedented professional success. In fact, by 2007, almost a quarter of wives were outearning their husbands.[4]

But this success is a source of our internal conflict. Women like Libby, flourishing in education-laden careers and amply rewarded for those investments, expect and *want* to remain part of the paid workforce after becoming mothers. In 2007, the year after Libby's first son was born, almost 63 percent of college-educated women with infants were working.[5] But many, accustomed to winning at work, were set on maternal superstardom, as well. They professionalized motherhood while they took some time off, filling their planners with swimming/music/dance lessons and playgroups where the hostess mothers routinely decorated cupcakes (peanut-free, of course) with each child's first initial. When these moms tried to plunge back into the workforce *and* keep up the standards they had set while at home, nothing seemed to work. And neither did the default strategy: to simply work harder.

A WINDING ROAD TO A NEW DEFINITION OF SUCCESS

But without a set of MapQuest turn-by-turn directions, how were we supposed to find our destination? Our mothers didn't know. They had either quit their jobs when we were born or had thrown themselves full force into their careers. Our employers also struggled, fumbling with halfhearted policies or punting with "case-by-case" decision making. In fact, when Hollee was contemplating what she would do after Gideon was born, she was shocked to learn that her law firm didn't have an official policy on part-time work—in 2003. In fact, as far as she could tell, she was only the second woman in an office of more than 200 attorneys to negotiate a part-time schedule.

Am I really such a revolutionary? she wondered. *Is it possible that only one other professional woman in this office is struggling with the thought of full-time day care? Did I pick a career where balance is impossible? And why didn't anyone mention this little problem when I was slogging my way through college, grad school and law school, always jumping the hurdles that were supposed to give me choices?*

No, we weren't finding the answers at work.

Yet somehow, individually, as we made the choice to become mothers and started making plans for that reality, we began feeling our way into a new world, a place where we would make sense of the ample inheritance the Boomers left behind. We schlepped to work on the bus, bellies expanding by the week, and came home to mailboxes stuffed with baby announcements. Each new baby meant another friend had entered motherhood (or waded further into it), and we couldn't help but wonder: What is *she* doing to make it work? We found our contemporaries in different spots in the same maze—some quitting work altogether, some postponing the decision until the last possible day (and praying that the job share would come through), some committed to returning full-time after finding the ideal nanny or day care. It was the first time we couldn't follow a single, clear path.

After her first daughter was born, Becky spent much of her yearlong maternity leave debating options with three other new moms from the newsroom. (Becky took advantage of a policy that allowed her to request up to a year of unpaid maternity leave.) First, she and another reporter tried to negotiate a job share. Denied. Then she tried the part-time routine that ended with her meltdown over avocados and astronauts. And even after she made that frantic decision to quit, it took her more than a month to pull the trigger and tell her boss, Don, an editor she deeply admired. She needed a solid game plan, so she wrote up a proposal to work as a consultant to the paper from home. The gig was riddled with child-care issues; somehow, she just couldn't pull it off. She thought she was doing everything she was supposed to do—things that seemed to work well for other women. And she couldn't blame it on the newspaper, either: Her boss had been accommodating and kind. But this wasn't like shopping for maternity clothes, where a one-size-fits-most selection often did the trick. Like so many in our generation, Becky realized that she was going to have to write her own, personal definition of what it would mean to be a success.

* * *

As we navigated this winding path, many of us felt desperate for answers, for someone to talk to—someone, perhaps, like Kimberly Oster Holstein, who exudes the serenity of a woman who is at peace with her life choices. Kim has three kids and a gourmet pretzel company that she and her husband, Scott, launched out of their Chicago apartment in 1995. Her life is the embodiment of her dreams—and the empowerment, freedom and passion she feels is palpable and contagious.

Her business is a success, to put it mildly: Kim & Scott's Gourmet Pretzels now has annual revenues between $10 million and $15 million and employs more than seventy people. Their pretzels are sold fresh in their own Chicago café and, among other places, can be found in more than 5,000 grocery stores across the United States, as well as in the expanding international market. Yet, despite the time and energy she devotes to work, Kim doesn't feel torn in the way other women described: She weaves her days to fit all her top priorities, and finds joy in simple things like bedtime routines and Girl Scouts and unexpected conversations that happen on the way to school. In fact, Kim describes her work schedule as a "creative full-time"; her life is so fluid and the pieces are so entwined that it is hard to define it in terms of traditional categories.

It would be easy to look at Kim's life and see something akin to perfection. But Kim has found her success in part by embracing just the opposite.

Kimberly Oster Holstein, 43
President, CEO and "Chief Inspiration Officer"
Kim & Scott's Gourmet Pretzels
Wilmette, Illinois
Mother of Sonia, Daniella and Aiden

You can't be doing it all at once, be 100 percent and be perfect.

It's all about accepting myself and loving myself for who I am—I think that speaks to how I want to live my life. I strive to be as good as I can be.

I prioritize what I want to do. I am not afraid to let go of the cooking—I'd rather my kids have a healthy meal made by the babysitter instead of me rushing home and making dinner. I'm not a martyr, and I'm not trying to do this in a Supermom way.

Sometimes, I don't do the greatest job [at balancing everything]. But I feel good about it.

Almost all the moms interviewed for this book conceded that they had paid some price for a satisfying life—there was a trade-off for gaining control. Some of us sacrificed money—and lots of it—to find new jobs or to secure flexible arrangements. The money mattered, but for many of our peers, a perceived loss of prestige stung much more than the whack to the wallet. Before kids, our success at work defined us, but now we wanted success on the home front, too—without completely losing our sense of self.

For Hollee, the moment of reckoning came when Gideon was less than a year old. Even before she became a mom, the law firm wasn't the right fit. Hollee felt desperate for something that didn't leave her writing "Sometimes I feel like I won't be able to make it through the day" in her journal. But when the possibility of escape became real, when she was staring at the offer for her first job in academia—with a lowly lecturer title at more than a 50 percent pay cut—she felt unsteady and unsure.

Everyone will think I'm crazy to walk away, she thought. On her last day at the law firm, an older partner congratulated Hollee for "taking the mommy track." Then, several of her new colleagues boomeranged the uneasy feelings right back at her. An adjunct professor she met at a computer training session put it bluntly: *You seriously left a six-figure job to teach legal writing in West Virginia?* Another new colleague introduced himself, then told Hollee she was overqualified for the position she had just accepted, shaking his head.

It bothered her—let's be honest, it made her feel stupid—but Hollee forged ahead anyway. She was a twenty-eight-year-old new mother, and she was ready to adjust her expectations, to explicitly acknowledge that while her children were young, her career path was going to veer off the linear course she had always planned.

LEARNING TO DANCE

And so it has gone, as the women of our generation, in growing numbers, have found the beginnings of the New Perfect. Contemplating our careers has taught us to listen to what we really want, not just to what we think we *should* want. And because our careers aren't our only jobs, it's a complicated equation. This was clear in our New Perfect survey—and several of the women we interviewed were frustrated to discover that merely cutting back at work didn't deliver that much-anticipated work/life balance; for some, the problem was that they'd cut back *too much* at work.

That's because the New Perfect is an attitude, one that includes a thought-out approach to work, marriage, parenting—and even ideas about how we use technology, how we define success and what it takes to make us truly happy. Good Enoughs know that their approach requires the ability to segue from one job to the next *even before the first one is done perfectly.* (Becky, who absolutely hates to leave the house in the morning before the kitchen is perfectly clean, has been known to struggle with this one.)

This secret, however, is an essential one because working moms dance a delicate ballet, replete with lots of costume changes. Many of us segue through life: Hollee can play mom in the before-school rush, professor for morning classes, writer in the afternoon, wife come dinnertime, and a combination of job titles (mom/professor/writer/wife) as the day draws to a close.

The slashes that describe our life's work matter; they speak to everything that we're trying to do well enough and at once. Our workdays don't start when we get to the office—assuming we even have an office—or end just because we have assumed the "mommy" role for a few hours. Our iPhones don't know when we're at the pool, and sometimes our clients or patients or even coworkers don't know it, either. When we do our jobs well—when we define *perfect* as simply doing our best without going crazy—it doesn't really matter. What does matter is whether we are able to maximize our time, stockpiling potentially wasted minutes so we can spend them on the people and activities we love.

Yes, it's sometimes an exhausting dance. But it can also be a thrilling one, especially when we feel satisfied and successful and in control. After all, when we actively choose our sacrifices, we often can temper them with our own creative adjustments.

When Hollee remodeled her second-floor home office space, she added an unusual feature that has proven to be the envy of her girlfriends: a washer and dryer. At first she worried that the machines would sully her decorating scheme, but she soon grew to love watching the clothes spin while she critiqued legal memos, the proverbial "two birds, one stone" in action. That decision took away a costume change, too: In these moments, Hollee can do a Good Enough job at being two people—laundry-laden mommy and law professor—at once.

Of course, being Good Enough isn't as simple as installing appliances in the home office. And rarely can it be achieved by just quitting a job or scaling back to three extracurricular activities per child. To fully understand the New Perfect, we need to understand more about who we are, where we came from and how the progress we inherited as modern women has given us both our greatest gifts and our most intractable challenges.

2

THE INHERITANCE

- If you give up something you love just because it's hard right now, you may be missing the big picture.

- Consider your history when making your choices—but don't let guilt or other women's choices dictate your own.

- You can "Have It All"—just not at the same time.

- Be willing to decide.

Hollee was sprawled on the brown shag carpet, singing along with the *Free To Be . . . You and Me* album spinning on her family's Fisher record player.

> *Mommies are people, people with children*
> *When mommies were little, they used to be girls . . .*

It was 1981, the year Ronald Reagan took office, Sandra Day O'Connor became the first female Supreme Court Justice, *Columbia* became the first space shuttle to orbit and return to Earth, and Neva Rockefeller became the first woman ordered to pay alimony.

Hollee was seven, and she loved music. She could listen to *Free To Be* for hours. Her mom, who graduated from an all-women's college in 1970, hadn't purchased the album for its feminist message. Like many her age, she bought it simply because Marlo Thomas—a favorite television star among Boomer women—had headlined the iconic Ms. Foundation project.

In that cozy family room with the black stovepipe fireplace, Hollee squeezed her eyes shut and tried to picture a land where the rivers ran free. Where women didn't have to marry (like the fictional princess in one memorable *Free To Be* story), and they weren't supposed to care if they were pretty at all (although Hollee sure thought Marlo Thomas was).

> *Some mommies are ranchers, or poetry makers*
> *Or doctors or teachers, or cleaners or bakers*
> *Some mommies drive taxis, or sing on TV*
> *Yeah, mommies can be almost anything they want to be.*

Hollee smiled. Her future was wide open.

* * *

Becky, meanwhile, was nine and hard at work on her newspaper career.

On the weekends, she could sometimes persuade her dad to take her into the newsroom of the *Times-Union*, the Rochester, New York, newspaper where he was the managing editor. She loved the inky smell of the hulking printing presses—always the first scent to greet her when she entered the building—and the rushed way some of the reporters talked, even on a Saturday. If she was lucky, her dad would set her up in front of a metal computer monitor, with its black screen and robotic orange text, and she'd type "By Becky Beaupre" over and over. Her byline.

"Hey, Dad," she whispered one Saturday. "How's this?"

The two of them were writing an obituary for her dead hamster, Otto.

"'We buried him in the backyard, by the swing set.' Is that a good ending?"

Larry nodded approvingly. He took her into the composing room to print it out.

At age nine, Becky was sure of two things: She would grow up to be a newspaper reporter, and she would someday have a daughter.

She was right on both counts. In fact, about thirteen years later, she would have a desk not far from the site of that early obit—and, a decade after that, she'd have two daughters. What she didn't predict was how impossible she'd find it to have *both* the desk and the daughters.

* * *

It seemed simple enough when we were little girls. More than any previous generation, we believed we could do or be anything. Girls born in the mid-1970s were more than three times as likely as women born at the beginning of the twentieth century to pursue their fathers' careers;[1] it didn't seem odd or unattainable to model our career paths after theirs. The bounty bestowed upon us by the women's movement was vast and we were the first to reap its full benefits. As children, we may not have understood advances like Title IX, which gave us gender equity in public education, including sports; or the Pill, which made it easier to delay having children; or the ascent of women into corporate boardrooms and governors' offices and behind television anchor desks. But we felt the ripple. Or tsunami.

We were raised beneath a splintering glass ceiling, and the deafening thunder of expectation that accompanied it echoed to our bones. There was an implicit message: You *can* succeed, so you *must* succeed.

But as we grew older, we began adding to those expectations all the things we *didn't* want. A historic number of kids from our generation grew up in single-parent or dual-career families.[2] Many of us had mothers who worked long hours at the office—then put in a "second shift"[3] of housework and child care at home in the evenings.

Some of us had mothers who had given up careers or had scaled back to less powerful, second-tier positions—the so-called mommy track—so they could be home with us. Although these scenarios represented choices, at times there was something vaguely unsettling about them. Were there options that didn't involve being exhausted or frustrated?

Suddenly, we were older, and it wasn't so simple.

Jen Canter, 38
Child Abuse Pediatrician and Owner of Educational Toy Company,
Play This Way Every Day
Westchester County, New York
Mother of two sets of twins

My parents divorced, and I saw a very hardworking single mother. I wanted more of a balance than what my mom had. So I strived for the balance I didn't have growing up. I became a huge overachiever. I wanted for my children a childhood without anxiety, and two parents who love each other.

Boy, I was really something else as a kid . . . I just knew that if I worked hard enough, I wouldn't have to have all the stressors my mother did.

And, you know, we're really happy at home. I never expected that for myself: I have what I want. I think I have methodically designed my life to make it what I want. But I worked really hard for it.

As simplicity gave way to reality, we began to make lists. All the things we wanted, all the things we didn't. Spoken, recorded, subconscious—it didn't matter. Nor did the specific details. We all had lists. Long ones that grew longer with each passing year. We had been told we could have anything we wanted, and suddenly, there was a lot to consider.

I want to be a lawyer, a doctor, a firefighter, a journalist, an entrepreneur.
I want to fall in love.
I want an MBA, a JD, an MD, a PhD.
I want to get married.
I don't want to depend on my husband for money.
I want to have babies, and I want to bake cookies and coach soccer.
I want to be the CEO, the managing partner, the editor, the owner, the boss.
I want to be home when my kids get out of school.
I want respect.
I want to have fun.

I want to be skinny and pretty and have really cool shoes.
I don't want to be judged by my looks or the price of my handbag.
I want to be successful.
I want to be happy.

It was the only way to mentally organize the buffet of choices that so vexed and invigorated us. The Baby Boomers and their mothers had left a generous inheritance, and we had to figure out what to do with it. It was like having a china cabinet filled with Waterford, then being handed a full set of Royal Doulton and our grandmother's antique Limoges. Pretty cool, but also a bit overwhelming.

Still, we were determined to have everything. Problem was, we couldn't be the best at everything all at once. So we put off motherhood to focus on our careers. Then we sidelined our careers so we could outdo each other with Olympic feats of maternal prowess.

Neither quite worked—and everyone seemed to notice.

Increasing demand for fertility treatments and rising numbers of successful but baby-free women prompted speculation of an "epidemic of childlessness" among professional women. Some of the Baby Boomers had put off having kids and had paid dearly for that; now, supposedly, our generation was poised to make its own version of the same mistake. In her 2002 book, *Creating a Life: Professional Women and the Quest for Children,* Sylvia Ann Hewlett, founding president of the Center for Work-Life Policy, wrote:

> *My concern is that many of today's young women seem convinced that their circumstances—and choices—are vastly improved. They believe that employers these days are more accommodating, that men are more supportive, and that women can rely on getting pregnant deep into their forties ... But is such easy confidence warranted? I think not.*

When the babies did come, the concern and disapproval only mounted. First, there were too many twins and triplets. Critics blamed the rise in multiple births, and the accompanying risks and complications, on increasing fertility treatments—and then blamed older mothers for that trend.

Then came the resurgence of at-home motherhood, the so-called "Opt-Out Revolution."[4] Suddenly, former executives were singing and clapping under parachutes with their kids in the middle of weekday afternoons. They were breast-feeding at Starbucks instead of pumping their milk in converted supply rooms (or bathroom stalls) at work. Graduate degrees were getting dusty in the closet. "Helicopter moms" were hovering and homeschooling and not earning a dime.

Even working women on popular television shows began abandoning careers. On *Sex and the City,* Charlotte York quit her beloved job at an art gallery when she got married. "The women's movement is supposed to be about choice," Charlotte told her friend Miranda, a workaholic attorney. "And that is my choice."

The numbers shocked commentators: After two decades of increase, labor force participation rates of married mothers of infants were actually declining. Was quitting work to stay home becoming *trendy?* In 1997, nearly 71 percent of college-educated, married mothers with infants worked; by 2004, that number had dropped 11 percentage points.[5] Although some have said this trend had more to do with the early 2000 recession than a sociological shift toward stay-at-home motherhood,[6] there was no disputing that lots of professional women were home—and the Baby Boomers had something to say about that.

The trend was decried as *The Feminine Mistake* in a 2007 bestseller by author Leslie Bennetts, who asked in her subtitle, "Are we giving up too much?"[7] To hear it told, the moms of our generation were a mess—we had inherited the china, then dropped it down the basement steps.

Or had we?

Somewhere in the middle of the chaos and crisis, something new began to emerge. The Baby Boomers' daughters began piecing together three generations' worth of dreams. We examined what we wanted and mapped out how to get it. We began to shift our expectations. We rethought what it meant to Have It All, and we abandoned the stuff that didn't work. Slowly, the Good Enoughs began to appear, acknowledging what we all should have known all along: We would never *really* Have It All. Not in the traditional sense anyway.

In some ways, we'd have even more.

The shift was at once groundbreaking and unremarkable. The New Perfect, in many cases, sprang forth from sheer exhaustion. Most of us didn't see this readjustment as the path to greater success—we were just tired of trying to do everything. We'd spent our lives trying to figure out how to spend all that feminist progress we'd inherited, and the fact that we finally discovered the secret was sort of an accident.

We didn't fully understand how we had ended up buried and exhausted and in need of such realignment. Why were we struggling with advances that should have been pure victory? A look back at the overwhelming and disparate nature of our inheritance offers some insight.

TWO BETTYS: YEARNING IN THE AGE OF THE FEMININE MYSTIQUE

Betty Ann Luker wanted to be a lawyer.

And not just any lawyer but a *good* one. A star. The kind with degrees from a big state university and an impressive law school, a respected esquire with a litany of dazzled juries and hard-won cases to her credit. She had what it took, she knew that much. She was smart and vivacious, ambitious and deeply creative. A great writer. Not afraid to speak her mind. Except, it would seem, to her father, who said women should not be lawyers.

It was the late 1930s. Betty Ann was never going to law school.

Instead, she did as expected: She packed up her dreams and enrolled at a small women's college in northwest Illinois, just a couple of hours away from her parents' home in Chicago.

It was the beginning of a decades-long tussle between ambition and tradition that would define the life of Becky's grandmother and countless other housewives-to-be. For Betty Ann and other "Yearners" like her, the lack of choices was demeaning, the expectations stifling. She would rail against them her entire adult life in every socially appropriate way she could find, enjoying meager successes but never truly knowing how much her efforts mattered.

It was a tough time to be a smart woman. In 1940, fewer than 5 percent of women between the ages of twenty-five and twenty-nine had earned a bachelor's degree, compared with fewer than 7 percent of men—a gap that would widen over the next two decades.[8] Women who attended college in the 1940s and 1950s tended toward certain traditionally female jobs, such as teaching, and for some, college was simply an opportunity for a privileged girl to find a well-educated husband, the so-called MRS degree.

That wasn't enough for Betty Ann, and she lasted just a year at Rockford College, which had once been named Rockford Female Seminary. For the rest of her life, she would refer to it as Rockford Female Cemetery—she felt repressed and suffocated, and she begged her father to let her transfer to the University of Missouri.

Eventually, he agreed. He even let her major in journalism, and he didn't stop her from feeding her ambition on campus. She wrote for the school newspaper, served on student government and was elected president of the Gamma Phi Beta sorority.

In many ways, Betty Ann was lucky. She went to college and earned a bachelor's degree. She married a man, Bob Haverfield, whose feminist mother had chaired the local school board and taught Sunday school to special-needs children while he was growing up. He was proud of his ambitious wife. After she graduated in 1942, while Bob was overseas in the U.S. Navy, Betty wrote and edited for two medical magazines, then served as managing editor of eleven suburban newspapers outside Chicago.

During this time, another Betty—a rabble-rouser with a bestselling book in her future—was also parlaying a hard-earned bachelor's degree into a writing career. This Betty was five months younger than Becky's grandmother and had grown up just 130 miles south of Betty Luker. Though the two women never met, they were a lot alike: Both were smart and strong-willed; each spoke her mind; each bristled at the idea of using college for nothing more than an "MRS." Betty Naomi Goldstein earned her degree from Smith College in 1942, and, afterward, she went to graduate school in California to study psychology, worked as a journalist in New York—and then, in 1947, married a man named Carl Friedan.

Two ambitious Bettys from Illinois—one stymied by tradition, the other destined to become a feminist icon. Neither would fully escape The Problem That Has No Name, the housewifely yearning for more that disheartened them both, but it made Betty Friedan famous when she chronicled it in her 1963 book, *The Feminine Mystique.*

For both Bettys, whose generation of women was only the second to attend college in significant numbers, futures of children and chores loomed as constant and almost preordained goals, even as they earned their degrees, graduated and began putting their education and talents to use. But most would only work at those first jobs until they became mothers. Betty Luker Haverfield became a mom in 1947, when Becky's mother, Judy, was born. Only 17 percent of married women with infants worked outside the home in 1948[9] and, unlike Betty Friedan, who continued to write freelance articles after having children, Betty Luker Haverfield wasn't one of them.

Instead, she had a second child and became a full-blown 1950s housewife with a lovely home, a bridge club and *her very own washing machine.* And she was frustrated. She threw birthday parties so elaborate that attendees still talked about them half a century later; she led the Campfire Girls with fervor; she served in women's groups and on local boards and, later, even went back to college to earn a master's degree in education.

She probably felt very alone, beset by this unquenchable thirst, always wanting to do and be more. But, the truth was, she wasn't alone at all.

It was Betty Friedan who saw it, not in Becky's grandmother individually, but in many housewives who were suffocating just like her. Wrote Friedan:

Each suburban wife struggled with it alone. As she made the beds, shopped for groceries, matched slipcover material, ate peanut butter sandwiches with her children, chauffeured Cub Scouts and Brownies, lay beside her husband at night—she was afraid to ask even of herself the silent question—"Is this all?"

For Betty Luker Haverfield, as it turned out, it wasn't all. In 1964, she finally came as close as she would get to a postmotherhood career: She was appointed editor of Gamma Phi Beta's national magazine, *The Crescent*. Her husband built her an office in a spare bedroom, and she put her journalism degree to work. She redesigned the publication. She took a stand against the Little Sister organizations at college fraternities, calling them sexist and degrading to women, and she refused to publish announcements about them in the magazine. She held the job for ten years before being named Gamma Phi Beta's international president.

By 1977, more than a decade after Betty Friedan founded the National Organization for Women, Betty Haverfield had finally found her groove: She had a son in college, a daughter with more choices that she'd ever dreamed, grandchildren and, at long last, professional satisfaction.

The next year she died of breast cancer.

* * *

She may never have known it, but Betty Luker Haverfield left her mark.

Bigger voices—Betty Friedan and other crusaders, like Gloria Steinem—moved things forward in more obvious, public ways. They wrote eye-opening books and articles, formed the National Women's Political Caucus, and led consciousness-raising protests.

But legions of housewives inspired progress simply by wanting more—and teaching their daughters to want more, as well. Their individual gains may have seemed meager, but their collective voice—the yearnings they would later recount to adult daughters, the ambition that would emanate when they led their women's clubs, their dogged determination to be more than a mom with a fancy new washer—would resonate for generations. Their unnamed Problem, and their willingness to admit it, gave the crusaders a reason to crusade.

So what, exactly, did this mean for us?

Well, for starters, guilt—the unavoidable demon of any heir. It hovered over us when we took our choices for granted or when we took a few years off to "just" stay home with our kids, instead of working outside the home as many of our grandmothers had longed to do. In some cases, it pushed us to achieve—and it contributed to our perfectionism. In the New Perfect survey, nearly one in five Never Enoughs said they felt obligated to work because previous generations had struggled for the opportunities. (Good Enoughs were half as likely to feel this way.)

When Becky quit the *Chicago Sun-Times,* one of her few pangs of regret came when she thought of her grandmother, whose name she'd given to her daughter, Elizabeth Anne. Betty would have loved Becky's job, and, given the choice, she probably would have kept it after becoming a mom. The opportunity to effect change from the city desk of a major metropolitan newspaper would have been a dream come true for Betty, an honor not to be taken lightly.

"Did you really quit?" an old friend asked Becky in 2004, when she called to reconnect after several years. "I can't believe it. This is what you always wanted."

There it was, Betty's face in the back of her mind. It made Becky worry, just a bit: *Did I take the honor too lightly?*

These bolts of guilt, appearing every now and again, have shaped our attitudes and kept history from receding too far into collective memory. Not that there's much risk that we'll forget how hard these women had to work for what they achieved and the legacy they left us.

How could we? Our mothers are Baby Boomers. Damned if they'd let us forget a thing.

The Yearners, after all, did more than inspire our occasional bouts of hand-wringing. They gave our mothers' rebellious, stalwart generation its start. The Boomers learned early to speak up and speak loudly. They fought for jobs in male-dominated fields and stood strong against judgment and ridicule. They chipped away at glass ceilings and walked uncharted paths. They were natural revolutionaries, blessed by large numbers and good timing, and they were determined to have everything their mothers didn't. By and large, they succeeded. And they made sure their daughters knew it.

Guilt and inspiration. The proud legacy of any mother.

THE EARLY BOOMERS: SEARCHING FOR BALANCE ON AN UNEVEN FIELD

One day in about 1972, Meta Levin, a rookie reporter for a small Kansas City–area newspaper, attended a coroner's press conference. She needed the lowdown on a corpse.

The story was horrific but standard crime-beat fare—a decomposing body had been found in the trunk of a car on a hot summer day; it looked like an execution-style killing. The reporters peppered the coroner with questions. Who was the victim? When did he die? What were the cause and manner of death?

When the press conference concluded, Meta approached the coroner to ask a few more questions. Suddenly, a detective grabbed her hand and pulled it behind her back. *Snap.* Cold metal clasped her wrist. The detective spun her around and grabbed the other hand. *Snap.* Handcuffs.

"We have something to show you," he breathed, pulling her into the back room. The room was cold. An unpleasant odor hovered. There, on a long metal table, lay the body. The detective laughed.

Meta swallowed. *I can't throw up. I can't throw up,* she thought to herself. She swallowed again, over and over. *I can't be weak and girly.*

She held it together.

It was a new world, and Meta knew she was being tested. She was not about to blow it. Already she'd been turned away by a newspaper because there were "no openings on the women's page," and she had endured a television job that didn't permit women to be on air. In 1972, the National Press Club had only been admitting women for about a year; the country had yet to see a female network evening news anchor, and Edna Buchanan had not yet made her mark as one of Miami's first female crime reporters.

No, Meta Levin would *not* vomit.

That's how it started for some of the Boomer women, especially those who chose careers dominated by men. When they became mothers, as Meta did in 1975, they were trying to find balance on an uneven field.

In 1975, women earned less than 60 percent as much as men[10] and were underrepresented in many professions. Women were only 24 percent of financial managers; 13 percent of physicians; 7 percent of lawyers; and 1 percent of engineers.[11]

The obstacles for women with children were even greater—but that didn't stop Boomer moms from streaming into the workforce in record numbers. In 1976, only 31 percent of married mothers of infants worked. But by 1984, that number had risen to 47 percent; by 1988, it was 51 percent.[12]

Meta worked on and off as she raised her children and followed her husband from city to city. She remembers this general attitude toward working mothers in the 1970s and 1980s: "If you were going to do it, okay, but don't ask me for any help."

The hurdles were many: Sexism. Judgment. The constant need to prove oneself. A dearth of suitable maternity leave policies or child-care options. Occasional pangs of panic: Am I doing the right thing?

Linda Morse, who worked as a university administrator and technology executive while rearing her children in the 1970s and 1980s, battled it all: "I had to prove myself over and over and over again, and I never made it as high as I could have." Her daughter's preschool teacher even once said: "Molly's only problem is that she has a mother who works."

Linda, who now owns an upscale knitting shop with locations in Manhattan, Greenwich, Connecticut, and online, laughed as she recounted that memory. Molly grew up to be a happy and self-assured mother of two—and a vice president in the antiquities department at Christie's auction house.

Linda Morse, 67
Entrepreneur and Former Technology Executive
New York City
Mother of Michael and Molly

I was the assistant dean of the faculty at Princeton and the first woman non-secretary to work in the administration building. In 1969, Michael was born.

I never thought about what I was going to do after the baby was born. I never talked to my boss about it.

I gave birth, and my secretary called and said, "We've packed up all your things and we've terminated you."

And I said, "Holy shit!"

At that second, I knew I was going to work for the rest of my life.

Linda called Princeton and said she intended to stay. When she returned, she wrote the university's 1970 maternity leave policy.

In 1975, the family moved to New York, and Linda had to find a new job. "I can't stand being dependent," she said. "The only way to have freedom is to make your own."

And so she started networking. The series of meetings that followed showed just what she was up against as a working mother. One man asked if her children were in psychiatric care because they "didn't have a mother." Another asked her to sit next to him on the couch—she walked out of that one. Another had his staff meeting at 7:00 p.m. every day.

So she went to Columbia as assistant provost for a year—and hated it.

Eventually, she joined American Management Systems, where she worked for twenty-five years, became a vice president and was part of the leadership team that helped build the information systems consulting firm into a multi-billion-dollar company. Later, she served as CEO of a dot-com.

"Yes, there was tons of judgment," she says. "But I never cared—I kind of liked it. I didn't want to be like [the other mothers]. I was glad to be who I was."

At one point, Linda tried to be an at-home mom. Michael had encephalitis—and when he recovered, she decided that she'd never work again. The family moved to Oklahoma: "We thought we could ride off into the sunset," Linda remembered, laughing.

She lasted a couple of months.

As it turned out, the life of a stay-at-home mom was as soon as you dropped the kids off at school you start calling around to all the other moms to talk on the phone or find out when the exercise class was.

If Molly had become a stay-at-home mother, I would have thought that was awful. Women need something to give them identity.

Now, there is a flip side to this. There is about a ten-year period where your life is hell. The only time when you're ever alone is when you're on the toilet, if you're lucky enough to close the door.

But if you give that up, you're changing your life [because of that one] very short period of time.

THE NEW GLASS CEILING: "WHAT DO I WANT MY LIFE TO EQUAL?"

By 1995, the Boomers had made some inroads. The wage gap had narrowed; women were now earning about 71 percent as much as men annually.[13] Although women were still underrepresented in certain jobs, the proportions had increased. Women were now 50 percent of financial managers (up from 24 percent in 1975); 26 percent of lawyers (up from 7 percent); 24 percent of physicians (up from 13 percent); and 8 percent of engineers (up from 1 percent).[14]

About 57 percent of all married mothers of infants were now working; among those with bachelor's degrees or higher, the number topped 68 percent.[15] Women were also rising to positions of power in corporate America. In 1995, about 9.5 percent of board directors at Fortune 500 companies were women; 8.7 percent of corporate officers in the Fortune 500 were women.[16]

Women employees had reached a critical mass. Just as many of our contemporaries were entering the workforce in the mid-1990s, some of the old barriers were falling, but balancing work and family seemed to be getting *harder.* Though women had greater professional opportunities and employers were becoming more flexible, significant obstacles persisted—perhaps none more powerful than the overwhelming psychological pressure to succeed. The more we heard about women who had made it to the top, the more we felt as if we should, too.

What's more, years of empowerment and expectation had made us over-achievers in every aspect of our lives—and raising children was no exception. Even before we had them, we knew our children would become a full-time occupation, even if we also worked outside the home. We knew we'd approach motherhood the same way we'd approached our careers: armed with exhaustive research and full schedules.

It was around this time that Hollee was beginning her career as a lawyer and, for the first time, beginning to wonder about the notion of Having It All. Up until this point, Hollee had given almost no thought to how she would balance kids and career—and, in fact, she hadn't always been sure she would even have children. Making partner seemed like the most logical goal: Hollee had graduated at the top of her class at Northwestern University, had received her law degree from Duke University and had always aimed to be "the best."

But when she started practicing at a large Pittsburgh law firm, there were few female partners and almost none of them were mothers. The lack of role models began to bother her. How would she keep up with the rigors of modern motherhood and still make partner?

Becky, on the other hand, had always been sure she wanted a family. By 1996, she was a reporter for the *Detroit News* and engaged to Pete, a law student at Georgetown University with a job waiting at a major firm in Chicago. Her first big choice between family and career had just landed in her lap with a thud: Leave Detroit or live in separate cities?

At the time, Becky's dad was the editor of the *Cincinnati Enquirer* and her go-to person for career advice. One day, on a drive to a Cincinnati grocery store, Becky asked her dad whether she'd be able to Have It All.

Larry didn't even stop to think about his answer: "No, probably not."

Becky flinched. She had worked hard on the belief that she could.

"But," he continued, "if you're smart about it, you might be able to come close."

Larry told her to think about Janet Leach. Jan Leach was the *Enquirer*'s managing editor and the mother of three. Becky knew she was well-regarded as a tough but fair journalist. She had built an impressive career, weaving it deftly around motherhood. Her two youngest were twins, born in 1994, less than two years into Jan's stint as managing editor. They had been born seven weeks early after Jan had spent nearly two months on bed rest.

Jan had come back strong, her commitment to journalism never flagging. Later, she would go on to become the first female editor of the *Akron Beacon Journal*. From Becky's perspective, it seemed that, by 1996, Jan had already come very close to Having It All. Becky imagined that for somebody as smart and kind as Jan Leach, that sort of balance must have come easily. And she figured that even if she wasn't quite Jan Leach, maybe, if she was lucky, she could do it, too.

So, inspired by Jan and a female managing editor she'd worked for a year before in Rochester, Becky took her dad's advice: Work as hard as you can right now, build the career you want, don't skimp on the personal things that really matter to you—and then stop worrying so much. So, after less than a year in Detroit, she took a job at the *Chicago Sun-Times* to be with Pete.

Years later, while researching this book, Becky gave Jan Leach a call at Kent State University, where she had been teaching journalism since 2003. Jan's story was, of course, more complicated than Becky's younger self had imagined.

Janet Leach, 55
Assistant Professor of Journalism, Kent State University;
Former Editor, the *Akron Beacon Journal*
Fairlawn, Ohio
Mother of Cara, Natalie and Monica

I never thought it would be twins.

The doctor did an ultrasound and said it was twins, and I just cried.

I didn't think I could handle it—I didn't think I could handle two babies at once. I thought it was going to change everything, and it would be terrible. It just threw me for a loop.

I remember thinking I probably wouldn't be able to be managing editor. I had worked so hard for this job, and I liked it. But I thought, "There is no way I can have three kids, including two infants, and this demanding job."

But I really liked my job, and I liked journalism—and I wanted to prove I could do it.

And Jan did. When she came back from maternity leave, her job was the same, and the newspaper hadn't learned to "get along without me," as she had feared. She learned to take things one day at a time—and she accepted that she didn't need to be baking cookies and reading stories out loud every night.

Three years later, she left Cincinnati for the top post in the *Akron Beacon Journal* newsroom. There were days when everything fit, and there were days when Jan was torn: "I would be in high heels and panty hose, strapping them into their car seats—I mean, jeez."

But she continued to take it one day at a time. She and her husband shared responsibilities. She assigned chores as the children became older. She brought in a cleaning service a few times a year, and she learned to ask for help when she needed it.

Still, the balancing act wore on her. In 2000, she made 118 speeches and appearances as the *Beacon Journal* editor—on top of her regular newsroom duties, parent-teacher conferences, soccer practices and other commitments.

In April 2001, extensive newsroom layoffs took an emotional toll; later that year, the terrorist attacks of September 11 compounded the stress as she practically camped out at work to oversee her paper's coverage.

In 2002, Jan was running around crazy. Her daughters were in fifth grade and second grade, her husband was working at a law firm in Cleveland. The children had Girl Scouts and piano lessons and soccer. "The schedule, you know, was just chaos. If you looked at my calendar, you would say some toddler scribbled on this," she recalled. "It just got to be frantic."

One day, Jan got so busy at work that she forgot to pick up Cara from a soccer game. "A friend called and said, 'You know, the game is over and there is no one to pick her up.' I just didn't make arrangements," Jan told Becky. "I thought, 'How could you forget your own kid?' I felt so guilty."

Finally, amid a cacophony of professional frustrations, including the unrelenting focus on the bottom line that had become a consistent challenge in many newsrooms, and exhaustion at trying to juggle so much, Jan went to her publisher. She said she just couldn't do it anymore. He told her to take two weeks to think about it.

Her last big story as editor was on February 1, 2003: The explosion of the space shuttle *Columbia*. The same story, oddly, that Becky had been covering when she decided to leave newspapers.

"On Monday, I came in and gave my notice," Jan said.

What it came down to, in the end, was one simple question: "What do I want Jan's life to equal?"

I know what the answer was not. I had this vision that on my gravestone it would say, "She got the pages in on time." I know it sounds so silly. But I wanted my kids to be nice people. I didn't want them interviewed one day on Oprah *saying, "My mother was never around." I kept looking at my kids and thinking, "This is not the mother I want to be. This is not how I want to live."*

And so she didn't. Janet Leach left the *Beacon Journal,* a newspaper she loved, to find her balance. And she did, a few months later, as a journalism professor at Kent State.

DAUGHTERS OF CHANGE: PLACING THE CHINA ON THE SHELF

In the shadow of these women, our generation of mothers began piecing together our legacy and making sense of our choices. By handing us such a large legacy, history set the stage for compulsive perfection—but it also set the stage for the New Perfect.

Our options have continued to expand. By 2007, the pay gap had further narrowed: Women were earning nearly 78 percent as much as men.[17] More than 15 percent of board directors and nearly 16 percent of corporate officers in Fortune 500 companies were women.[18]

Since becoming mothers, our job has been to figure out how we fit in, what we will do to continue the progress—and, most important, what works best for our families. We are learning to embrace our inheritance—and to define it on our own terms.

Molly Morse Limmer, 37
Vice President and Head of Department for Antiquities, Christie's
Armonk, New York
Mother of Rosey and Lily
Daughter of Linda Morse

I never at any point pictured not having a job. It wasn't in my vocabulary.

My mother was an executive in a software company. I was always proud of her. I never felt an absence.

I understood [that] my mom had an important job. I heard stories in my childhood where she was questioned [as a mom] for having a job. My parents always pushed me to do what I loved. I loved art history.

I love my job. I don't really understand making these sacrifices otherwise. I love the objects, I love the people, I love the travel.

But I never feel 100 percent anything . . . I guess that comes from being a perfectionist. I've always been that way. My mom is that way.

But I control it. I make sure I get what I want. I'm not afraid to speak up. If I need to leave [the office], I can.

My mom was home [in the evenings] . . . and I decided it would be that way [for me], too.

She decided.

A rich inheritance, proudly displayed.

THE NEW MOMMY WARS

- There are a lot of "right" ways to be a good mom.
- There's nothing wrong with "easy"—just because something's hard doesn't mean it's more valuable.
- There's a difference between being the best and doing your best.
- Be yourself.
- Ignore the "eyes on your back."
- Balance isn't about having perfect harmony each day.

And so Molly Morse Limmer proved her preschool teacher wrong.

Not only does she travel to Europe several times a year to appraise ancient Greek and Roman art, but she's home many nights to hang out with her daughters and tuck them into bed. In the evenings, they'll play cards or read out loud; Molly loves serenading them with "Alligators All Around," and "'A' You're Adorable," a song her parents used to sing to her.

Molly's favorite part comes a couple hours later, just before she goes to her own bed: "I go and peek at each of them, and I give them kisses.

They are just so sweet when they're sleeping peacefully," she said in a gentle voice. "I love that."

As modern moms, nothing is stopping us from creating full lives. Our big challenge is that we have so many choices. Many of us grew up following obvious, well-marked paths to success, only to become mothers and find ourselves surrounded by a thick forest of other "right" answers. Even the categories that we expected to find—the "working moms" and "at-home moms," who were supposedly vying for superiority in the Mommy Wars—have blurred, largely because the boundaries that once separated them have vanished. Today, a burgeoning middle ground is filled with women who inhabit both worlds at once. And this seems like pure upside, until we look around and can't find anyone else who seems to fully understand our experience. All this custom-tailoring has left many working mothers feeling lonely and alone.

Even a woman like Molly, who has worked a demanding full-time job with Christie's since having children, can look at another successful "working mom" and struggle to find common ground. Molly's career certainly shapes her identity; it's easy to see how she's different from women who have opted out of the workforce altogether. But Molly hasn't worked from home or scaled back her hours (as Hollee did); she didn't take a few years off when her children were babies (as Becky did).

When we interviewed successful women, we couldn't help but notice how often we heard this phrase: "I'm not like the other mothers."

It was these words, spoken over and over, that revealed our generation's new Mommy Wars—a battle that is far more emotional and isolating than a clear-cut debate over working versus staying home. This war is one we fight alone, and mostly with ourselves, as we try to figure out where we fit in. (The conflict we'd expected—the old Mommy Wars—at least gave us a "side" we could join, and the camaraderie of other women who'd made the same decisions.) Now, we struggle to make sense of our options, defending one priority one day, and another priority the next. We steel ourselves against the cacophony of messages about what we "should" want, and stave off competitive inclinations that sometimes lead us to pursue someone else's idea of success.

And that's when these new Mommy Wars exact their greatest toll—when they make us forget that what's good enough for someone else isn't always what's good enough for us.

Shawnna Durand Snodgrass, 39
Adjunct Clinical Faculty Member and Hospital Shift Nurse
Loveland, Colorado
Mother of Lauren, Grey and Aidan

Women need to trust what is best for them. What worked for our mothers may not work in today's world. Some women should never be at home—it makes them miserable. Some women would kill to stay at home.

Look, it's a struggle and women have an extremely difficult job. We need to cut each other some slack and stop being so judgmental. Can't we support each other? That's the only way we'll find any peace.

* * *

Hollee worried most about failing in the eyes of . . . her mother-in-law. In part, it was because Loranne, John's mom, could seriously have medaled in the motherhood Olympics. She had six kids (identical twins to cap off the crew), and she dedicated her life to them. Completely. As her babies started having babies (she's up to sixteen grandchildren), Loranne became the exalted family expert on child rearing, a font of wisdom. She made it to almost all the births, then stuck around to help the sleep-deprived new parents through the early days. Anytime a kid-related question popped up, she could reference the latest studies or statistics (on top of her three decades of personal experience). And, unlike Hollee, she seemed to love nothing more than just hanging out with infants and toddlers. She served casseroles, cheerfully played Candy Land on the floor, remembered and recorded every milestone in each of her six baby books.

Hollee looked at Loranne and knew there was no way that she would stack up in the Mom Department. Not with her job. Not with her lack of talent in the kitchen. Not with her impatient nature. Her mother-in-law had given birth to six children without complaint; Hollee was so petrified that she wouldn't make it through childbirth without catastrophe that she hired a personal coach to help her get by.

And, as she'd feared, Hollee wasn't really cut out for the early years; she didn't operate well without at least eight hours of sleep (and her kids weren't those perfect ones who slept through the night at two weeks). So Hollee spent much of her time counting down the minutes until bedtime, then feeling guilty that she wasn't appreciating her little men. As they got a little older, she searched for ways to kill time. She took the longest possible route to the grocery store. She knew it wasn't good for babies to watch TV (they really shouldn't watch at all until they're two, Loranne gently reminded her), but she couldn't figure out how to fill the hours without *Blue's Clues* and *Lazytown*. She would even take her toddlers to the law school to wander the halls when her husband, John, taught night classes; she couldn't stand the isolation of staring at the same walls, talking to people who were too little to answer. Perhaps it was because she was trying to work a full-time job without enough child care; or maybe it was because she didn't know anyone else who was fitting the puzzle pieces together in exactly the same way.

Hollee imagined that at-home moms, like Loranne, spent more time thinking about motherhood, more time reading about it; surely at-home moms were rarely in the frenetic state Hollee was always in, rushing between work and home and never having any time for herself. Hollee's reasoning was simple: Loranne had never worked outside the home, Loranne was the time-tested authority on parenting... and therefore, Hollee concluded, Loranne would always be the better mom.

* * *

Becky, on the other hand, was determined to *win* the motherhood Olympics.

She opted for a long maternity leave so she could give Elizabeth her full attention, and, almost immediately, she became obsessed with baby classes. She was addicted to signing up for the endless offerings available to infants and new moms throughout Chicago: Gymboree, Kindermusik, Wiggleworms, baby yoga, swimming lessons, mom-and-baby strollercise—Elizabeth did them all before she turned one. By the time she was two, her dossier had expanded to include fairy-tale ballet and toddler art. Like any self-respecting urban baby, Elizabeth also belonged to several playgroups and had "coffee dates" so often that she could recognize the Starbucks logo before she could talk.

During these early years, before Katie joined the family, Becky ran her life much as she'd run her career. She immersed herself in mountains of research on breast-feeding, sleep patterns and brain development, and she kept her calendar filled with appointments. She had goals and daily to-do lists (although, admittedly, in the early days of motherhood, those lists sometimes included line items like "shower" and "eat"). Becky liked having an agenda; she *needed* to have an agenda. For a while, the whole type A thing made her feel invigorated and in control. Plus, once she left the *Sun-Times,* it allowed her to justify her lack of a paycheck: There would be no mistaking her contribution to the family.

It also distracted her from the identity issues she had with being "at home." She loved spending the day with her baby; cuddling with Elizabeth or watching her master some new skill was worth every byline she'd given up. She would sometimes lie on the couch with her sleeping baby in the middle of the afternoon, just watching the small face cradled on her chest, and feel a peace she'd never known before. But even though she'd thought hard about taking a long, unpaid maternity leave—and then, later, about quitting altogether—Becky didn't want anyone to think she was "just a mom." In retrospect, she'd feel ashamed for having felt this way, and she'd realize that it stemmed from insecurity more than anything else. But, back then, the bias was so strong that she routinely hedged when asked what she did. Instead of saying, "I'm a full-time mom," she'd typically start by describing what she'd done *before* becoming a mom. Later, she'd wonder why she'd done that. She didn't think less of her other at-home friends; why did she feel such conflict about her own choice? Feeling embarrassed and fraudulent, she'd commiserate with her friend Tracey, a friend and former *Sun-Times* colleague who was experiencing a similar internal struggle.

"I did it again," Becky would tell Tracey, cringing as she admitted this. "I gave the 'I used to be successful' speech."

Tracey would nod sympathetically. She knew the speech; she gave it sometimes, too. "We need to stop doing that," she'd say.

Becky would agree, but, deep down, she still felt torn and confused. Back then, in the early 2000s, the Mommy Wars were receiving a lot of media attention—and Becky had no idea which "side" she really wanted to take. She didn't feel any particular camaraderie with the conventional description of either group, yet she still ached to belong somewhere.

So she threw herself into being the best, most productive, most dedicated mommy *ever*. She figured she could fit in with the stay-at-home set and still feel "productive" if she turned the job into something really challenging. She signed up for more classes. She read more books. She played games on the floor until she thought the boredom of toddler toys would kill her.

This approach worked beautifully.

Until it didn't.

* * *

Who would have thought the latest iteration of the Mommy Wars would be so heavily soaked in identity crisis? *Do we stay at home, work full-time, work part-time, work from home, or do something altogether different—and what kind of mother will this make us?* Even once we'd begun to make peace with the choices we'd inherited from the Baby Boomers, the women of our generation have deliberated and wrestled, turning everything over and over *and over and over* in our minds. ("You all think too much," one Baby Boomer told Becky.) Many of us were surprised by the uncertainty and isolation we felt, even as we figured out ways to make things work. With so many of us facing the same challenges at once, and with so much freedom to choose, it was hard to understand why each of us felt so . . . different.

Hollee remembers attending a late-summer birthday party populated by a swarm of four-year-olds and their impressively toned at-home mothers. The moms were sipping wine in their sophisticated outfits (some laughed about the preschool bash being a chance to dress up), and while Hollee (sort of) looked the part and tried to join the conversation, no one ever asked about her work. She didn't share the same circle of friends or daytime activities; she knew she wasn't really part of their crowd.

And yet at work, she sometimes felt that same sense of isolation. Most of her female colleagues didn't have young children, and they always seemed to make time for midafternoon colloquia or extra moot court coaching sessions or late-night speeches that she couldn't attend without burdening John or missing something with the kids. As a professor, Hollee had crafted a life that straddled both worlds—yet still left her feeling lost in the middle.

Much later it occurred to her: Maybe some of the moms at the birthday party or on her faculty felt the same way, but just couldn't find the words or the opportunity to express that unsettling emotion. Was this all just an unspoken truth? Did all mothers feel as if their lives didn't quite match anyone else's?

The feeling of "not-quite belonging" was a common theme in our New Perfect interviews, even though most of these mothers had active social lives and friends they cherished. Women expressed it in different ways: "It's a little different for me." "Nobody else really understands." "I'm not like the other moms at school." "People just don't get it." But the feeling was pervasive. When we hosted a roundtable discussion with twelve of the working mothers who appear in this book, one of the women later confessed that she'd felt like the "odd woman out," like she hadn't quite fit with the rest of the group. And then, a few weeks later, a second woman said the same thing. And then a third.

In interviews, we heard "I feel alone" from women who were working part-time in an office and from women who were working full-time from home. We heard it from those with flexible scheduling, and from those with demanding, full-time, high-level jobs. Some women were lonely because "I feel like I'm the only mom who works in this town"—something we heard repeatedly, even from women who lived in the same town.

Some moms experienced outright judgment; some expressed it. But many more described a subtle chafing—a mild but consistent disconnect that ulti-mately conveyed just how different mothers' lives could be. Often, it wasn't that a specific moment or encounter had devastated these women; it was the accumulation of misunderstandings, failed connections and hints of disapproval that rankled over time. Many found it hard to articulate why it mattered so much, but it did. They'd gotten tired of having to explain their choices, and even more tired of issuing the same silent reminder to themselves: *It doesn't matter what anyone thinks.* Some simply missed the camaraderie they remembered from their days before kids. One woman matter-of-factly described a friend: "She's not like me. She's basically a *stay-at-home mom*—she works from home." The comment didn't come from a place of condemnation; it was merely an acknowledgment that the two mothers faced different challenges.

And being creatures of affinity, some moms couldn't stand not fitting in. Many were so used to (and sometimes even dependent on) a steady stream of approval that they hated being thrust into a game that didn't offer a single "winning" solution. Sure, most could identify women who shared their approach in several areas—but in all of them? There simply wasn't one right way to assemble this puzzle. Sometimes, we couldn't help but wonder: *If we'd done things right, wouldn't everyone else be doing the same thing?*

A WHOLE NEW BATTLEFIELD

We had expected the debate over the infamous Mommy Wars, which were basically about two choices: working or staying home. Many of us had been primed by media coverage that seemed to suggest a more easily recognizable divide—and more overt strife—than what we encountered. Instead, as we waded deeper into motherhood, many of us found that debate to be meaningless and unproductive; the to-work-or-stay-home decision was only a sliver of the equation. And just because it was easy to create two sides didn't mean we really cared to duke it out. We had bigger fish to fry—and eventually we began to make that clear.

By 2009, attempts to reignite the Mommy Wars were met with disdain. In October 2009, a blogger and at-home mom drew ire when she spoke out, on a *Dr. Phil* talk show episode titled "Guilty Moms," against mothers who chose to work. The message in blog posts that followed—including one by Leslie Morgan Steiner, editor of the 2006 bestseller *Mommy Wars: Stay-at-Home and Career Moms Face Off on Their Choices, Their Lives, Their Families*—was clear: We are sooo over this.

And with good reason: It had become increasingly obvious that neither choice claimed an across-the-board superiority. What's more, it was hard to debate "at-home" and "working" when so many moms lived somewhere in the middle.

And that was really the kicker. We had moved on—but the discussion hadn't. In interview after interview, mothers told us that they were eager to talk about this next phase of the work/life conflict, but couldn't find a forum, or sometimes even a fellow mom, who would dive into the discussion.

So when Hollee got the chance to interview Ellen Galinsky, who has been studying work/life and parenting issues since the 1970s, the challenges modern moms face in balancing work and family was the first topic she brought up.

Ellen wasn't the slightest bit surprised that moms were feeling so "hush-hush" about the latest twist in the work/life dilemma. "Until very recently," Ellen told Hollee, "this conflict was assumed to be a 'private' issue that shouldn't be publicly discussed or debated, much like The Problem That Has No Name that Betty Friedan described in *The Feminine Mystique*."[1] In fact, as Ellen conducted research for her own books in the 1970s and 1980s, the women she interviewed were similarly reluctant to share their secret thoughts about blending family and career.

"But," Ellen told Hollee, "the 'very slow cultural revolution' over the past forty years has picked up steam and may be reaching a turning point." It was the spring of 2010, shortly after Ellen had helped organize the White House Forum on Workplace Flexibility and published her latest parenting book, *Mind in the Making*. She noted that work/life was finally becoming a main-stream issue for two big reasons.

First, it's no longer just a problem for moms; men are starting to feel the pain, too. Ellen's research shows that "changing gender roles" have contributed to a significant rise in work/life conflicts for men over the past three decades—from 34 percent in 1977 to 45 percent in 2008.[2] Second, Michelle Obama's interest in the issue has put work/life conflict on the national radar as never before. A vocabulary has even emerged: phrases like *the time bind* and *time squeeze* (from one of the foundations supporting the Forum) to *juggler families* and life as a series of *high-wire acts* (from President Obama in his closing remarks).

"It really meant something that Michelle, with all of her advantages, admitted the work/life challenges affected her, too," Ellen told Hollee.

After the Forum, Ellen wrote about the "mismatch between the workplace and the workforce" in a *Huffington Post* column—how there is a gap between what people want life to look like and how it really looks now. Ellen talked about the traditional family of the previous generation, and how, as we have moved toward an economy where both parents work, there are "still the same family responsibilities—just less time to meet them."

And that's why personal definitions of success, and a willingness to choose Good Enough over Perfect, can make all the difference.

Ellen Galinsky, 68
President and Cofounder of Families and Work Institute
Author, *Mind in the Making: The Seven Essential Life Skills Every Child Needs*
Mother of Lara and Philip

You have to learn to deal with the grayness of life. When you don't know what to do, when you don't want to make the wrong choice, it can be really helpful to ask yourself, "How will I feel about this in five years?" Sometimes it will be clear that you should go to the work thing or that you can't miss the ballet recital. Whether it will matter in five years is really personal, and you need to listen to what matters to you—not what your friends say or the books say.

We all muddle through.

There is no perfect path in parenthood. You've gotta live with the grayness and learn to be a good problem solver.

* * *

When Becky first interviewed Jennifer Pate in August 2008, the Los Angeles mother of two was straddling the traditional categories: She was home with her kids, but was about to launch her next professional move. A former casting director for television and film, Jennifer had enjoyed a robust career before kids, cofounding and managing a casting agency. She had planned to continue her career (her second; she'd already spent ten years as a professional dancer), but two months after she returned to work, she was pregnant again. At that point, working just "felt so wrong for me."

Had someone tried to categorize Jennifer during the more than five years she spent home with her children, she might have been pigeonholed as part of the "Opt-Out Revolution," the controversial spate of professional women leaving careers to be at-home mothers.[3] But that label would have covered only a fraction of Jennifer's life, and it would not have accounted for the astounding professional evolution that unfolded in the year after Becky first interviewed her. By the next fall, Jennifer had become the cohost and co-executive producer of a successful internet-based reality/talk show about moms—and was earning more than twice what she had in her previous career. And because she had so much control over her time, she *still* didn't identify with either group: "I'm sort of a stay-at-home-working mom."

But, in that first interview, Jennifer was still on the brink, full of optimism and excitement—even a touch of uncertainty—as she described how the web series, eventually named *Jen and Barb: Mom Life,* had come together. She and her partner, Barbara Machen, had met while taking their children to a class at a kids' gym. "We found each other and we hung on for dear life," Jennifer told Becky. Their experiences as moms convinced them to create their show: a series of five-minute segments taking on contemporary motherhood. Their tagline: *We're all in this together.*

"I felt like there was a common thread, no matter who I talked to—whether she was a stay-at-home mom, a working mom, somebody who's trying to balance it all—everyone was having a bit of an identity crisis," Jennifer told Becky. "There were very few, if any, women I knew who weren't struggling with, 'How do I make this work?' There was a real common thread of, 'Who am I? I'm confused. I'm not doing it right.' That's when I thought: *People need to know that they're not alone."*

Of the women we followed, Jennifer was not the only mom whose work arrangement changed substantially in the two-year period when most of the interviews took place. Nor was she the only mother to describe herself as a hybrid. In the New Perfect survey, nearly three-quarters of the women had changed their work arrangement after having children, but their new roles were so diverse that more than 20 percent of the women couldn't say yes to any of the ten arrangements that we described on the questionnaire. (This may be further proof that what the work/life experts say is correct: True flexibility isn't something that can be attained—or even described—by checking a box.)

Some of the women surveyed had taken advantage of flexible hours, others had begun job shares. Some had become freelancers or independent contractors, others had cut back their hours. Some had quit and found new jobs that allowed them part-time or more flexible hours, others had started their own businesses. Some, like Jennifer, had temporarily opted out, only to opt back in a few years later. (The majority returned to work in two and a half years or less.)

Even the words that mothers use to describe their professional lives have become so varied that Molly Morse Limmer, the Christie's antiquities expert, found that she needed to adjust her own definitions when she started a "working moms' group" within the preschool association in her children's school district. "What was really interesting, and I had to work on not being judgmental, was that on our membership form you just had to check off: Are you a working mom?" Molly says. "And it turned out, I was getting lists of women who taught one exercise class a week and considered themselves working moms. And so it really took a while to understand that it's a mentality as much as anything else. . . . You don't have to be going to an office every day to be considered a working mom." Molly's group embraced the broader definition—and grew into a strong committee.

* * *

Still, as the labels peeled away, many of us remained desperate to classify ourselves and each other—and, perhaps, to reassure ourselves that our way was the best. As one woman noted: "We're all different, and we're all looking around and judging everyone else." Many sensed judgment regardless of which path they had chosen—there was always someone who didn't understand. Some women, particularly those who were further along in motherhood, trained themselves to ignore it. And as the years passed, the less it seemed to rankle—either because the judgment had subsided, or because they'd simply stopped noticing or caring.

That was the case for Cathy Calhoun, a single mother and top executive at a leading public relations firm. When Cathy became a mother, she had already built an impressive career that included helping launch the "got milk?/milk mustache" campaign. Now, as president of Weber Shandwick North America, she oversees operations in twenty offices across the United States and Canada. When Becky first interviewed Cathy in her Chicago office, she was confident and thoughtful as she described how her life had changed in the dozen years since the birth of her daughter, Sophie. It hadn't always been easy—for starters, Cathy never married Sophie's dad—but she learned to roll with the punches and allow herself some imperfections.

Early on, there had been occasional comments from other mothers, particularly when Cathy was flying across the country for work, but it was hard to tell whether the other moms were disapproving, envious or just plain curious. Cathy felt some women were reacting to their own choices, and sometimes, Cathy admitted, her own doubts may have clouded her perception.

Cathy Calhoun, 48
Public Relations Executive and President of
Weber Shandwick North America
Chicago, Illinois
Mother of Sophie

The trick with my job is that I travel. That's what freaks out all the other moms. I've always felt a little judged by other mothers on that because I'm gone at least one night a week. It averages out to three or four trips a month. Which means I'm away from her. I've been doing that since she was [about] 4 months old.

I've heard, "How can you leave her? How can you do it?" But I don't have a choice. This is the job I have, and I have to do it. And [when I'm gone], she's with her father. She's never with a sitter at night—she's always with a parent.

But they still would judge that. When she was little [other mothers] would say stuff or I'd get the [disapproving] look. But just innocent, not meaning to be malicious. And then sometimes it would be almost a little jealous—like, "Oh, you get to go and have a hot meal and sleep."

So I never really knew where it was coming from. Also, I think I felt bad. I felt a little guilty leaving a baby. But, at the same time, I'm the primary breadwinner in our household. It's just a part of the deal. And [Sophie has] always known it. She's so used to it now, she doesn't even blink.

In fact, Cathy's choices have conferred many advantages: Sophie has grown up with a sense of independence and an ability to adapt. She still has two parents who love her—and she knows it. She and Cathy are close and honest; Cathy is up front when things are hard. "To have the relationship I have with her, I feel so lucky every single day," Cathy says. And because of this closeness, Sophie doesn't believe that she's somehow deprived because her mother has a demanding job. When Cathy bought Sophie designer shoes—a $180 pair of Tory Burch flats to wear with her school uniform every day—Sophie accepted it for what it was: an unusual splurge. And when another mother asserted, in front of Sophie, that Cathy "*has* to buy her things because she works," Sophie was indignant. "No, she doesn't," she told the other mom. Cathy tells this story matter-of-factly and without resentment: The other mom, she says, meant well. She was just shrugging off pressure to buy pricey shoes for her own child.

To a certain extent, Cathy accepts these remarks as a part of the working-mom package. And it's subsided, too, now that Sophie is older. Still, guilt and self-doubt occasionally creep in. When she feels she's fallen short, Cathy indulges these feelings briefly before she moves on. "I try not to play Monday-morning quarterback," she says.

But many of the women interviewed said this letting go took tremendous effort, especially because we're faced with so much information about what defines a "good mom." Many of us have found ourselves trying to filter the messages, searching for guidelines to live by. Can we take fewer than ten mommy-and-me classes and still be good moms? Leave town once a week to travel for work? Bottle-feed our babies? Let the nanny take them back-to-school shopping? Limit playdates because of our hectic schedules? Sometimes we secretly wonder: At what point do we become *bad* moms?

Because no matter how confident we are in our choices, deep down, we all want to be perfect mothers.

THE MYTH OF THE PERFECT MOM

We see her everywhere, that specter of maternal perfection. She's at Gymboree, asking sweetly, "How much sign language does Carter know? Landon can sign apple, kale and toilet—and he's only nine months old!" And at the playground, smiling serenely as she passes a slice of organic pumpkin millet loaf to her toddler while we dig through our own bags, praying for a stray granola bar or a bag of chips to satiate our own child. We see her at school, shepherding her tightly braided and well-matched kindergartner into the classroom while she signs up to run the Halloween party *and* the book fair. (We're sure she never forgets to turn in field-trip money or send sneakers on gym day.) And she's at work, exuding the healthy glow of a woman who has never arrived in the office with Cheerios in her hair and someone's empty juice box in her handbag. It doesn't matter that this woman exists only as a composite. In our minds, she's there, and she's succeeding where we fail.

The myth of the perfect mom haunts us, making it harder to develop personal definitions of success. It has driven us to strive for maternal superstardom at times—and not always because those efforts reflected our greatest priorities.

Hollee once spent two hours turning a bag of Oreos into miniature spiders, complete with pretzel-stick legs, so she could wow Gideon's kindergarten classmates (and, let's be honest, their mothers) with her competence and energy. At the time, she felt guilty for missing a class field trip, and she didn't want to further reinforce the working-mom stereotype by sending a store-bought snack. So she labored over the spider-cookie recipe that Gideon had picked out of a *Highlights* magazine, cursing when the pretzel legs kept snapping. She felt ridiculous later when John, munching on one of the broken-legged spiders that Hollee had rejected, wondered aloud whether the kids had even noticed.

In interviews, even mothers who were confident in nearly every other aspect of their lives confessed to their maternal shortcomings. The confession would often come out in the second or third interview, and it usually went something like this: "I shouldn't even tell you this, but I don't like reading out loud to my kids." Or "I don't schedule a lot of playdates because it's too complicated." The confession wasn't that they didn't ever read out loud or schedule playdates—it was that they didn't do it as often as they thought they should or, worse, that *they didn't enjoy it*. As if being a good mom meant they not only had to accomplish, and even micromanage, everything on the checklist—they had to love every second doing it, too.

And that was where our inner Supermom tripped many of us up: We couldn't satisfy her demands without driving ourselves crazy.

* * *

Becky, as it turned out, couldn't hack it as Supermom. Which was too bad: She thought for sure her type A tendencies would make her a shoo-in for maternal superstardom. But the list of requirements was too long, and when she actually achieved one of them, it wasn't nearly as satisfying as she'd imagined. When she threw her energy into managing her daughters' nutrition—trips to Whole Foods for organics, from-scratch cooking (even though she doesn't enjoy cooking), the fruitless efforts to avoid the scourge of, *gasp!*, juice boxes—she'd wind up feeling deficient in another area. She'd realize that she hadn't spent enough time playing games on the floor. Or that the digital pictures still hadn't been uploaded, captioned and emailed out to the grandparents. Or that her rush to get on to the next task had caused her to leave a sippy cup of spilled—and spoiling—milk in the backseat of her car. (Side note: Spoiled milk is an expensive smell to remove from a car.)

There were plenty of things Becky loved doing, but those things came too easily to consider them to be parental victories. She'd breast-fed both daughters for more than a year, but did that count if some of her reasons were, well, selfish? She'd been partly motivated by ease—getting up to prepare bottles seemed like a lot more work—and nursing relaxed her. Becky was also quite the cruise director: She loved Chicago and effortlessly found time for trips to the Shedd Aquarium, the Museum of Science and Industry, Millennium Park and Navy Pier, not to mention children's museums, beaches, playgrounds, nature centers and zoos. And she loved reading aloud; it wasn't hard to spend an hour reading E. B. White and Dr. Seuss, and later Roald Dahl and Madeleine L'Engle, aloud.

Yet, none of these things made Becky feel like as if she'd mastered motherhood; she just liked this stuff. It wasn't until later that she realized that even the fun things counted—and that these same easy "victories" inspired guilt in other women, moms who maybe excelled at cooking and board games and organizing their digital photos.

But it was hard for Becky to remember this, to allow herself to do what, essentially, felt like slacking off. She was starting to feel as if the only way to be a good mother was to make it a full-time job. But what would she have to show for it if she made mothering her only priority? Did she want her daughters to grow up thinking they needed to quit work to be good moms?

Perfect, she began to realize, wasn't quite so . . . perfect.

THE NEW PERFECT

The new Mommy Wars bestowed some gifts: As we wrestled with our priorities, many of us finally began to define life on our own terms. We figured out which battles we actually wanted to fight, and which we wanted to surrender. We began to hear our own voices above the din, and we quelled the inner voice that said we needed to be "the best" at every single thing. This is where the "I Quit" moments came in. After all, not everything was worth it.

We started listening to our guts. And it worked. The Good Enoughs in the survey were much less likely to say that the pressures they felt came from external sources such as friends, family and society—28 percent compared to 41 percent of Never Enoughs. Our interviews also confirmed that the most satisfied women had stopped caring so much about external approval; they learned to identify their priorities and then protect them from the onslaught of contradictory messages.

But it took discipline—and that discipline took time to develop. Many of the women we interviewed said they had to *learn* to remain true to their own definitions of success. Even Molly Morse Limmer, who exudes the calm, controlled confidence of a woman who knows what she wants, didn't miss a beat when asked how she'd become so adept at protecting her priorities: "Practice."

Molly Morse Limmer, 37
Vice President and Head of Department for Antiquities, Christie's
Armonk, New York
Mother of Rosey and Lily
Daughter of Linda Morse

It really sucks at the beginning. I mean, when Rosey was an infant, I was so torn. I didn't know which way was up and how I was supposed to feel and what I was supposed to do. I always felt like there were eyes looking at my back when I was leaving [work]. And there probably were. But . . . I've just made it clear: This is it. This is what I do. It's not up for debate. When I know I have to work late—five or ten times a year—I'll do it. I know how to prioritize. But on your average day, I'll go home.

I've given up on trying to be a Supermom. I can't do everything, and I now know that. And I think every year, I get more comfortable with that. And I get more comfortable with myself and where I am as a parent. And as an employee. I don't feel that pressure now.

I had to learn it, for sure. I wanted to be able to do everything and do every-thing well. And it took, I mean Rosey's six and a half, and it has taken until now to get to a place where I'm totally comfortable not being perfect, and not being everything to everybody.

I'm still a perfectionist in every way. I'm a perfectionist in my job. I'm a per-fectionist as a mom. I beat myself up when I don't know what they wore during the day; you know, I leave when they're in pajamas, I come back and they're in pajamas. I'm a perfectionist as a friend and as a family member.

But, I don't have to be the best.

For Molly, being mediocre would never fly and, frankly, the words *good enough* make her uneasy. She equates it with settling, and that's something she never wants to do. She expects the best from herself in almost every arena, and that's one reason she has been so successful. Molly has learned to use perfec-tionism as a strength—squeezing out the good parts but turning away before the urge pulls her under. She's learned to be a perfectionist *without being per-fect*. There's a difference.

Perhaps most importantly, women like Molly have learned to focus on their passions.

"Having a daughter makes me want to love what I do," a female tele-vision executive told Becky. "If I don't love what I do, why am I away from her?"

For many women, following their hearts made everything easier. As attor-ney Libby Windsor describes it: "The secret to having it all is loving it all."

But loving it all doesn't always come easily, especially because so many of us grew up thinking that anything worth doing had to be hard.

* * *

When Alexis Martin Neely was in law school, she took the hardest tax class.

Not because she loved it—she didn't—but because she loved being the best in the hardest class. Winning, after all, felt good. The tougher the win, the better. After a while though, Alexis discovered that the effort it took to conquer something that didn't come naturally left her feeling exhausted and unfulfilled. She wondered, why wasn't it enough to work hard? Why didn't the pride and fulfillment automatically follow?

It wasn't until later—after she'd become a mother and joined a big law firm and discovered, to her shock, that the most prestigious legal venue did not offer the kind of life she wanted—that the lightbulb went on. Gradually, she began to rethink her strategy.

She quit the firm. And, in 2003, the same year her second child was born, she started her own estate planning practice. She consulted career and life coaches, and studied other successful entrepreneurs. Following her gut and applying what she'd learned, she crafted her business model around the idea of engaging clients and building lifetime relationships.

The climb was hard. In 2006, the same year that Alexis and her husband divorced, her business hit $1 million in revenue for the first time. Later that year, she launched the Family Wealth Planning Institute to share her approach with other lawyers. Two businesses, two kids.

Eventually, life started feeling crazy. So, in 2008, Alexis sold her law practice—and continued to fine-tune her attitude. "At some point," she said, "I learned that I can't be the best at everything."

To her surprise, her success—at work and at home—grew with this revelation. In 2008, the Family Wealth Planning Institute did just over $1 million in revenue; in 2009, it did about $1.5 million. She appeared on the *Today* show, *Good Morning America,* and CNN as a national expert in estate planning. What seemed miraculous to her is that by strategically adjusting her expectations, she had reaped more success. But it took some internal battles to figure it all out.

Alexis Martin Neely, 36
Lawyer and Entrepreneur
Boulder, Colorado
Mother of Kaia and Noah

I've only recently gotten in touch with my drive to be "the best." It's a positive thing because it's what drove me [to do so well in law school]. But when I'm not conscious of it, it's what makes me a workaholic and makes it hard for me to relax. How can you be the best without going overboard?

My style has shifted a lot. In the past, it has always just been: "Just do everything you have to do." There's not ever this need to stop and slow down. I can work nonstop for hours. But it's not good. It's not what I want in my life. I'm a "get it done" girl. It has served me in many ways, but it also didn't serve me in other ways. It was an escape.

[Now] before I say yes to something, I ask, "Is this something I'm just doing because of the challenge—or is this something I'm doing because I'm passionate about it?" If I'm only doing it for the challenge, I'm starting to say no. I try not to feed my ego. There's a big process of becoming aware of when I am being driven by the ego and not being driven by my higher self. . . my higher self that wants happiness and harmony and fun.

You have to let go of the things that you're not ever going to be the best at. I always had this underlying belief that I'm shedding now that something is only good if it's hard.

That's one of the biggest things I'm trying to work on with my kids: Life can be easy.

* * *

It can be a tough concept for a generation so accustomed to constantly raising the bar.

When Hollee joined the legal academy, she was convinced by her Baby Boomer mentor, Grace, that she should "walk like a duck." The phrase, common in the legal writing community, meant that Hollee should do all the same things the other tenure-track professors did; rather than be herself, she should follow a formula and, essentially, mimic her way to tenure.

So she tried. She wrote three long law review articles with hundreds of footnotes. It was hard (mostly because she was forcing herself to learn about areas of law she wasn't passionate about) and, worse, completely uninspiring. And then she found out that only a handful of people would ever read the articles. *Great,* Hollee thought, *I slaved over those footnotes for nothing.* It was not the writing career she'd had in mind. Still, Hollee continued to struggle, trying to convince herself that she needed to be at the highest rung, even if it meant forsaking her true passions and talents in favor of something that felt arduous and unnatural.

Much later, at an Association of Legal Writing Directors conference, she met several other thirtysomething women who shared her passion for legal writing and were equally serious about law school teaching—but didn't want tenure or its arcane scholarship requirements. They knew there were other ways to showcase their talents and make a mark. Buoyed by the unexpected camaraderie over this mutual frustration, the women vowed that they'd be quails, not ducks, and do it their own way.

PEACE TREATY: FINDING FREEDOM BY TAKING THE LONG VIEW

As our children grew, many of us found our internal battles giving way to the bigger-picture view. As we refined our priorities and grew more experienced as mothers, we began to see individual choices as less important than our overall record, rough patches less meaningful than our sense of fulfillment. Recognizing that we could mold a series of less-than-perfect days into something that balanced out in the long run made it easier to miss the first day of camp because we needed to be at work, or to accept that it was okay to take a few years off if that felt right. It was like the difference between viewing an impressionist painting up close—where all we would see is a jumble of seemingly incoherent dots—and stepping back to view it as a breathtaking scene.

Cathy Calhoun finds tremendous comfort in stepping back: "If you saw my calendar sometimes, you'd think I was going to Mommy Jail," she says, laughing. But the point is, it doesn't always look that way—and that's how she's built a successful career and raised a well-adjusted daughter.

Rarely, we've discovered, is a single day the perfect mix of family and work. Instead, work and the rest of life tend to move in seasons. We've found this to be true in our own lives. When we first signed a publishing deal for this book, we had to accept that our lives would be focused on work for the next seven months. Despite the book's title, settling for anything less than our best effort was unthinkable. But the New Perfect didn't require us to shortchange our work; it merely required us to focus our perfectionist tendencies in the areas that mattered most.

So Becky's typically insane standards for domestic neatness were going to have to sink. The dishes wouldn't always get done right away, not if a chapter needed polishing or she hadn't gotten enough time with Elizabeth and Katie that day. Hollee wouldn't donate her annual dinner party for the law student public interest auction; she'd go on fewer class field trips and give up her weekend routine of inviting her close friends for Sunday dinners.

Ten years from now, would anyone really judge us based on seven months of dirty dishes or remember that we'd only chaperoned one field trip? Would it matter that our husbands made all the school lunches (and all the breakfasts, too)? The choices seemed life-changing at the beginning, but as time wore on, we began to see that we couldn't define ourselves by seven months of work imbalance—just as we couldn't define ourselves by our career choices. It was possible that, in the end, these extremes would make for a richer picture of what our lives had been.

That's what we told ourselves, and each other. And, right then, it was enough.

THE GOOD (ENOUGH) WIFE

- Sometimes, the biggest problem is lack of time. Solve, don't blame.

- New jobs often mean readjusting the division of duties at home.

- Don't just focus on chore division; work on truly sharing with your spouse by investing equally in parenthood and housework. Share the "power."

- Sometimes our spouses can be our greatest assets.

Libby Windsor wasn't prepared for the stresses that came with the birth of her second son: the sheer exhaustion, the anxious jealousy of toddler Will, the feeling that she'd never have enough hours in the day to succeed as an attorney and a mother of two.

But what surprised her most was the bitter, aching strain that took root in her marriage to Ben. Reluctantly, Libby cut her hours at the law firm to 80 percent, trading salary and prestige because she felt so desperate to improve the situation at home. But relief just didn't come.

It was as if the things Libby loved about Ben—his sentimental yearning to watch their wedding video over and over; his willingness to drop everything to find the keys or the BlackBerry that she was constantly misplacing; the way he always "smelled like home"—were fading as she struggled to make it through the days.

She started focusing on her complaints, including her resentment that Ben seemed to need constant instruction when it came to caring for their expanded family. She had become his boss, meting out orders just to accomplish the domestic tasks that accumulated around them. And while Ben was willing to pitch in—coming home early if needed, changing the baby's diapers—Libby grew increasingly tired of having to *ask* for his help.

Worse was the internal drama that simmered after she'd finished billing her at-home hours each night. She'd forage for something to eat (the nanny took care of feeding the kids but the couple hadn't worked out a system for feeding themselves), then drag herself to the bedroom to claim a few hours of sleep before her sons' endless roulette of nightly wake-ups began. As she drifted off each night, Libby steamed over two inevitabilities: The first cry always seemed to come at the very moment she fell asleep—and Ben would most likely sleep through the entire thing on the brown velvet couch downstairs. In her mind, he simply didn't want to deal with "the nighttime drama of the two-year-old and the baby waking up and wanting to be in our bed at the same time."

And so Libby began to confront Ben, pleading with him not to leave her with "these two maniacs during every night shift." He offered some excuses the first three times; finally, he said he just couldn't help it and shouldn't be held responsible. Her anger, fueled by extreme sleep deprivation, began to boil over.

In September 2009, after a night in which she'd been up for almost five hours while Ben dozed a floor below, she delivered an ultimatum: Go to counseling with me to learn how to be more helpful—or I'm leaving you. She drove downtown to her office and spent the day fuming, stewing and exhausted. She called Ben and asked him to meet her at a park near their house after work; she called her nanny and asked her to drop the kids off at her mother's house.

Libby was prepared to make him suffer; Ben couldn't stand for anyone to be mad at him, and she could be stubborn.

But the second she saw her Ben—the effortlessly stylish man who had won her heart years before—she knew he was sorry. They talked for forty-five minutes, and Ben listened in a way that showed his regret over leaving Libby with so much of the responsibility. They resolved to go to counseling to learn to undo the bad habits they'd fallen into after fifteen years together, then walked to a restaurant for a glass of wine before heading home.

Just three months later, the incident seemed like a faraway memory, something that Libby almost couldn't believe had happened. "When you're in that period and not sleeping and trying to work, you're really at the end of your rope," she said. But she couldn't imagine how her life would have changed if she'd carried through on her threat. "I felt I didn't have the support I needed, but it turns out that I did."

Ben stopped falling asleep on the couch, Libby learned not to stew—and Will and baby Andrew started sleeping through the night.

Relief had come.

* * *

Our big effort to make work and family fit often hinges on the dynamics of our marriages. Marriages that, women will confess in hushed tones, aren't always so easy to nurture once they've had kids.

We heard it over and over in interviews: Women knew that strengthening their marriages would make things easier, but, frankly, some were too maxed out to do much about it. Even women who had strong marriages could rattle off examples of friends whose marital struggles had hampered their career options and, in some cases, kept them from working at all. One told Becky that she had friends with Ivy League degrees who looked at her with "such envy" because their husbands didn't want them to work.

In our survey, more than one in ten mothers said their *greatest* sacrifice had been their marriage or partnership. In their comments, some of these moms confessed that marriage had taken the bottom spot on the to-do list because there was just too much to sort out—division of chores, parenting techniques, even broader ideas about what role each partner should play in the family.

Modern marriage often feels like another game that we've been asked to play without a rule book. Many of us, like Libby, have found ourselves navigating what feels like barely charted territory; we're grateful that mothers' roles are no longer so strictly defined but unsure how to write the job description for a contemporary wife. Are we supposed to celebrate our femininity and relish all that makes our gender unique, or strive for absolute equality? What if we want a little of both? Can we have our proverbial cake and eat it, too—frosting and all?

Nikki Adcock Williams sure thought so when she met her husband-to-be, Tom, at the University of Kentucky School of Law in 1999. Nikki was a year ahead of Tom in school, and when he initially spotted her in the student lounge, he was struck by her confidence and assertiveness.

"Of course, I thought she was really cute," Tom told Hollee. "And she was also nice as can be. But it was clear that she was going somewhere."

Nikki's mom often jokes that her daughter majored in extracurricular activities as an undergraduate—she had been a student orientation leader, the social chair for her sorority, the president of the Greek honor society, and a member of a university choir that traveled to France and Belgium to perform.

That outgoing nature caught Tom's interest, and though it took some time to convince Nikki to go out for a cup of coffee, after that first date, they were "pretty much inseparable." By the time the pair got married in 2002, they seemed to have every advantage—a deep love, impressive degrees, exciting job prospects.

They knew they wanted kids, and they knew they both wanted careers. But not once during their dating years did they discuss how two ambitious lawyers were going to pull that off.

Things were different two or three generations ago. Through marriage, men and women gained efficiency by sharing production, with one (typically the wife) assuming responsibility for the home and children, and the other (typically the husband) supporting the family financially.[1] But, gradually, time-saving technology such as dishwashers and vacuum cleaners erased some of that economic benefit, and opportunities for women outside the home expanded. So marriage shifted to what some economists call a "consumption-based" model. People now tend to marry for love and companionship.[2]

So, as with other aspects of our lives, we find ourselves faced with more choices and, once again, wanting *everything*. We want independence combined with the nurturing support of a husband. We want an equitable division of household responsibility coupled with an ability to claim certain aspects of parenthood as our sole domain. In our interviews, moms repeatedly said that while they wanted their husbands to do more around the house, it was hard to not to jump in and make sure they did things the *right way*. Many almost reflexively referred to their husbands' role in housework as "helping"—and said that no matter how hard they tried to recast their thinking, they just couldn't shed the idea that the domestic buck stopped with them.

Our gains as wives are undeniable: Husbands *are* doing more housework and spending more time with their children; technology has continued to reduce the overall burden of household chores; and we have more freedom to choose when we have children and how we structure our families.

And yet some of us have found that reality hasn't meshed with our expectations; quite a few mothers we interviewed were surprised to find themselves grappling with domestic issues that seemed so . . . 1970. Study after study has shown that even though men are stepping up at home, women still do far more housework. Even in families where both parents have full-time, paid jobs outside the home. Even when the wife earns more.

But there's no simple solution. For many of us, hammering out an equitable partnership can be like solving a Rubik's Cube: In order to complete one side, we wind up throwing the other five out of whack. Getting it all to align can be frustrating and difficult. After all, we aren't the only ones redefining our roles, or the only ones feeling tapped out. The men of our generation grew up being told they could play with dolls and they grew up to be daddies who were willing to change diapers. But men, on average, still devote more time to paid work than women. What's more, when both paid and unpaid work are counted, mothers and fathers on average have the same weekly workload.[3] Increasingly, our husbands are asking: *Shouldn't we be allowed to combine work and family, too? What about us?*

Which sometimes leaves us twisting that Rubik's Cube—trying to reallocate our time, which we don't have enough of to begin with—and feeling as if we can't possibly get it all right. Sometimes we've wondered: *Does anyone have the answer?* In our research, we found that the women who were most satisfied with their work/family fit also tended to be the ones who described strong, equitable, communicative marriages. The survey backed this up: The women who felt they had "sacrificed too much at work or at home" were *more than twice as likely* to rate their ability to connect with their partner as a "disaster" or "not very good"—36 percent compared with 17 percent of women who felt their "sacrifices reflected their priorities."

But that brings us to the proverbial "chicken and egg" question: Did weak marital communication cause wives to sacrifice more than they wanted, or did their imbalance and exhaustion cause the communications breakdown? Anecdotally, the two factors seemed to interact symbiotically, creating a tightening spiral of discontent. To some, it was an unavoidable consequence of having taken on so much: Their marriages simply didn't make the cut when it came to doling out time that was already spread thin by jobs and children. This was the blunt calculation from three moms we surveyed:

Time spent with my husband . . . now goes to work. Relationship with my husband suffers. More stress at home.

My husband and I work different shifts so we can avoid the use of day care/babysitter. This also means we sacrifice most of our time together during the week.

My husband and I have opposite schedules now so our son is always with one of us.

One mom confessed in an interview: "You can't drop the ball on the kids part or the client part—and I shouldn't on the husband part, but it's the easiest thing to give."

Not surprisingly, the mothers who expressed the *least* frustration over division-of-labor issues were those who were lucky enough to hire help with cleaning or cooking—or who had simply let go of certain tasks or made peace with the house being less than perfect. Many of these women and their husbands still worked hard to divide the remaining duties equitably, but once they'd addressed the shortage of time even that was a bit easier.

But still, it wasn't a simple negotiation. For so many of us, marital triumphs and struggles are an inextricable part of our journey, both speeding and slowing the search for peace in our professional and personal lives. But one thing is for sure: Some of us prioritize our marriages because we have yet another huge legacy to overcome.

DAUGHTERS OF DIVORCE

Our childhoods weren't *all* girl power and go-get-'em. We grew up surrounded by failing marriages. Between 1965 and 1980, the annual divorce rate more than doubled, hitting a peak in 1981—and leaving a searing imprint on the girls and boys who would become today's parents.[4] Although researchers never pinpointed a single reason for the increase, the skyrocketing divorce rate coincided with the elimination of no-fault divorce in many states, the sexual revolution and the rise in women's workforce participation.

Divorce emerged as a consistent theme in our interviews. For the mothers who had experienced a parental split, either as children or young adults, the shadow of divorce lingered, influencing their attitudes about family and work, sometimes in seemingly contradictory ways. Not only had their experiences fostered a deep desire to create marital harmony in their own lives, but it had also made them crave personal and financial independence. In our survey, more than half the respondents said they worked so they wouldn't have to depend on their husband or partner for money.

One Massachusetts attorney, whose parents had gone through a bitter divorce when she was fourteen, told Hollee that she'd experienced an internal struggle over whether to change her name when she married. On one hand, she was eager to ditch the last name of a father who was no longer a part of her life. On the other, she knew that marriages didn't always last, and the "strong feminist" in her was reluctant to take her husband's name and give up a piece of who she'd been for twenty-six years. In the end, she took her husband's name, but used her maiden name as a middle initial: Danielle G. Van Ess. To her relief, Danielle found that she grew into the name—it became hers, not something that felt wrapped in her husband's identity.

Other women worried about losing their identities in more than just name alone. Some had seen their mothers struggle in the wake of a divorce, hampered by years spent out of the workforce, and these girls grew into women who were never going to depend on a man—for money or for their sense of self.

Julianne Lagerstrom, 35
Independent Consultant and National Vice President for a Network
Marketing Company
Mission Hills, Kansas
Mother of David, Reagan and Caroline

I think that my mom feels like she poured herself into our family, and now she doesn't have a whole lot to show for it. Now she's divorced, we're grown and we have our own lives. And I think that's very hard. She was a nurse before she had my sister. . . but then she was a stay-at-home mom.

I did think, I'm going to make a conscious effort to . . . not ever feel like everything revolves around my husband and my kids. I need to have stuff outside, for sure.

I knew that was critical for me. It's an identity issue.

Reconciling our competing needs for independence *and* happy, stable marriages convinced many of us that finding the right fit for both work and family was imperative. We knew we couldn't sacrifice too much of our professional selves, and we knew we needed to invest time in our marriages. Too many of us had seen firsthand the consequences of forgoing one or the other.

As Becky navigated her own choices, this became a recurring theme: Her mom, Judy, had given up too many dreams as a young woman.

Like her daughter, Judy had grown up dreaming of a journalism career, as a newspaper reporter or author. (As a teenager, Judy even envisioned her pen name: Allison Hall, after the Northwestern University dormitory she'd lived in during a high school journalism program in the summer of 1964.) She worked for her school newspapers in high school and college, studied journalism at the University of Missouri, and spent her summers interning at newspapers in St. Louis and Rochester. When she graduated, she had offers from several newspapers, including a plum job at Long Island's *Newsday*.

But she was also engaged to Becky's dad, Larry, a reporter at the *Times-Union,* the evening newspaper in Rochester. So Judy turned down *Newsday* and returned to Rochester as a reporter for several months before the wedding. It was a great time to be in a newsroom: 1969 was the summer of the moon landing, Woodstock and Ted Kennedy's car crash at Chappaquiddick. But those were also the waning days of Judy's newspaper career: Just before Thanksgiving, she left to get married, and though she'd intended to return to her career, things didn't go quite as planned.

For starters, Larry had been drafted into the U.S. Army, so after the wedding, the couple headed to Fort Sill in Lawton, Oklahoma, for ten months. Judy worked for a newspaper there and planned to reclaim her job in Rochester when they returned. But just before it was time to head back, the *Times-Union* sent a letter: Larry's job had been held during his military assignment, as required, but Judy's had not. The newspaper cited a nepotism policy that prevented them from hiring spouses. Larry went on to cover the Attica prison riots, and he began ascending the ranks, eventually becoming the paper's managing editor.

Meanwhile, Judy looked for a writing job, but with little luck. One employment agency steered her toward a receptionist position. She wasn't interested. So instead, she had babies: in 1972, Becky; in 1976, Peter. Judy loved being a mom, but felt a void in her life. She knew she was missing out on the writing career she'd planned. Still, she never really spoke up and, instead, fell into a traditional role. The choices, however, took their toll.

In 1993, when Becky's dad was being transferred to another city, Judy didn't want to give up her new career directing grants and sponsored programs at a local college. Other issues contributed, of course, but Judy's disappointment at having given up a career still lingered, and she couldn't bring herself to do it again. So she asked for a divorce.

When Becky struggled to make her own choices about work and family, she found herself mentally rehashing her parents' split. How, she wondered, would she avoid the regret her mother had felt but hadn't fully anticipated twenty years earlier? How would she ever reconcile her longing to be home with her babies with the knowledge that giving up too much could have devastating effects? Both Judy and Larry assured Becky that she was different, that times were different—and that their divorce, like most, was far more complicated than one decision. (And both wound up fine: Judy traveled the world and pursued her career; Larry built a happy life, remarrying and rearing two more daughters.)

Judy told Becky that the mere fact that she was thinking about these issues gave her a leg up. But, still, Judy's regret haunted Becky, and when she left the *Sun-Times,* Becky knew she'd have to tread carefully to avoid a similar fate. She felt sure she'd made the right choice for that moment—but she also knew she'd have to work on plan B.

And she'd have to do it soon.

* * *

Years later, Becky asked her mom what she would have done differently. Judy considered it for a moment and said, "I would have taken the job at *Newsday,* and I would have waited to get married." In retrospect, Judy figured she could have at least begun her career at *Newsday* while Larry was in Oklahoma; she could have had a longer engagement. But times were different. Only Judy's paternal grandmother, forward-thinking Mabel (the one who had chaired her local school board in the 1930s), expressed some worry at the timing: "She's still going to do her career, right?"

By the time we married our husbands—just two months apart in 1998, Becky at the age of twenty-six and Hollee at the age of twenty-four—women *were* waiting longer. Between 1970 and 1998, the median age of first-time brides rose from 20.8 to 25. By 2008, it had risen to nearly 26.[5] For many of the women interviewed, waiting to marry and have children—something most described as only partly intentional—offered an opportunity to build professional clout before facing the issues of blending work and family. When it came time to ask for a flexible schedule, these moms had already proven their worth; when they decided to switch jobs or start a business, they had years of work experience on their resumes. Some of the women (including both of us) had even "test-driven" marriage with their future husbands by living together first.

Some researchers believe the trend in delaying marriage has contributed to the decline in divorce: By 2007, the divorce rate was at its lowest point since 1970. The marriage rate also fell, but the couples who did tie the knot were more successful. Among men who married in the 1970s, about 23 percent had divorced by their tenth anniversary. The ten-year divorce rate for men married in 1990, however, was only 16 percent.[6]

But avoiding divorce wasn't the only item on our long list of expectations. Many of us entered marriage determined to find a level of equality we had not seen growing up. And though many of us found ourselves with husbands who shared this goal, putting it into practice—especially when it came to child care and housework—was often harder than we'd imagined.

SHARING ON THE SECOND SHIFT

It's easy to look at Kim Holstein, the pretzel company entrepreneur, and think that everything that seems *so right* about her life has just fallen into place. Maybe it's her easygoing demeanor or the fact that she seems so centered and self-assured. Maybe it's because she can readily articulate what makes her happy. Either way, it's a theory Kim is quick to debunk: Yes, she is happy. But, no, that didn't just happen, and it isn't an every-second-of-the-day kind of thing. Kim and Scott have worked hard for what they have—a life that fulfills them professionally, emotionally and spiritually. They talk. They work with a life coach. And they try to find solutions to time pressures, rather than blaming each other for the things that don't get done.

These efforts—and the freedoms that come with owning a successful business together—have bestowed an additional advantage: They are able to evenly share parenting and housework; both Kim and Scott richly experience family and career. In our survey, having a husband or partner who "helps enough at home" was among the factors that *most* contributed to the mother's ability to juggle work and family, ranking nearly as high as "an efficient and organized work style" and a "willingness to make sacrifices." And it was the factor about which moms were most emphatic: Nearly 43 percent "strongly agreed" that spousal support helped them juggle competing demands on their time.

Kimberly Oster Holstein, 43
President, CEO and "Chief Inspiration Officer"
Kim & Scott's Gourmet Pretzels
Wilmette, Illinois
Mother of Sonia, Daniella and Aiden

This is what I wanted in my life, to have a partner like [Scott]—it just feels right. I just feel like I can relate more to him, he can relate more to me. He understands what it feels like—and I know how he feels. It helps us to have a deeper relationship, and to be on the same plane. We try to help each other out.

Scott is a fabulous dad. He's fun and he's loving, he's caring. Especially as a dad with girls, he's really perceptive and sensitive. He's thoughtful. He's not perfect, but when he messes up, he's willing to apologize. He has a lot of fun with Aiden, doing a lot of "boy" things, playing baseball. He's just really involved in their lives.

Scott has really set out on a mission to be different [from his dad's generation]. He's just willing to grow.

We both feel there's a limit of time. But he has the same priorities as me. We have this passion to build this company, and we have this total passion, too, to build this family, and to be with our kids and have a good time.

Day to day, picking up, doing dishes, we just do the best we can. We don't really look at who's doing what. We used to have conflicts like that. But we realized, when we had our babies and we would have some conflict over something, that what it was really about was that we didn't have enough time. So instead of attacking each other, [we learned to say,] "What are we going to do about this?"

The mothers who described strong, egalitarian marriages told us that they worked very hard at it. After all, the shift in attitudes about gender roles hasn't been perfect or immediate, and it hasn't erased conflict over the division of household labor. Though men's contributions have increased, the infamous "second shift" of household chores that has dogged women since they entered the workplace still exists. Women are still doing about twice as much work around the house—even in families where both parents work.

Check out these findings from recent studies:

- In families where both parents were employed full-time, mothers spent an average of 2.1 hours per day on household activities (including housework, cooking and yardwork), while fathers spent about 1.4 hours doing those same things. However, fathers in two-career families spent more time at work—an average of about six hours per day compared to about five hours for their female counterparts.[7]

- Married mothers with full-time jobs were more likely to do housework on a given day than married fathers with full-time jobs: 56 percent to 18 percent.[8]

- Both at-home and working mothers are more likely to do jobs such as cleaning bathrooms and doing laundry, while fathers tend to do jobs like mowing the lawn and taking out the garbage. Mothers are much more likely than their male partners to be responsible for taking care of sick children, planning birthday parties and handling medical appointments.[9]

- Some 58 percent of women say the division of labor is not fair to them; 11 percent of men say the division of labor is not fair to them.[10]

What's shocking about that last statistic, is that *more* women don't say that the division of labor is unfair.

"When you look at most of the social institutions outside family, the opportunities for women have been increasing dramatically," explains Sampson Lee Blair, an associate professor of sociology at the University of Buffalo, who studies division of labor. "But inside the family, it's still just so traditional that it just boggles the mind. It is just so blatantly, so patently unfair that it's ridiculous."

What's more, he adds, the numbers don't even tell the whole story. They don't account for the fact that women tend to multitask their way through several jobs at once (often with a child in tow), while men tend to do one job from beginning to end. They don't account for the physical and psychological differences in the types of tasks women and men tend to do, which also tend to be imbalanced. (Women are more likely to shoulder the more grueling and boring "drudgery work.")

Researchers have various theories for why the inequality persists. But the most likely culprit, many say, is our own deeply ingrained social ideas about what makes for good mothers and fathers.

Sure enough, we spoke with many mothers who had found themselves inexplicably gravitating toward conventional gender roles, regardless of whether they worked outside the home. Even the Holsteins haven't escaped a slight but curious tug toward traditional roles. It isn't enough to cause conflict, but it does catch Kim's attention. Best she can figure, it's a reflection of the models she and Scott saw growing up.

"I will feel like a comment about our house is a criticism of me as the 'mother of the house,'" Kim told Becky one morning, as they sat at Kim's kitchen counter. It was a quiet Tuesday in December 2009, and the kitchen, which Kim had warned Becky was "a mess," didn't feel cluttered or sterile, just warm and welcoming. Sunlight poured in, and a big, white goldendoodle named Otis roamed about. ("He tends to eat everyone's shoes, and he'll ruin toys," Kim told Becky. "It's taught the kids that you can't take things so seriously. One minute you have something—the next, it's devoured by Otis.")

Kim reflected for a moment on the messages that she's somehow internalized about domestic responsibility. "There's that old message ingrained: I should be home nurturing, doing the scrapbooks, having everything in order; I should have all the clothes in the right age group. So, yeah, there's a little bit [of a draw to old ideas]. And I struggle with that conflict within myself."

"But—" and Kim smiled as she revealed the next part "—there's a part of me . . . I mean, when [the kids] are sick or hurt, I'm always the one front and center. And I love that. You know? I'm the Mom."

Some mothers, though, resent having adopted a greater responsibility for the housework, and several were frustrated by how hard it seemed to be to escape those tendencies. Some admitted that they had helped perpetuate that expectation, often taking the responsibility on themselves and refusing to give their partners an equal role. One mother, an executive who outearns her husband, admitted: "I don't want to be the only one taking care of things, but, at the same time, I'm territorial."

Several women said the issues emerged over time, particularly when the division of housework didn't automatically adjust to changing family dynamics. That was the case for Jennifer Pate, who began reexamining her domestic life after she returned to work.

* * *

Certain household duties come naturally to Jennifer: She enjoys cooking for her husband and takes great pride in nurturing her family. When her children were little, Jennifer loved being at home with them—caring for them all day, taking them to mommy-and-me classes—and she didn't regret leaving her job as a casting director to do it. But then the family moved for a year to Wilmington, North Carolina, where Jennifer's husband, Jonas, a director, writer and producer for television and film, was creating the TV series *Surface*. Before long, Jonas started talking about moving to North

Carolina permanently and, suddenly, Jennifer's feelings began to shift: "I went, *Oh my God . . .* I felt very sort of off my center. I felt like, *Wait a second, I'm now a stay-at-home mom, and I'm moving to the South, and I don't have a job. And I don't have my own identity.* And definitely that threw me. That was a hard time for me."

The Pates moved back to California, however, and a couple of years later, Jennifer found her groove again when she and Barb Machen launched their web series about motherhood, *Jen and Barb: Mom Life.* The show took on topics that genuinely interested the two women: marital communication, playdate etiquette, reentering the workforce, "having it all," stay-at-home fatherhood, sibling rivalry, in-laws, postpartum depression, body image. They featured guests like Paula Deen and author Ayelet Waldman, plus a variety of experts—pediatricians, psychologists, life coaches. And Jen and Barb willingly displayed their real selves. They discussed marital rough patches, showed footage of themselves without makeup and bantered in a playful way that revealed the closeness of their friendship. It felt *good* to Jennifer right from the start: She loved working with Barb, she loved creating something designed to bring women together, she loved "letting it all hang out."

The show—distributed by digital video company Broadband Enterprises, launched with major sponsors like S.C. Johnson and Kraft—was profitable from the day it went live.

It was also a fantastic fit: Jennifer's show allowed her to work on something that fulfilled her deeply and, because she had control over her time and was attuned to her priorities, she still found time to devote herself to the household tasks she loved. She reveled in being *both* an earner and a domestic caregiver. "I believe that women are nurturers. I believe that it shows our love to our family," she told the women at a roundtable we hosted to research the book. "I know for [my husband] that being cared for and cooked for makes him feel loved, and so I do it lovingly."

That didn't mean she enjoyed every aspect of domestic life—she loved being a wife and mother but disliked the mundane aspects of housework—or that she was equipped to carry a full load while also building a new career.

After all, *Jen and Barb: Mom Life* took off in ways even Jennifer hadn't predicted. By November 2009, the first fifty episodes of *Jen and Barb: Mom Life* had been viewed approximately 67 million times. A second season was in production, Jen and Barb had been filmed for an episode of the *Rachael Ray* show and the roster of sponsors was continuing to grow.

As her success, and duties, grew, she also realized this: She and Jonas weren't entirely prepared for the rigors of becoming a two-career family again. Jennifer had a lot going for her: Jonas was deeply supportive from the start, and the two were able to pay for help with cleaning and certain other household jobs. But there were plenty of duties that weren't, and wouldn't be, outsourced—and those fell most heavily on Jennifer.

Jennifer Pate, 43
Co-Executive Producer and Cohost of *Jen and Barb: Mom Life*
Los Angeles, California
Mother of Cooper and Lilah

It's been a big challenge, especially because I went into the traditional role for a while. My husband is an amazing guy... I really love him and we have a great partnership. But, I have to say, it has taken some real work to shift back because, when I was a stay-at-home mom... he really expected if he was making the money then I'm cleaning the house and doing the laundry, making the dinner.... He definitely expected me to be the "domestic person." He was the "working person." That I resented horribly. Of my stay-at-home motherhood time, I actually loved being with the children. But I hated being a "housewife."

It's been a little bit of a battle to make him understand: I'm working, too, now.

Now I am the "domestic person" and the "working person." There was this realization for me. When I went to New York to [be on] Rachael Ray a few weeks ago, I left pages: The kids need to be here, this is what they're doing, this is the class they take, this is whose house they're going to. This is my itinerary, this is the hotel I'm staying in. The whole thing, right? [But when] he goes to

Vancouver: A town car pulls up the driveway, and he jumps in and leaves. And I was like, "Wow, what different lives we have."

I said to him, "This is really getting unbalanced." And he's trying . . . But it's been a struggle to communicate with him nicely—I mean, I can be a little bit of a bitch about it and get really annoyed.

Other moms described a struggle that stemmed from not always sharing with their husbands the same domestic standards. Hollee's husband, John, a journalism professor and book author, wrote a humorous guest post for our blog, asserting that men tend to be more laid-back at home:

If you're married, chances are you have a Good Enough role model right in front of you.

Your husband.

Watch him. Study his child-rearing habits. He picks the kids up from school right on time (or a couple minutes late), instead of showing up fifteen minutes early to get an update from the teachers. He doesn't worry about whether the peanut-butter sandwich is sliced—choking on a little crust will only toughen up the kid, he reasons. He may believe that corporal punishment is ineffective, but he can forgive himself for swatting a kid's behind from time to time.

Even the man who is a perfectionist at work tends to slide smoothly into Good-Enoughness at home. It just comes more easily to us. We're naturals.

And one female reader, Melissa, responded:

That cracked me up! But perchance husbands are able to be "good enough" because they know their wives will pick up the slack . . .

That comment, though intended partly in jest, was another reflection of the ingrained social attitudes—and it reminded Becky of the games she and Pete sometimes played. When the girls were babies, Pete often expressed utter befuddlement at the assortment of matching Gymboree outfits in his daughters' nurseries. Becky rolled her eyes at this and wondered how a smart guy with an advanced degree couldn't figure out how to properly dress a baby. (Later, this developed into "The Daddy Special," which was Pete's name for the messy, lopsided ponytails he created when brushing his daughters' hair.)

Becky also found herself falling into an exhausting pattern with housework. Frustrated that Pete didn't clean the kitchen the "right way," she'd often push him out of the way and do the job herself.

And then complain that nobody helped.

That tendency, she later learned, reflected a somewhat controversial concept known as "gatekeeping" in which the mom controls her husband's level of involvement by essentially refusing to share the workload, insisting that things be done a certain way and adopting the role of "expert parent."

Becky began to wonder whether it really made sense to kick Pete out of the kitchen just because he didn't value streak-free stainless steel or perfectly swept floors the way she did. Was she keeping the kitchen clean—or creating a dangerous pattern? Did she really need to be the Queen Bee *that badly?* And what about all of the other smart women out there who were still fighting the urge to rule the domestic roost?

To help her better understand the forces at play, Becky turned to Francine M. Deutsch, a psychology professor at Mount Holyoke College and the author of *Halving It All: How Equally Shared Parenting Works*. Right off the bat, Becky learned that this push toward traditional roles, the ingrained attitudes other experts had referenced, could be seriously hard to avoid. Partly because they're *everywhere*—and partly because they tend to sneak up on us when we're not looking. Our language, our attitudes, even our little jokes push us subtly toward these roles. Like when someone asks a new mom what she plans to do about work—and nobody thinks to ask the same question of her husband. Or when we use the word *help* to describe men's contributions around the house. (This was a word we admittedly used in our survey and later regretted: "My husband/partner helps at home" was an answer choice when women were asked about the factors that helped them juggle competing demands on their time.)

"Women have internalized the idea of what it means to be a 'good mother,' and that often means being the 'number one parent,'" Francine told Becky.

"We often underestimate the relentless pressure on both women and men to play out these traditional roles. The expectation that the woman is the one in charge [at home], that the man is incompetent—it's relentless. And these social pressures are often invisible. People are being subjected to these pressures, but they almost don't realize what's happening, and they experience it as internal, as choice, as preference."

This helped explain why some of the smart, strong women we interviewed had found themselves surprised and disappointed to be falling into traditional roles they'd planned to reject, and why it took real work to overcome these tendencies. Francine's explanation also offered more insight into why we'd adopted these I-Must-Do-It-All attitudes.

But she had some good news for Becky, too: The movement toward equally shared parenting appears to be picking up speed. (To be sure, we interviewed a lot of women who were sharing equally, or at least working very hard to do so.) But, for many couples, it requires certain conditions. For instance, parents should have jobs of equal value—not necessarily in terms of salary, but in terms of respect. "Each person should be honored for the work they do outside the home to same extent," Francine said. They should be equally committed to sharing both the work and the "expert parent" role—and they should surround themselves with others who share, or at least support, their views.

The rewards, Francine told Becky, are immense.

"When I was writing the acknowledgments for my book, I wrote something like, *I don't have to thank [my husband] for sharing equally because he got to have the kind of relationship with my son that I have,*" she said. "Who would trade that for anything? It's like the best-kept secret that mothers get to have these deep relationships with their children that fathers often don't get to have."

And there's another benefit of shared parenting that Marc and Amy Vachon, two passionate advocates of the approach, told us about—more time for each parent to have some fun. The Vachons, authors of *Equally Shared Parenting: Rewriting the Rules for a New Generation of Parents,* entered parenthood determined to be peers in child care, career, housework and—yes—taking time for themselves. They believe that egalitarian parenting offers a solution to the frustration many working parents face because couples using their technique share in the work of parenting *and* the joy.

Their strategy touches on four main areas—child rearing, breadwinning, housework and recreation—and focuses on intentionally *sharing* rather than trying to divvy up tasks.

"There's a danger in scorekeeping—it turns everything into drudgery," Amy told Hollee. "What we tell people to do is step back and think about what they want their relationship to look like over time. This gets them on the same side of the solution. If they've got that mind-set, then deciding who does dishes on Tuesday becomes more than simply looking at that task."

"The key," she said, "is to focus on sharing power. There must be a two-person board of directors rather than one CEO and one underling," she said.

Some of the practical tips Amy and Marc shared:[11]

- When you are both home, trade off who's in charge of the kids and who is free to wander away to do chores, errands, or check email.

- You should not have to prepare for your absence when you head off for fun, the Vachons say: "Do not precook meals. Do not leave lists of things to do. Do not call home just to check on things; call home to say 'hello' and 'I love you' and to share your day, but not to make sure the kids are bathed."

- Try not to remind each other about child-care tasks. "If one parent begins to own all the remembering, the other will eventually abdicate this duty and dumb down."

- When dividing up housework, a couple should reach agreement on three basic points: (1) what needs to be done, (2) when it needs to be done, and (3) how thoroughly it needs to be done.

Finally, they added, letting go of perfect is an essential part of becoming equal sharers.

Marc Vachon, 47
Information Technology Specialist and Author
Watertown, Massachusetts
Father of Maia and Theo

I did not sign up for this lifestyle to do more dishes! We wanted to enjoy our lives like we did before we had kids. We had fun playing tennis and going hiking and with weekends away and we didn't want to give up what we had.

Let go of the definition of what you think perfect should look like, but don't let go of your ideals. If you think you want equal partnership, that ideal is worth holding on to. . . . It's not always easy, but it's worth the struggle.

THE NEW MARRIAGE: A CALM WITHIN THE STORM

Given what we know about social pressures and the difficulties we still encounter when dividing parenting and household chores, it's no wonder that the women we interviewed couldn't talk about work without referencing their marriages. It's all part of the same story.

But it's a story that wouldn't be complete without discussing how our husbands make things easier and, sometimes, *possible*. Modern marriage, after all, is more than a thorny thicket of conflicting gender roles and unwashed dishes. Some women interviewed singled out their husbands' support—emotional and otherwise—as the *one thing* they couldn't do without. For some of us, our husbands—and the dynamics of modern marriage in general—have been our greatest advantage.

Just ask Jen Canter.

* * *

The first thing you should know about Jen: There aren't many women in the world quite like her. She has two sets of twins and more than one career. She testified before Congress when she was seventeen. She's not afraid of the things that make most people turn away in discomfort or denial; she tends to look the ugliness of life right in the eye—and she has a hard time understanding people who won't.

As a teenager growing up in Rockville Centre, New York, Jen launched a grassroots effort to have warning labels put on alcohol bottles—and wound up meeting Senators Strom Thurmond and Al Gore, testifying before a U.S. Senate committee and playing a role in the passage of the Alcoholic Beverage Labeling Act of 1988. (One of Jen's favorite stories involves a Washington, D.C., lawyer calling her mom to explain that she couldn't ground a teenaged Jen because she might be needed to testify at a Senate hearing.)

When she became a doctor, Jen chose child abuse pediatrics, a specialty that requires her to confront the effects of cruel acts. As director of a medical child abuse program in Westchester County, New York, she's seen children who have been beaten, starved, locked away, sexually assaulted and murdered. Her job includes speaking the unspeakable: She regularly testifies about her findings in court. She tends to downplay the dramatic aspects of her job when she talks about it. She also teaches, focuses on prevention and is often in a position to reassure parents that an injury or behavior *isn't* the result of abuse.

Jen's story, in many ways, reflects our generation's collective journey. She leapt into adulthood determined to make the most of the choices she'd inherited from her predecessors, throwing herself full throttle into a medical career, motherhood and, eventually, the founding of her own educational toy company.

And, largely, she's succeeded, even though it has meant precariously riding the waves (and occasionally being pulled under) as everything in her life surged forward simultaneously. Despite her discipline and motivation, Jen is occasionally forced to acknowledge that she's, well, human: She can't always do everything she wants to do, and pitfalls sometimes throw her unexpectedly off course. Sometimes it feels like this period in her life is the one that will define her as a mother, a doctor, an entrepreneur, a wife. Yet, at her core, Jen is a problem solver who tends to forge ahead even when life ebbs instead of flows, who readjusts when she finds herself stymied or stuck or simply exhausted.

But there's a reason her story picks up here, in a chapter about marriage: For all her independence, one of Jen's greatest assets in riding these waves is that she hasn't ridden them alone. At the center of her chaotic and exhilarating journey is her husband, Wade. It is because of Wade that Jen has the room to flex her ambition without worrying that she'll drown; it is with him that all things feel possible.

Jen Canter, 38
Child Abuse Pediatrician and Owner of Educational Toy
Company, Play This Way Every Day
Westchester County, New York
Mother of two sets of twins

I don't have a husband who needs me to cook for him every day. I don't have a husband who doesn't want a strong, successful woman as a partner. I don't have a husband who is intimidated by my success, which is a huge thing. Thank God. . . . I put really high standards on myself, things I want to accomplish. And I just feel really run-down sometimes, and really, really overwhelmed and tired. It's a joke that I finished my [child abuse specialty] board exam that I've been studying for for a year and, all of a sudden, I only have four kids, a husband, my business and my full-time job to deal with—and I feel relaxed. It's kind of comical.

Thank God for my husband. I mean, I think with this kind of life, having a really strong marriage where we are totally best friends [makes a big difference]. We are interested in the same kinds of things. We love watching reality TV and zoning out and going to a movie, we just like to do the same things. He's my best, best, best friend.

And if I didn't have him, forget it, I would just be so lost. . . . We roll with the punches. We talk things through. We have a great way of laughing at whatever it is.

For us, success isn't money, it's stability. And whatever that means, we are in it together.

When Becky interviewed Jen, that commitment to stability and harmony was revealed in the moments when she spoke about her husband and kids, and her typically bold, hurried voice would soften and slow with unbridled affection. Suddenly, it was easy to see how *ambitious doctor* and *loving wife and mother* could coexist so seamlessly in one woman.

Jen and Wade are not the "perfect couple." They sometimes irritate each other or squabble over the division of labor. But, in the end, they *get* each other in a way that gives them shelter in the maelstrom of life. And that makes all the difference. Wade can make one simple statement, like "Jen, it's not the end of the world" or "Jen, just relax." And it will be just what she needs at that moment.

I don't have to check with him about how he's going to think about certain things. I kind of know—I think we get each other. I really have a partner. I'm really thankful that I have somebody who is on my team.

There's times . . . when we'll look [at one of our kids], like the other morning, we're looking at one of our sons . . . and we're both kissing him. And I said, "You know, isn't it so nice to both be the one who's most in love with this baby?" And that's what it is: We both have a common goal. We love these four awesome kids, and we both want what's best for these great kids.

No matter what it means, no matter what house we have to live in or how long we have to work, or how much one of us might not be happy at work for a period of time . . . It's not just about us, it's about our family. And we both have that focus.

The shared focus gives them the room to weigh risks and ideas as a team—rather than adversaries bent on swaying the other to a "winning" point of view. Wade, a lawyer working in the financial industry, spent years listening to Jen's entrepreneurial musings; once she wanted to sell homemade farmer's cheese; once she devised a plan to open a gift shop. Thoughtfully, he'd assess what Jen calls "my harebrained schemes"—and she respected his judgments. He would tell her it wasn't the best idea, and Jen would know he was right. It wasn't a threat to her autonomy—it is hard to imagine Jen forgoing anything that means a lot to her—it simply was feedback from a deeply trusted source.

But then, in 2008, Jen had a sudden brainstorm during their son's speech therapy sessions. She decided that she'd create a durable play mat with interchangeable cards that could be used by parents with their toddlers, or by speech and occupational therapists. And she'd shape it like a U, so the child could be in the center. Wade saw the potential right away—and, together, they set about making Jen's vision a reality.

I always felt the speech therapist had ways of playing with my child that I didn't. Play didn't come naturally, and I wanted to be better at it. I thought . . . maybe I could develop something that could help parents like me.

We started from scratch, reading books. We'd put the kids to bed at night and work on it.

I realized my excitement early on was not as exciting for everyone. But Wade—he totally got it.

Together, Jen and Wade developed the concept for the U-Play Mat, the product that would launch their toy company. They hired a law firm to complete a patent application, and they found a designer and a manufacturer. Soon, they also had a publicist and a website. And, of course, naysayers: Not everyone believed they'd succeed. A few well-meaning friends thought it was impossible.

By fall 2009, Play This Way Every Day was accepting orders for the U-Play Mat online and Jen and Wade were officially in business.

In many ways, it wasn't surprising: The first time Becky had interviewed Jen, she could tell the energetic doctor felt supported and secure. The way she spoke, the stories she told—it was clear that she wasn't afraid to risk failure.

"I know I'm walking on a tightrope," Jen told Becky. "I have to accept that I'm going to fall sometimes. But I'm a mother, so I have to get back on. . . . I don't have the need to be perfect. I have the need to be real."

It is plain to see why the tightrope isn't so scary: Jen has Wade to catch her if she falls.

5

FINDING THE RIGHT FIT AT WORK

- One size rarely fits all.

- Determine what you want.

- Figure out what *you're* willing to do to make it work—and remember what you bring to the table. Flexibility is a two-way street.

- Consider all the obstacles.

- Don't make choices based on guilt and fear.

- Think big.

- Do what you love.

Becky was lying in bed, staring at her pregnant belly bulging under the thick duvet. She'd jerked awake a few minutes before and had been startled to see the right half of the bed still empty. It was 2:00 a.m., the wee hours of Christmas Eve, 2003.

Pete was still at work.

She'd kissed him goodbye sixteen hours earlier, in the hallway outside her obstetrician's office. They'd just seen their second child on the ultrasound monitor, another girl. Two-year-old Elizabeth had been with them, and she'd jumped out of Pete's lap upon hearing the news: "We'll call her Baby Katie!

Look, it's Baby Katie!" And Becky and Pete had agreed: Katie it would be, short for Katharine.

Becky had spent all day calling family members to share the news—and trying, in vain, to prepare for Christmas while chasing an excited toddler around the house. Relatives were coming over to celebrate after church and she figured she'd clean the house and make food on Christmas Eve morning, when Pete would be home.

But now it was just thirteen hours before they needed to leave for Mass—and his pillow was still cold. It had been less than nine months since Becky had left the *Sun-Times,* and, already, she knew that quitting hadn't solved everything. Even though she wasn't "working," she was always behind, and she had become increasingly convinced that she'd never be able to fit *any* kind of paid work back into her life.

Becky reached in the dark for the phone and dialed Pete's office. "Where *are* you?" she asked when he picked up. He sounded tired—and, he told her, not even close to done. She told him to drink coffee and hurry.

Two hours later, she called him again.

His voice was considerably more alert. "Baby, I'm on *fire,*" he practically shouted. He was overtired and completely jacked up on caffeine.

"Hurry," she told him.

When Becky got up with Elizabeth in the morning, Pete was *still* at work. He called a couple of times with updates, his voice becoming progressively more hollow. When he finally pulled up in a cab early that afternoon, he was wiped out—and Becky was in a messy kitchen, frantically rolling green olives into some cheddar dough that was absolutely the wrong consistency. Elizabeth was cranky and bored and weaving a path of destruction through their house, which still wasn't fully unpacked from their move just a month before. It was almost comical to think back on it years later: Becky had been *literally* barefoot and pregnant and covered in cheese, while her child ran wild and her husband worked late. Not the life she'd envisioned while earning that Northwestern journalism degree.

Pete took off his coat. "Your mom said you should skip church and take a nap," Becky told him.

Pete shook his head. He preferred to spend Christmas Eve playing with his daughter. And he wasn't interested in missing anything else, including Christmas Eve Mass. So he took Elizabeth to church while Becky stayed behind and did the best she could with what were turning out to be fairly limited domestic skills. Later, when their guests had left, Pete stayed up with Becky to prepare the living room for Christmas morning before finally heading to bed, forty hours after he'd left it. It was a much-needed prize: A full-night's sleep followed by a quiet Christmas morning.

Except a few hours later, Elizabeth crawled into their bed, laid a feverish cheek against Becky's hand—and threw up all over the pale green duvet.

* * *

This is how it was for the first decade of Pete and Becky's marriage. Pete was an associate at a major global law firm, doing what was necessary to keep the partners happy—working late, working weekends. As much as she valued the opportunity to spend her days with the girls, Becky was more exhausted and overwhelmed than she'd anticipated. Becky and Pete knew they were *very* lucky; and complaining made Becky feel guilty. For a long time, this guilt—and a mild fear of change—kept her from acting: *What right did she have to expect better for herself when she already had it pretty good?*

What bothered Becky, when she let herself think about it, was that she'd started out making what seemed like a *choice.* And now she felt trapped by it.

How had she wound up here? She felt as if she and Pete had jumped into a wagon that was now careening downhill, completely out of control. Becky began to wish for some way—any way—out.

In 2009, she got it. The economy tanked, and thousands of big-firm lawyers lost their jobs. Pete was one of them.

WHY "FLEX" OFTEN ISN'T GOOD ENOUGH

As Becky began learning more about work/life flexibility, she realized that she and Pete had made a mistake in always considering their careers as isolated choices. They had failed to look at them as pieces of the same puzzle.

In fact, Becky was guilty of more or less the same thing that has kept major companies from successfully implementing flexible work/life options: She was thinking about her career as an all-or-nothing proposition (work or stay home) with a few limited possibilities (working two or three days a week in the same job she'd had before kids) in between. Even when she looked at more creative options, she found herself stuck because she'd failed to consider her entire reality; she just wasn't seeing the big picture or thinking enough about what *she* needed to do to meet her own definition of success.

So here's our generation's big work/life revelation: We can't pluck a "flexible" option from a limited rack ("I know, I'll work part-time!") and expect it to fit like a handmade gown. What seems like a miracle solution for one woman is a disaster for another. After all, we have different lives, different jobs—even different reasons for wanting to work. (In the survey, the leading reasons women worked were financial necessity, a desire to feel accomplishment outside the home, a desire for financial independence, passion for their jobs, and needing a "break from being a mom.") We sometimes talk about "part-time" or "work from home" as if these arrangements have only one shape, and we try to squeeze ourselves into categories without realizing that what we really need is a little tailoring—and a better understanding of our individual priorities and limitations. One size or style can't possibly fit all.

It just winds up feeling a little like . . . Mom Jeans.

Remember those? From the *Saturday Night Live* commercial parody? The sketch depicted a group of women bouncing out of their minivans in unattractive, high-waist, elasticized jeans—apparently the only decent fit available now that they'd given birth. But it wasn't just the hideous pants that made the sketch so funny, it was the voice-over: "She'll *love* the nine-inch zipper and casual front pleats.... Give her something that says, 'I'm not a woman anymore. I'm a Mom!'"

It might have been even funnier if it didn't ring true. Let's face it, there's a parallel here. Like jeans, our jobs don't always fit once we've had kids. And, often, in lieu of better choices, we take flexible work arrangements that are sort of like, well, Mom Jeans. They don't really fit, and they practically scream, *I'm not a woman anymore. I'm a Mom!*

No wonder so many "work/life balance" opportunities have been under-utilized, rejected for their poor fit or morale-busting powers. They leave many women feeling like "square pegs in round holes," as author (and mother) Kristin Maschka describes it in her book on "remodeling" motherhood, aptly titled *This Is Not How I Thought It Would Be.* Our needs go beyond what any checklist of simple "accommodations" could possibly provide.

But a revolution is under way, and the New Perfect is part of it. As working mothers continue to integrate and customize our lives in ways our predecessors could never have imagined, we are changing the professional landscape and bringing new rules to the game. Increasingly, we've refused to settle for one-size-fits-all policies that leave us feeling "mommy tracked" or undervalued. After all, taking more time with our kids doesn't preclude us from contributing at work in meaningful ways that actually *enhance* our careers. We just don't always want to take a traditional linear path; these days, we are just as apt to scale a "corporate lattice"[1] that lets us move up, down and sideways as we fit together the many pieces of our lives.

We're leveraging our talent and experience—and all that professional capital we earned pre-kids—to lobby for flexible options that *actually work.* When we've found them, we've shown that we know how to work smarter rather than longer. And when we haven't gotten what we needed, some of us have quit and sought better ways to fulfill our personal definitions of success.

Not that it has been easy. Some, like Becky, have struggled to see the big picture; others have wrestled with guilt or other Never Enough tendencies that have us saying "yes" to just about everything. And not every workplace has implemented a successful flexibility strategy, which means that some of us have had to work particularly hard to get what we need.

Tory Johnson, 39
Founder and CEO of Women for Hire and Author of
Will Work from Home
Workplace Contributor, *Good Morning America*
New York City
Mother of two

It's so easy to give lip service to the idea that we should lift our voices and flex our muscles, but the reality is that . . . some workplaces are not open—it takes more work. [That] doesn't mean you shouldn't speak up, but it's going to be an uphill battle, and you prepare differently for mountain climbing versus taking a walk.

It is completely based on the culture of where you work—even more so than the work you do. It's the people you work with, how tolerant the culture is.

In some ways, it's difficult because of this. You wish you could get a cookie-cutter formula for doing it.

Some have struggled because companies fear being perceived as "unfair" if they deviate from a fixed policy, or afraid that a change for one employee will either be abused or lead to a cascade of requests that can't be filled. In Becky and Hollee's study, about 26 percent of women said their ability to juggle work and family was impeded by a job that wasn't flexible enough.

Early on in her research, Becky interviewed a Los Angeles attorney who was commuting an hour round-trip each day because her firm had refused her request to work from one of their other offices, just ten minutes from her home. That extra time would have made a huge difference: The woman could have spent it with her two young children, or even billing clients. But the firm didn't want to set a precedent of people "switching offices for reasons of personal convenience," she told Becky, the bitterness still evident in her voice. "It was such a small token they could have thrown my way."

That firm wasn't the only company to shy away from customization: In one survey, 45 percent of chief financial officers reported a concern that any flexible arrangement had to be offered to either all employees or no employees.[2]

Other women had options available, but felt they would be—or had been—penalized for taking advantage of them. In our survey, one woman wrote: "I am still a partner in my law firm, but I don't feel like I am as respected as I used to be because I don't work as hard as I did before children." Studies confirm that women who work reduced hours face a "flexibility stigma" or "career penalty"; one study showed that 43 percent of working parents believed that working flexibly would jeopardize their job advancement.[3] And that's why, as we push toward a real integration of work and family, we need to see what Becky couldn't when she slipped on her part-time "Mom Jeans" and then melted down because they didn't fit.

Flexibility is part of something much bigger—and it isn't just about *moms*.

CREATING A WORK/LIFE BALANCE THAT WORKS FOR YOU

Cali Williams Yost has been saying that for years.

A work/life flexibility strategist who has successfully fit a big career and motherhood into her own life, Cali treats flexibility as part of an overall business strategy, not just as policies and perks aimed at women. True, mothers leaving are often the motivator because maternity is a more visible life change than, say, the man who needs to leave work early because his dad has Alzheimer's. "But," Cali said, "making flexibility a female issue actually hurts women."

"I try very hard to keep it about everybody—and I do that because it's the truth," she says. "What's happening is, because we keep making this about women, it's reinforcing a bias that's not accurate . . . which, in turn, is hurting women. So managers think if they hire a woman, she's going to have kids and she's going to leave. [They think], 'If I hire everybody else, they're going to stick around.' And that's not true necessarily. It helps women much more if we keep this about all of us—and about women having babies as just one of the many transitions we all have to manage."

So Cali advocates policies that allow employees, both men and women, to tailor their jobs to meet the unique realities of their lives and their careers—and to alter them as those realities change. For companies, this means having a culture that embraces flexibility. For employees, this means doing what the Good Enoughs in the New Perfect survey did well: Knowing your priorities and revising your thinking to achieve them.

How do you go about this? As Cali advises, figure out what you really want, come up with a realistic plan and present it to your manager. Her advice:

- You have to define what it is you want. "Most people will spend three hours telling me what they don't want," Cali explains. "But when I say, 'Okay, but what *do* you want?' they really don't know." It's essential to determine what you want in order to structure a situation that works best for you.

- Break out of all-or-nothing thinking. In her practice, Cali finds that people tend to be very extreme in their thinking, "Either I'm in or I'm out." But that's not necessarily true, nor will it help you structure a work/life balance that really works. Instead of focusing on what you *can't* do—focus on what you *could* do.

- Be flexible in your definition of success. Often, this means adapting your pre-baby ideas to feel okay about what you're doing now. "You may not be gunning for CEO for the next few months, but you're hanging in there. And that's okay," Cali says. This can be hard for high-achieving people, she adds. But it's worth it.

- The final step is having a clear plan and then presenting it to a manager. "It is not them coming to you," Cali says. "They do not know your life, and they probably do not know how you are doing your job."

Cali herself has been very specific in setting her goals and acknowledging her priorities and limitations. When she can't volunteer at school, she doesn't feel guilty about it. Sometimes, she's really busy at work; other times, she's managed her work/life fit so that she has more time to spend at home.

Cali Williams Yost, 45
CEO and Founder of Flex+Strategy Group/Work+Life Fit, Inc.
Author of *Work + Life: Finding the Fit That's Right for You*
New York City Metro Area
Mother of two daughters

It's an active, ongoing, everyday process. I saw pretty early on in my work that the people who managed their work/life fit successfully were the people who were active in how they managed their definition of success and got rid of the guilt. They were pretty clear in what they could and couldn't do. And most of them were just fine in terms of how they thought their family lives were going, they just made peace with what they were going to do.

I found [that for] the ones who kvetched and felt bad about it all the time, it wasn't working. And it wasn't going to work.

After speaking to Cali, Becky couldn't help but reflect on the narrow view she had taken of work/life fit in those early years of motherhood. Back then, she hadn't stopped to spell out her personal definition of success. In retrospect, that definition seemed simple: She wanted more time at home to enjoy motherhood, she wanted control over her schedule—and she wanted to write stories that would allow her to immerse herself in data, research and people's experiences. That last part was what brought her alive professionally.

But she hadn't sat down to figure out how on earth she'd fully immerse herself in people's stories while working only two days a week. If she had spelled out her specific goals back then, she could have assessed whether a newspaper was the best place to accomplish them, given her circumstances. Instead, she analyzed her professional possibilities through a single lens: the number of hours she would be working each week.

And, clearly, that wasn't the only issue that needed to be considered. Because in 2010, as Becky was writing this very chapter, she was working at least three times the number of hours—and, because it was exactly what she loved doing, it was a perfect fit.

* * *

The fact is, a lot of factors go into figuring out what works—and that part was evident as we interviewed moms and discussed their choices. Those who had found the right mix hadn't necessarily found it immediately. But they knew what they wanted, and they hadn't been afraid to admit when something wasn't working.

When Gena Gerard's first child was born in 2002, she had been putting her master's degree in public affairs to good use for five years. She was heading a Minneapolis program to combat street crime and her job was her "other baby," a giant source of self-fulfillment.

She wasn't interested in a drastic change—and she certainly wasn't interested in quitting—so when she came back from maternity leave she asked whether she could reduce her work hours, just a little.

Her "Wednesdays off with Claire" routine worked for a little while, but as the organization grew, so did the demands on Gena's time. After her son was born in 2004, she tried to manage the competing responsibilities, often cramming in unfinished work after putting the kids to sleep. That's when she started feeling really pinched; it just wasn't working anymore.

So Gena, who describes herself as a "bit obsessive and happy to work hard on something I love," decided to make another change. She started focusing on a business idea that had been brewing in her mind since Claire was a baby. It would take some trial and error to go down the entrepreneurial path she was imagining, but Gena was passionate, gutsy and determined.

Which was a good thing because—as we'll describe later—fate was about to pave the way for Gena to leap feetfirst into her new dream.

That was a common thread for the most successful women: They'd been willing to take action. Their secret wasn't that they'd avoided sacrifice—it was that they'd *chosen* the sacrifices that best suited their priorities. Instead of trying to squeeze themselves into an ill-fitting pair of Mom Jeans, they'd found the solutions that actually worked.

And some of them did this by cashing in the professional capital they earned back when they firmly believed they could Have It All.

LEVERAGING OUR POWER: REPUTATION AND PASSION COUNT

There are a few things you should know about *New York Times* reporter Rachel Swarns and how she wound up covering First Lady Michelle Obama despite working only four days a week.

First of all, Rachel is disciplined, she knows how to use her time effectively and, if work needs to be done on her day off, she just does it. Also, she "love, love, *loves*" her job. (This last point is a big one: The most successful and satisfied women we interviewed described immense passion for their work and cited this as a tremendous advantage in choosing how to juggle work and home life.)

When she became a mother at thirty-seven, Rachel had racked up a couple decades' worth of accomplishments. She'd worked hard in school and learned Spanish, a skill she later used as a reporter. She'd majored in Spanish and minored in African and Caribbean studies at Howard University before going on to earn a master's degree in international relations at the University of Kent at Canterbury in the United Kingdom. Ambitious from the start, she'd climbed quickly from the *St. Petersburg Times* in southwest Florida to the *Miami Herald* to the *New York Times*.

She'd traveled the world as a reporter: Haiti, Cuba, Russia, Africa. She'd spent three-and-a-half years as chief of the *New York Times* bureau in Johannesburg, South Africa, and covered immigration out of the Washington, D.C., bureau. By the time she had kids, she'd built a reputation. People knew her work ethic.

Still, when she asked to take a year of maternity leave after the birth of her first child in 2004, she approached it "with some trepidation." She knew her editors didn't have to say yes. But they did.

Near the end of her leave, she asked to return part-time, and that request was granted, as well. It helped, she says, that her bosses had experience with other part-time reporters. "They had seen [that] these situations could work." She continued to cover immigration and then, after the 2008 election, was assigned to cover the First Family—a beat that eventually led to a book deal.

Though she had always planned to be a devoted mom, Rachel never really thought about how career and motherhood would fit together. Looking back on it the day after her oldest son's fourth birthday, Rachel laughed at her own "haphazard" approach: "It all just sort of worked out."

But the truth is, although she didn't draw up a detailed plan for achieving a good work/family fit, Rachel made a lot of conscious decisions that contributed to her flexibility. She and her husband aggressively saved money while on assignment in South Africa because the possibility of taking time off from work after children was floating in the back of her mind. She demonstrated reliability: She almost always travels when needed and jumps in willingly, and often, on her day off. (She and her husband, a *Washington Post* reporter, employ their nanny five days a week to make this possible.)

"Whenever I need to work, there's never a question," she says. "I always work when I have to because I never want the fact that I'm working four days to become a problem."

In other words, Rachel came into the situation with a lot to offer—but then did everything she could to ensure that her arrangement worked. When John McCain selected Sarah Palin as his running mate, Rachel was called over the weekend to help write about mothers' reactions to the pick. Her babysitter wasn't available, and she had family in town. So she worked during naptime and after bedtime—in her characteristic style, she just got it done.

She also strategically pursued beats that allowed her more flexibility: "I'm not covering Congress or the White House or the State Department. I really felt like I wanted to be realistic about what I could do."

Her dedication continued to pay off: In late 2009, a story she wrote about Mrs. Obama's ancestry—a complicated lineage with roots in slavery—resulted in an email from HarperCollins asking if she had considered writing a book on the subject. By January, she was on sabbatical from the newspaper, fully enmeshed in research—and still trying to make the most of a Tuesday-to-Friday workweek.

And here's the thing: It's doubtful that anyone handed Rachel Swarns a flexible schedule just because she was a mother—they did it, most likely, because they wanted to keep her on the staff.

In other words: Flexible work arrangements are often (and should be) two-way streets. Both sides get something out of it.

In fact, studies have shown that companies with the highest representation of women in top management perform better financially.[4] Claire Shipman and Katty Kay said it well in their 2009 bestseller, *Womenomics*:

> *It's clear: A company "allowing" you to work the way you want isn't doing you a favor; it's making a strategic decision. Businesses want employees who boost profits. . . .*
>
> *So next time you're sitting at your desk far too long, are missing soccer practice for the forty-third time, are dreading your child's face as you show up late, and are wondering whether it is finally getting to be too much and whether tomorrow is the day to hand in your resignation, don't despair. Stop. Take a deep breath and remember pink profits. You know the expression—"Every good career woman is just one bad day away from quitting"? Well, it doesn't have to be true. You don't have to quit.*

THE RIGHT KIND OF CUSTOMIZATION

The key, of course, is assembling the individual puzzle pieces in just the right way. Rachel's arrangement worked because it acknowledged the unique circumstances of her life: It gave her the extra time she wanted at home with her two sons during the week but also made room for the unpredictability of the news business. (Rachel said she wound up working on Mondays, her day off, about 60 percent of the time before leaving to write her book. And she was okay with that.) Rachel chose her sacrifices in a way that reflected *her* top priorities. She wasn't biding her time in an unfulfilling job; she was still writing stories that she wanted to write.

Similarly, one of Hollee's dearest friends Lisa Tannenbaum, thirty-six, has a job arrangement that reflects the seams and stitches of good tailoring. And like any good fit, Lisa's position probably doesn't look exactly like anyone else's, though it closely resembles the work arrangement of her Deloitte Services job-share partner, Sandy Francis, thirty-eight. Together, Lisa and Sandy fill a single human resources manager position within a company that has become well-known for its career customization.

At Deloitte, employees work with their managers to adjust their career paths as their lives evolve. Instead of a single option to move in one direction—up the corporate ladder, working full-time and continuously—employees are able to scale a corporate lattice that allows them to move up, down and sideways to fit their personal and professional goals. There are boundaries, of course, and a formal structure—one that encourages continual collaboration. Unlike flexible work arrangements, which are often seen as exceptions to the norm, this system is part of the corporate culture. It also provides for multiple ebbs and flows, as opposed to providing single, short-term accommodations for specific events. Deloitte calls it "Mass Career Customization."[5]

In Lisa and Sandy's case, this customization looks a bit like a two-headed monster; that's how people sometimes see them. The two moms split their days evenly. (Lisa works Mondays and Wednesdays, Sandy works Tuesdays and Thursdays, and they both work Fridays.) They each have access to the other's email accounts, update each other via long voice mails at the end of each day, and text throughout the day. People often interchange their names, which merely reassures them that they've created a seamless arrangement.

But here's the best part: Lisa and Sandy even managed to snag a promotion as the "two-headed monster"—coordinating their resumes together, posting for jobs together and even interviewing together.

"To my knowledge, it had never been done before, so people didn't know how it would work," Lisa explained. "We had to prove ourselves in the interview process, and we reached out to people who had worked with us in the past and knew what a good deal it was to work with us as a team."

While the promotion isn't without sacrifice—Lisa can't completely "check out" on her days at home, as she used to, and she and Sandy have to coordinate more than ever—it was the right time for the pair to advance, and she feels lucky that her workplace took the risk.

"We knew it would work, and we were happy to be given the chance to prove it," Lisa said.

Deloitte, of course, isn't the only company that has taken a customized approach to managing employees' shifting needs. Cathy Calhoun, the frequent-flying PR executive from chapter 3, has spent years considering the ways to mesh life and career. She's learned a thing or two about what works and what doesn't, and she's a big believer in the important roles that communication and teamwork play in figuring this all out. "Rigidity," she says, "is the enemy here."

As Cathy shared her insights with Becky in the fall of 2009, she couldn't help but note its particular relevance. Work/family fit was unusually high on Cathy's radar right then.

* * *

That was the year the Chicago office of Weber Shandwick experienced the baby boom: thirteen women expecting a total of sixteen babies.

Which meant about 5 percent of the Weber Shandwick workforce in that city had to figure out—at roughly the same time—how to fit their careers with a new or expanded family.

As the global PR firm's North American president, Cathy wasn't the one directly negotiating family leave and flexible scheduling; Chicago is only one of the twenty offices Cathy oversees in the United States and Canada, though it happens to be her home base. Still, the situation drew her attention: She has been a leader, and a working parent, long enough to understand well the complexities, and importance, of managing the evolving fit between work and family.

Keep in mind the variety in Cathy's vantage points: She's the mom who hops on a plane several times a month so she can meet the demands of her job and provide for her daughter. (As a single parent, she's had the "advantage" of not really having a choice in the matter; this has excused her, in a sense, from the hand-wringing that has plagued some of her contemporaries.) She's the mom who tries to leave work at 5:45 p.m., who makes a point of being in town on her daughter's birthday, and who cashes in those frequent-flier miles so she and Sophie can explore places like Italy, Argentina and France together.

She's been the employee who had to walk into her manager's office and say, "I'm pregnant," and the manager who has listened as valuable employees have come to her with the same announcement. She *gets* it, and, as she talked about the 2009 baby boom and her approach to creating a work/life–friendly environment, her wide perspective was evident. Weber Shandwick is a people-driven business that thrives on creativity, and Cathy believes in fostering a culture that engages people and places value on life outside of work. (Weber Shandwick routinely ranks high on lists of "the best places to work.")

Making it possible to change the shape of a job so it fits someone's evolving life is simply good business. As Cathy says, "I can't imagine not doing it. It's never occurred to me that we would say, 'Here's the deal: Nothing changes when you have a kid. It's just the same.' People would run—and they would run to my competitors."

Over the years, Weber Shandwick executives have undertaken a bit of trial and error in this regard. They've fine-tuned their approach, and they've developed a process that includes both structure and freedom. For the most part, it works.

Which isn't to say that sixteen new babies in one year didn't feel like . . . *a lot.*

Cathy Calhoun, 48
Public Relations Executive and President
of Weber Shandwick North America
Chicago, Illinois
Mother of Sophie

First of all, when we find out these women are pregnant, we're really happy for them. We're a close-knit community here, people are friends . . . so we're always really happy for people, not to overstate the obvious. But, at the same time, [we're thinking], Oh, my gosh, what are we going to do? How are we going to get through a client-service business with that many fewer people?

And not only that many fewer people, but the uncertainty of whether they're going to come back or not. So, it's a lot to manage in terms of moving those chess pieces around.

Years ago, when we were at the beginning of this whole debate about "work/ life balance" . . . we were cutting all kinds of deals with people. It was insane—we couldn't keep track of who was working on what day, what they were doing, who was home, who was here. It was not manageable. We got crazy. That's why we pulled back and said, We have to frame this out.

We know now, from that experiment, where the tipping point is. We say: This is what we have to work within. *But which days, and how we do it, and, in some cases, even where you live—we can figure that out. We have gotten to a place where we have a framework—but there's still a lot of freedom within that framework to accommodate what people need.*

When it gets messed up is if there's no communication. It takes a lot of team-work, and a lot of mutual understanding.

Over the years, Weber Shandwick has standardized its flexibility options to reflect the realities of its business. The company generally requires a certain number of days of "face time" per week, depending on the person's job; and travel, for most, is a must. But the policy isn't so carved in granite that there are never exceptions. Instead, it becomes an ongoing conversation. "What's happening today is you have to customize to the employee and the business need. It's matching those together. Right now, in the workplace, you have to be fluid and fair," says Weber Shandwick executive Susan Howe, president of the Chicago office.

Some job-tailoring has fallen outside the usual parameters: If a situation fits both an employee and the job, Weber Shandwick is willing to experiment. One employee, a mother of two who technically reports to the Chicago office, works part-time from her home in New Hampshire. "She's someone who is incredibly reliable," Susan says. "I've always known if I needed something, she'll be there for me. I have incredible trust." Susan herself spent several years working remotely from Seattle after her husband took a job there.

Often, flexibility results from the general attitude that family needs *matter*. Little adjustments can be made as opportunities arise, Cathy says, and that makes a difference:

This morning, I had a client who wanted to start a meeting—one that we have in a few weeks in Key West, Florida—at noon. I have four people going to that, and one of them has twins in first grade—and a husband who travels a lot for work. And I looked at that, and I looked at the flights, and I thought, We're all going to have to go in the night before. *But, if you move that meeting . . . we could come in that morning. And that's an extra night at home with your kids, putting them to bed.*

So I went back to the client and I said, "You know what—if you move it an hour and a half, we can come in that morning and you'll save the hotel money the night before." Everyone wins, right? And they said, "Sure, we can do that." And they moved it. It's those kinds of things. And God bless the client, who is a mom.

For those who navigated the Weber Shandwick baby boom, 2009 was a reminder that the work/life puzzle has a lot of pieces—and it was evidence that the company's "freedom within a framework" works. In the end, the flexibility requests were "pretty simple": reduced hours, schedules that included some work from home. There were a few, too, who decided not to come back.

"It's really a dance and a balance for me personally and professionally," Susan Howe told Becky. "You have to keep flexing both sides of your empathy, in terms of the business side and the human side, to make it work."

* * *

In many ways, we were lucky: As we navigated our own work/life issues, we were actively researching the topic, chatting with top thinkers, listening to the stories of smart and successful women. We heard different perspectives and philosophies, from employees like Rachel, to employers like Cathy and Susan. And so, as this book came together, we found ourselves continuing to fine-tune our own attitudes.

Becky, in particular, benefited from this wider view.

PAINTING A PICTURE
MADE FOR TWO

As it turns out, the work/life conflict Becky and Pete faced in those early years of parenthood was a common scenario facing college-educated professionals. Overworked husband, wife who can't figure out how to be completely flexible and still have a job that doesn't feel "mommy tracked." This was the picture painted by a 2010 study that examined work/family conflict across three different socioeconomic groups and included this bit of data: Having a husband who works more than fifty hours a week increases the odds of a woman quitting her job by 44 percent. Having a husband who works more than sixty hours a week increases her odds of quitting by 112 percent.[6] The report went on to mention that, in one study of highly educated women who had "opted out" of the workforce, more than 60 percent cited their husbands as a key reason.

Professor Joan C. Williams, one of the studies' authors and the director of the Center for WorkLife Law at the University of California–Hastings, had touched on this issue when Becky interviewed her a year before for an *ABA Journal* column on two-lawyer families.[7]

"In many workplace environments, particularly law firms, *full-time* is defined as sixty to seventy hours [a week], and for one parent to do that, it means the other is functioning as a single parent," she'd told Becky. "Two parents doing that is beyond the imagination of many parents."

The 2010 study had noted that only 6 percent of married professional families had two parents working fifty or more hours a week. In most cases, the husband worked the long hours and the wife scaled back. And Becky, of course, understood the ramifications of that perfectly: Many of them, like her, probably found that they had to reduce their hours so much to make up for their husband's long hours that they found it hard to find real satisfaction at work.

Something else caught Becky's eye—a section about overworked men, especially those in jobs where long hours are "a badge of honor." Because, in the end, Becky truly had not felt "forced out" by the *Sun-Times* when she quit . . . she'd felt "forced out" by the realities of her own life, and the realities of Pete's job. He wanted to be home more, but he also wanted to make partner. There was no way he was going to walk into a partner's office and say he wanted to work fewer hours.

In our survey, 70 percent of respondents agreed that "a woman who makes lateral career moves or downshifts to a less demanding position while raising children can still be viewed as serious about her career."

But when asked that same question about men, only 51 percent agreed.

Of course, not every family falls into these clichéd patterns. Becky has long admired her friends Patrick and Noelle McWard because they address their careers, and all the other elements of their lives, as complementary parts of the same machine. For them, life isn't an all-or-nothing proposition where work must be sacrificed for family or family must be sacrificed for work.

Instead, they've made deliberate decisions that have freed them from having to choose among their most important priorities. Both Noelle, a therapist who works with individuals and couples, and Patrick, an executive coach and professional speaker who has addressed more than 1,200 audiences on business growth and work/life balance, are self-employed. That means they've given up employee perks like paid vacations, subsidized health benefits and stock options in exchange for freedom. Much like Kim and Scott Holstein, this also means the McWards *both* experience the benefits of balance.

Not that it's been simple. Sometimes, it has meant letting go of traditional ideas to stay true to their own vision of success.

"I wanted to be able to feel a rhythm in my life," Patrick told Becky. "There are times when I want to work really, really hard, really intensely, because I love what I do. But there's other times when I want to just ... do nothing. And for me, doing nothing would be doing yoga and meditating and having coffee with a friend. And that is definitely not the [traditional male].... I see that as a very empowering thing to be able to say I'm going to take the day and go to yoga class. But even at the yoga class, there's like three guys out of sixty. I kind of had to let go of the facade of being a traditional male—and it's the best thing I ever did."

Sometimes remaining true to their vision has meant staving off fear. In December 2008, as the economy was flagging, Patrick's speaking business suddenly dropped off. Companies were canceling annual meetings and had stopped bringing in speakers. As the fear over lost income began to settle into the McWard home, Patrick was offered a three-month contract to do outplacement training. The catch: He would have been on the road almost the entire time. Noelle especially felt fear over their shrinking income, but, in the end, the opportunity simply didn't fit their vision.

So Pat said no. Business picked up; within a few months, everything was fine.

Noelle McWard, 41
Psychotherapist
Chicago, Illinois
Mother of Kayla and Connor

At the time, it was an opportunity to make some money for a few months, and I was ... in a lot of fear about what was going to happen. Then he went for one day and said, "I'm not doing it," and I was actually relieved.

It worked out. That was a good decision to make.

I do think whenever you make a decision based on a fear, it's not likely to be a very good one. You really need to focus more on your values and your vision of what you want your life to look like.

And that, of course, is one of the great lessons of the New Perfect: focusing on the vision of what we want our lives to look like. This involves seeing the big picture, which includes understanding all the realities that play a part in custom-tailoring a career: understanding how it looks from the perspective of our companies, figuring out how the unique circumstances of our family lives impact our choices and knowing what we bring to the table to make this custom-tailoring possible. It also includes knowing what we want—and not being afraid to take that risk to get it.

* * *

When Pete first left his old firm, Becky would often lay awake at night, consumed by the knot of worry that had lodged itself deep in her throat. It felt as if someone had reached in and was squeezing, just above her heart, as if she might burst into tears at any minute. And then life—mercifully—began to fall into place again. This time, it better fit the vision she and Pete had for their lives. Pete joined a new law firm, one in which he enjoyed the work but could still carve out a life at home. And a few weeks later, she officially had a book deal for *Good Enough Is the New Perfect*.

Beginning almost right away, things began to shift at home. Pete still worked hard, but he was home more—and he now took on a role that extended far beyond "helping." Now he was firmly *in charge* of numerous jobs. He not only made the breakfasts, but he took over the entire morning routine, including packing the lunches and quizzing Elizabeth on her spelling words. On the weekends, while Becky holed up in her home office to write, Pete did the grocery shopping and cooked the best meals the family ate all week. At one point, Becky realized that she no longer knew whether the kids were running low on oatmeal, lunch-box snacks or the vitamins they took at breakfast. Pete also took over many of the kids' weekend activities, including keeping up with the schedules.

Pete also began joining Becky for morning drop-off at school. Soon, he was signing permission slips, rummaging for lost homework and chatting with the teachers and other parents at school.

It was exactly what Becky had always wanted. Except for this: It was now clear that she wasn't the only one capable of running the house. And, at first, this was disconcerting and disappointing.

But then it was comforting. Truly, unbelievably comforting.

Because Becky had a book to finish—and, for the first time since having kids, she had a work routine that really worked.

6

MOTHERHOOD IN THE AGE OF TECHNOLOGY

- Technology requires boundaries and self-control. Be willing to set limits.
- Not everyone is suited to working from home.
- Facebook and Twitter are not substitutes for face-to-face communication.

Rebecca Molloy sees no reason why she can't help save the world, part-time, from home.

After all, the counterterrorism researcher and Arabic linguist from New York has highly specialized skills, a high-speed internet connection, and a full-time nanny to help with her four kids. She makes it work, so the Combating Terrorism Center at West Point, which contracts Rebecca to train FBI agents several times a year, does, too.

At five foot three, Rebecca is outspoken, has a keen sense of humor, a deep intellect and no problem walking into a room of male

FBI agents to lecture them on Arabic name analysis. She was born in New York, but she spent almost her entire childhood in Jerusalem, and served in the Israeli military between the ages of eighteen and twenty. Frankly, it's hard to picture Rebecca not getting what she wants.

Her approach to working motherhood represents our time in history. She has leveraged technology to blend career and family in ways previous generations could never have imagined. When she's not on the road conducting trainings (roughly six one-day trips a year), she's working in her second-floor home office—aided by the internet, email and her home computer—and seated just a quick shout from the four people whose childhoods she doesn't want to miss. From that room, she says she's translated declassified terrorist documents, planned curricula and pored over research.

Technology is a critical piece of our story as modern moms because it has extended our boundaries in ways nothing else could. The women's movement may have broadened our choices, but it's the internet, email, personal computers and cell phones that have given us the ability to telecommute, launch businesses from home and leave work before our clients call back. It has extended the definition of *at work* and given us access to massive amounts of information. And, of course, it has enabled us to take multitasking to a whole new level.

We google our children's symptoms and email our clients from the treadmill. We text our babysitters. Spend entire piano lessons in the car making calls, cross-checking our work calendar with the baseball schedule and remotely setting TiVo to record *The Wizards of Waverly Place,* just so we'd have a decent bribe to get us through that evening conference call. Our BlackBerries and iPhones and laptops have helped us squeeze work into the tiniest crevices of our days. Portions of this book, for instance, were written in the back of a Chicago church; on the sidelines of flag football, soccer, basketball and baseball practices; at a hotel in midtown Manhattan; and in various waiting rooms.

Which brings us to another big point about technology: It can sometimes incite our overachiever tendencies, dangling familiar promises ("You *can* do it all!"), tempting us with new obsessions and forcing us to reel ourselves back to that elusive "middle ground."

And that's what makes it so double-edged: Technology is, at once, an irreplaceable asset—and an extra opportunity for our perfectionist selves to go overboard. When it comes to technology, it can be tricky to strike that Good Enough balance.

* * *

The scene was Nobu Fifty Seven, a swank Japanese eatery in midtown Manhattan, and we were meeting Jen Canter and her husband, Wade, in person, for the first time.

Laptops were back in the hotel and mobile phones were tucked quietly into handbags. Since arriving in New York City, we had been obsessively answering emails, updating our website and listening to a Blog Talk Radio interview we'd given earlier in the week. But now it was time for face-to-face interaction, and we were prepared to unplug.

Except before the first round of tuna maki had been set on the table, Becky's iPhone was out and so was Jen's BlackBerry. (Hollee and Wade managed a bit more restraint.) Reflexively, Becky and Jen acknowledged their meeting via Twitter:

@beckyandhollee: H and I are at Nobu with @playthisway, sitting one table away from Ivanka Trump.—B

@playthisway: At nobu w @beckyandhollee and ivanka is at table next to us—gorgeous....

Jen pulled up pictures of her four children on her screen, and Becky did a quick check of email, voice mail, Facebook and text messages, just to be sure she hadn't missed something from Pete and the kids. Later, as Jen was talking about a business decision she'd been pondering, the solution came to her and, just like that, she whipped out her BlackBerry and sent an email. ("That's it. Decided. Done," she announced before returning seamlessly to the conversation.)

Setting aside judgment on this table-side etiquette (Was the tech use inappropriate and tacky or impressively efficient?), the scene reeked of modern working motherhood. For many of us, technology is the golden key to managing our intricately layered lives, the magic serum that allows us to be in many places, and be many different people, *all at once.* ("Without my BlackBerry," Jen told Becky in 2008, "I'd fall apart.")

In our survey, more than three-quarters of respondents agreed that technology helped them juggle work and family. But more than 10 percent *disagreed* that it helped, and another 14 percent were "unsure," perhaps reflecting some of the ambivalence regarding technology that emerged in interviews. Although many women identified technology as a prized luxury, many also admitted that, at times, the constant connectivity made their worlds more exhausting and even harder to manage.

After all, technology can connect us to other people *and* isolate us from real human contact. It can promise efficiency, then give us even more to do. And it can further thwart our attempts to "be present," something that many women cited as one of their most elusive goals.

For some, the intrusion wasn't just about the calls themselves, but the anticipation—a sort of "availability anxiety" that made it hard to effectively switch gears. As a doctor, Jen knows the feeling. When she's on call, she'll sometimes find herself thinking, *When is it going to happen? Am I going to have to go into the hospital?*

"I've accepted that that's what my job is," she says. "The reason it's hard for me is, I have four children. I always have to think, 'What do I need to set up if I need to go in?'"

Jen typically comes up with a solution, but she never quite knows when she'll find herself stuck, paying someone (anyone?) to fill in as a babysitter or, worse, out of options entirely. And so, for her, each ring of the BlackBerry is accompanied by a low-grade tension, the possibility that she'll need to scramble.

Some women have felt virtually *shackled* by the BlackBerries knocking around in their handbags, drawn into a continuous "on" state in which they are always available, always thinking about work, always waiting for the next call or email to come through. Nikki Williams, the outgoing attorney who married a fellow University of Kentucky College of Law alum, told Hollee that her relationship with technology soured after she had received the BlackBerry she'd long coveted. As time passed, she began to feel "leashed" to the large law firm where she began her career. The device had promised liberation—but then, seemingly, had stolen it away.

Nikki Adcock Williams, 33
Attorney
McDonough, Georgia
Mother of Anna and Liam

I was gleeful the day my BlackBerry was delivered to me—fully charged—and felt a sense of freedom that night as I made the drive home.

I quickly realized it was not really fun to be accessible all of the time. I began checking my BlackBerry while in the car, at the dinner table, at the movies with my husband, Tom, and even during intermission at the opera.

Tom disliked my BlackBerry and really loathed it the night I got a whole series of emails from a partner who was traveling in Europe and needed me to "think" about some legal issues. My BlackBerry vibrated whenever I received a new message. When I did not initially respond [because I was sleeping], he sent me several more emails to inquire why I had not yet replied to his first message. The ensuing vibrations literally bounced my BlackBerry to the floor. The traveling partner had forgotten there was a time difference and later apologized for waking me at four in the morning. Tom never got an apology for the interruption of his slumber.

Tom and I talked about how he felt I was less present now that I had a BlackBerry. That is when I really began to resent the invasion of technology into my life.

It's a complicated relationship we have with our ever-evolving gadgets, and we fall prey to their seductions to varying degrees. It is impossible, however, to deny the gifts they've bestowed. Becky, for instance, can't quite imagine juggling the pieces of her life without her iPhone, which serves as a sort of hub for her entire life. She has found herself obsessed at times or, sadly, paralyzed by her dependence. That was the case, once, when her iPhone malfunctioned just as she was placing an emergency call to the pediatrician. "My phone's not working! I can't even look up the doctor's number!" she'd panicked, after rushing to the school to investigate her daughter's bumped— and, as it turned out, concussed—head. For a brief moment, she'd been literally frozen, unsure how to proceed without a functioning touch screen in her palm. "They probably have Dr. Lechman's number on file in the school office," her friend Emily had said patiently. "And there are phones attached to the wall."

But, for the most part, technology has drastically improved options for modern mothers whose work/life fit depends on portability, flexibility or, at a minimum, the ability to work from home.

Which brings us back, for a moment, to counterterrorism expert/mom Rebecca Molloy.

THE WORK-FROM-HOME REVOLUTION

Rebecca worked hard for her doctorate in Middle Eastern studies and Arabic linguistics; she has invested in her education and her career. But she doesn't want to get up and go into an office every morning—not right now, anyway.

"I wanted to bring people into the world, and I wanted to be there," she told Becky during an early interview in 2008. "But there's always a little part of you that just wants to be you."

Working from home gives her that opportunity. Her work is cyclical: Sometimes she's contracted for projects on top of her regular FBI trainings, and she'll find herself working full days upstairs in her office, breaking only to eat lunch or hug her kids. (When they were younger, she'd also take short breaks to breast-feed.) Working from home suits her: She has the ability to tune out and just *focus;* she doesn't tend to get sidetracked or distracted. When she's concentrating, she barely hears what goes on outside her office door; in fact, she barely gets up from her desk. This isn't something she's had to cultivate, either—as a child, she was extremely focused. "It's just the way I am," she says. "If I know I need to do something, I do whatever it takes to get the job done."

When she's not on a big project, she focuses on writing articles, ones with names like "Deconstructing Ibn Taymiyya's Views on Suicidal Missions." Training sessions are often out of town, but they are scheduled, so she's able to plan around them. She only travels to places that are within a two- to three-hour flight each way so she won't be gone overnight. The schedule gives her the freedom to participate in the day-to-day tasks of mothering, like dropping the younger ones at preschool or playing in the yard or practicing martial arts with the kids.

"For me, the balance and the calm and doing what I think is important—that's perfection," she says.

One brisk morning in January 2010, as Becky was interviewing Rebecca in the dining room of her Westchester County, New York, home, one of Rebecca's daughters walked into the house. Without missing a beat, Rebecca excused herself from the conversation and leaned down until the two of them were eye to eye. She spoke quietly to her daughter in Hebrew for a moment, then kissed her, her eyes locked and focused on the little face.

"It's nice," Rebecca said, "to have those moments."

* * *

Those moments are what many moms are after when they choose to work from home. And, even for those who don't have doctorates, technology has created what work-at-home expert Tory Johnson calls a "golden time" for employees looking for home-based work. The latest advances—most notably the relative ease and low overhead required for online stores and consulting firms—have created work-at-home options for women exploring a wide range of opportunities. (Even though traditional direct sales companies, like Tupperware, Mary Kay and Avon, repeated historical growth patterns during the latest recession, they represent just a sliver of today's work-at-home options.)

The notion of working from home struck a dreamy chord with many of the moms we interviewed—from entrepreneurs scheming to launch big ventures, to lawyers forging home-based practices, to mostly at-home moms looking to caulk family income gaps.

Tory Johnson founded her own women's recruiting company from home, and now she touts the advantages of home-based work during her regular spot as a workplace specialist on *Good Morning America*. The biggest sells: no commute, less predawn rush and the opportunity to make money without (always) getting dressed.

The problem, Tory says, is that many women have a romantic vision of children playing quietly on the floor while they build empires from their laptops on the couch. (Insert laughter from moms who have tried this.) "Women can succeed in home-based work by leveraging technology," she said, "but first they need to assess their work-at-home readiness. Not everyone, after all, finds home to be the optimal work environment."

Rachel Swarns, the *New York Times* reporter, had considered working from home when she started her book-writing sabbatical. Initially, she thought she'd clear out the guest room and set it up as an office for digging into Michelle Obama's ancestry. But her husband dissuaded her, pointing out that even with a nanny at home, it would be hard to stay focused with their two young sons at home part of every day.

As tempting as it was to ditch the commute, Rachel knew he was right. So, instead, she set up shop at the Smithsonian. That meant she had to spend some of her precious work time commuting—but it also meant that when she was at work, she could truly be *at work*.

It's that separation between work and home that has been at the root of our generation's struggle with technology. We are grateful, on one hand, for the dissolving boundaries that allow us to do so much. But it has also taken some real effort to figure out when to let go, or to recognize when we've gone too far. The intrusion, after all, doesn't always come from overzealous bosses or impatient clients.

The internet has put an entire world, filled with a seemingly endless supply of information, news, entertainment and people, right at our fingertips. And sometimes we can't help but invite it in—even when we know it's keeping us from the real people in our lives, the ones who matter the most.

INFORMATION OVERLOAD

For a long time, Hollee's interest in technology had been vague and utilitarian. She'd never wanted a BlackBerry or an iPhone. For years, she didn't even carry a cell phone; when she was working in her office, her kids were at home with a babysitter who could easily call her work phone.

But eventually the kids entered schools that essentially required parents to be available by mobile phone, and Hollee succumbed—but *that was it.* She saw technology as a distraction; it annoyed her when her students were checking email and surfing the web while she was trying to present her lessons. She banned laptops in her classroom because she was "sick of teaching to eyebrows" and shook her head when she saw other academics texting around the clock.

Until she started working on this book.

As first-time authors, we knew we would need to build a website before we circulated our book proposal, and we spent the first half of 2009 hammering out our concept. When we launched our website in August 2009, the plan was to blog on occasion; we just wanted to prove our web savvy to potential publishers. In fact, early on, Hollee resisted setting up a personal Facebook page ("My students might try to 'friend' me!") and had been skeptical when Becky's sister-in-law, Anya, suggested Twitter.

Then she joined both, and they sucked her in. Facebook became an opportunity to reconnect with old friends and contacts, to promote the blog—and to chat in real time. Sometimes this saved time: Becky and Hollee could exchange quick messages via Facebook chat while writing and avoid the need to interrupt the process with phone calls. Other times, well, it provided the distraction Hollee had feared. That was nothing, however, compared to Twitter. (John told her that his journalism students agreed with her; they called Facebook a mere "gateway drug," compared to the "crack" of Twitter.)

Her type A tendencies came out in full force. Hollee couldn't just post a blog entry—she had to update her Facebook status, tweet about it, and ask close friends to comment. She installed Google Analytics to track traffic, and she studied the results compulsively. After she put the kids to bed, instead of hanging out with John, she'd head to her computer, attending "Twitter parties" and commenting on blogs in hopes of building readership. When our web server went down for forty-eight hours, Hollee called or chatted online with our web host at least a dozen times; she couldn't stand the idea of the site being down.

Hollee couldn't stop, and John got mad.

"You would rather spend time with people you don't know than me," he yelled one night in December.

And it was true. The book project made her feel out of control—the deadline felt too tight on top of her full-time job and family responsibilities—and the nights on Twitter gave her a sense of comfort that she was contributing something more to the book. Still, even with this recognition, it was hard to scale back. Cultivating a network was important for the book but it was hard to temper that interaction and find a middle ground.

And so, despite numerous conversations in which Hollee pledged to tweet less, not much changed. Hollee kept tweeting, pretty much around the clock.

TURNING IT OFF

For many of us, setting limits was the trick to enjoying the benefits of all of this technology without letting it drive us crazy. Once again, the concept of Good Enough—taking things to just the right point instead of all the way—was essential. The most satisfied women we interviewed had defined for themselves how much computer or smartphone time was good enough—and then had taken responsibility for the times when they overshot.

"If I'm going to be honest here, it's me that's the problem," Jen Canter once told Becky. "If I handled [technology] better, I don't think it would be a problem." So Jen—ever the problem solver—began working hard to temper her use, trying to calibrate it to an amount that truly gave her freedom. She stopped checking her BlackBerry as often and she removed its Twitter application. She also set limits, asking people from work to limit after-hours calls to emergencies.

In the first interview, Jen had been enthusiastic about the multitasking abilities conferred by technology, telling Becky that she could write a "perfectly spelled email while running on the treadmill." But, nearly two years later, she was proud to have scaled back her use. In a private message sent via Facebook, she told Becky:

> That's the evolution for me—that I can only do so much and have to focus on my little boys, my little girls, my husband and save some energy for ME (even if that is as simple as staring at the wall for ten minutes)! I still would be a wreck without the BlackBerry, but lately it is in the locker room at the gym rather than with me on the treadmill!

This ability to adjust technology use—and to ensure that it doesn't take us away from our personal relationships—can be an important consideration in today's world. Therapist Noelle McWard sometimes sees this while counseling couples: One will complain that the other's technology use is intruding on their lives.

"There are so many ways that you can get all your energy and focus into Facebook or your email or other things where you're not actually connecting with another human being," she told Becky. "And even Facebook is not a real connection with another human being. It can be a problem for families and couples because all that time could otherwise be spent face-to-face, interacting with each other. Even if it doesn't go into the spectrum of addiction, it takes you away from one another."

What it comes down to is setting boundaries and communicating. Which isn't always easy, Noelle said, because "it's not a solid line most of the time."

Even Tory Johnson, the work-at-home expert, has trouble breaking free—she struck a deal with her children when planning a cross-country vacation. They were traveling first to the Red Rock Mountains, where her son wanted to golf, and then on to Los Angeles, where her daughter wanted to see where Kim Kardashian lived—and the kids were worried about BlackBerry distractions. So Tory promised to check in with work only once a day. The shock: *Nothing horrible happened while she concentrated on enjoying her vacation.*

In contrast to fellow attorney Nikki Williams (whose story unfolds a bit later), Libby Windsor learned to set limits once she was a little further along in her career. She knows which clients, cases and partners require an immediate response and which can wait until she has finished dinner. She knows her priorities—and she trusts her ability to prioritize.

Libby Windsor, 34
Employment Litigator for an International Law Firm
Mt. Lebanon, Pennsylvania
Mother of William and Andrew

There are plenty of days when I'm tied up in a deposition or at a hearing and I know that, if it's an emergency, someone will find me and tell me so.

I try to have the same attitude with my personal time. Of course, as I said, you just can't have that attitude all the time—you have to be aware of what is going on with work and prioritize.

I like to think that I don't feel leashed by my BlackBerry, but my husband will probably tell you that there has been many a dinner or afternoon running errands when I've checked my email, announced, "Shit!" in response to something that is on there, and then jumped on my cell phone for the next twenty minutes about it without missing a beat. It happens.

But all of this makes me think that, at least in this line of work, all of this is only really possible if you have some perspective and experience on what you're doing. For the first few years as an attorney, you really don't have any sense of priority about the way things progress, which clients expect immediate turnaround—and which ones won't look at your work product for months.

When you are starting out, you are more likely to be dropped into projects and cases that you have only a very small sense (if any at all) about what the project is about and what the big picture is and, because of this, it is hard for a junior associate to be able to be untethered.

* * *

Hollee eventually hit her groove with Twitter, in part, by getting a better glimpse of the big picture and zeroing in on her priorities.

She reset the Twitter application so it no longer beeped every time a new update was directed her way, and she limited herself to checking messages several times a day, instead of leaving the application open all day on her desktop.

Now, when she tuned out, she also tuned in—this time back to her family. John was happy to have her attention back, and Hollee was happier, too.

Although, sometimes, she can't help herself: She likes to share that happiness with her friends via . . . a status update.

I'M THE BOSS OF ME

- Entrepreneurship is a path to control, but it's not a simple solution.

- Support networks, mentors and coaches can make the entrepreneurial path less lonely.

- Experienced entrepreneurs learn to self-moderate business growth so that they won't be consumed by their businesses.

Gena Gerard's big idea struck while she was walking on a treadmill, trying to regain a semblance of her pre-kid life while her infant daughter was in the gym's child-care center, just a room away.

It was 2003, and Gena, who had founded a nonprofit organization after earning her master's degree five years earlier, was determined to avoid the isolation of new motherhood. She didn't want her house in suburban Minneapolis to feel like a prison, so she forced herself to get out—she registered for a parenting class, joined a book club for moms and made her way back to the gym.

And that's where her entrepreneurial vision first took shape. On the treadmill, she started dreaming about a space where she could offer new moms the support system she had begun cobbling together on her own. What if, Gena wondered, there was a one-stop shop where moms could bond while taking fitness or art classes—with the bonus of on-site child care and salon services?

At the time, it was just a passing thought. When her maternity leave was up, Gena returned to the job she loved, heading up the citywide expansion of a mediation program that allowed nonviolent offenders to make amends to the community by working with citizens who had been affected by their crimes. Gena was a successful grant writer and manager, and the organization grew quickly—within a few years, more than a dozen neighborhoods had joined her initiative.

Her organization was thriving, but Gena was exhausted, and she wondered why no one had warned her that she might struggle to Have It All. For years, she had heard that the "best" thing to do was to go to college, find a good job and start a career.

"No one ever warned me that at some point I would probably have kids, and that having babies would hugely interfere with my work life, creating a tug-of-war that you have to work out all by yourself," she told Hollee. "It's the elephant in the room, the thing nobody talks about with teenage girls and college women. My feeling was, 'Why didn't anybody tell me this?' 'Why was I so unprepared?' I felt completely blindsided."

The Mommy Wars that were playing out in Gena's mind started taking a toll. She was angry about the mixed messages she had received. First, it was: "Go to school, study, get good grades. Good for you, you got a job!"

But as soon as the babies were born, she felt as if society was delivering a louder communication: "Stop what you're doing! Stop right there! You have children now, and your children need you. How can you leave your children? Shame on you!"

So Gena decided to dial back her hours at work, and that's when she felt yet another voice creeping into the conversation: "How can you leave your job early today to pick up your kids? If you don't care about your job, someone else will be happy to have it!"

And just when the ideal worker versus ideal parent battle was reaching its peak in Gena's mind, divine providence stepped in (at least that's how she sees it).

Her father died in the spring of 2007, leaving Gena enough seed money to start the business she had been thinking about for years. In the wake of her father's death, she felt as if someone was saying, "Here's the money, and here are your children, and I'm giving you what you need—so go for it." She quit her job and started drafting a business plan.

Gena thought she had the business background to make a smooth transition into entrepreneurship; she had managed ten employees at the nonprofit.

And in May 2009, she launched her "Mother's Day" lifestyle center in suburban Minneapolis, pouring all of her inheritance (and more) into the business. She didn't skimp on a thing. The final space exceeded her expectations: a welcoming, open studio in a building with salon services right next door—a space where she could hold fitness and art classes and set up tables for moms to enjoy wireless internet access while she served complimentary pastries and provided child care. A place where they could take Pilates or yoga or scrapbooking classes and remember what it felt like to be a woman without a toddler dangling off the hip.

* * *

In creating her enterprise, Gena joined the legions of women who have started businesses in the United States as a means of gaining flexibility and control. The nearly 8 million women-owned enterprises in this country (which account for 23 million jobs) pack a $3 trillion annual impact.[1] In fact, women own nearly 20 percent of businesses with revenues over $1 million,[2] and more women than ever are starting businesses in America.[3] A *Catalyst* study showed that even in the wake of the economic downturn, a substantial percentage of alumni from leading MBA programs started their own businesses—and in the study, more women than men took the entrepreneurial plunge.[4]

For moms looking to take control, entrepreneurship makes even more sense. More than 20 percent of the moms in our survey owned their own businesses or worked as freelancers or independent contractors. Here's why, according to two survey respondents:

Originally I started to work from home as an employee. About sixty to eighty hours per week later, I realized that I needed to get out and become the master of my own time.

I initially quit to stay home and raise my kids, but one income was difficult and with divorce I had to reenter the workforce. Now I am working on developing my own company to allow more flexibility in my job schedule and more time with my family.

Entrepreneurship puts us in the driver's seat, allowing us to dictate our own schedules and escape jobs that, perhaps, never quite fit the way we needed them to. The economic crisis that began in December 2007 only accelerated the trend.[5] With dads making less or getting laid off—men accounted for the vast majority of layoffs during that recession—moms jumped in, trying to plug the family income gap.[6] (In fact, in 2009, women were poised to outnumber men in the workforce for the first time in history.)[7]

But as with every other aspect of this grand chess game we call working motherhood, it's all about custom fit. Some women negotiate deals as independent contractors, others open private practices in their current fields. And many launch brand-new ventures—everything from kitchen-table sidelines to multimillion-dollar enterprises. And with every move, these moms have had to learn that, in business, there are some things you can control, and some that require a different discipline: The ability to forgo perfect.

WHY GOOD ENOUGH IS PERFECT FOR ENTREPRENEURS

Once upon a time, Kim Holstein (of Kim & Scott's Gourmet Pretzels) wanted to be a weatherwoman. Or an anchor on the *Today* show. Or, maybe, a rabbi.

"I wanted to inspire people," she told Becky the first time they talked, on a crisp autumn day in 2008.

Meteorology and theology dropped off the dream board, but, now, the inspiration part is written into her title: She's the president, CEO and "chief inspiration officer" of the multimillion-dollar company she runs with her husband.

"I am calling the shots in my life," Kim said.

That's why she and Scott became entrepreneurs: They love living by their own rules. Kim can't describe an "average day at work" because she's never really had one. She has structure—she meets weekly with her leadership team, for instance—but she plans her weeks around the needs of her business *and* her family. Her weekly planning list always has two columns, work and personal, and she does her best to create days that reflect those priorities. She heads to her downtown office when she needs to meet with her team, but the rest of the time, she works on her laptop from home, in her favorite room: the kitchen. But there was a time, before Kim had children, when work wasn't quite so energizing and inspiring. For much of the 1990s, even as she and Scott were first launching their company, Kim worked in advertising. And it wasn't a good match.

"I will never forget the day I quit, when I walked in there and gave my letter," she told Becky. "I just felt like I was saving my life. I was just suffocating. . . . You know, making a commercial for a company that wasn't even going to air it. It just didn't mean anything to me, and it was so unfulfilling and painful."

Being an entrepreneur is different: Kim has choices and passion—and she knows she could never go back to her old way of life. She and Scott work according to their strengths, which happen to be complementary: Kim is great with ideas and strategy; Scott excels at execution and details. And because it's their company, they can infuse it with things that are important to them, like spirituality and social consciousness. Their "Pretzels with a Purpose" program includes initiatives like "Pretzel Dough," which, in the 2009–2010 school year, gave schools $1 for every Kim & Scott's UPC box flap collected; and "Pretzels for Peace" that has donated pretzels and proceeds to organizations like the Special Olympics, breast cancer walks and food banks for the hungry.

"There's a much deeper reason we're building a business," Kim says. "It's not just about money."

The first time Becky interviewed Kim, she was struck by two things: the freedom Kim experienced as an entrepreneur—and the role "good enough" played in her success. Kim thought "good enough" described her attitude well—she loved how liberating it was to accept imperfection. In fact, Kim loved freedom in general: the ability to follow her dreams, to reject fear, to create *exactly* the life she wanted.

Kimberly Oster Holstein, 43
President, CEO and "Chief Inspiration Officer"
Kim & Scott's Gourmet Pretzels
Wilmette, Illinois
Mother of Sonia, Daniella and Aiden

I think it's something I've worked on a lot through personal growth: What do you want in your life—and how are you going to create it? What's going to get in the way of that—and how are you going to not let that get in the way?

I think that, growing up, there were plenty of times I felt hopeless and not trusting and . . . just trapped. And somehow through a lot of personal growth work, I've [come to feel] like anything is possible. And once you've gone there, there's no room to let the fear overwhelm you. I feel like I can't let that get in my way.

Growing up, I was a huge perfectionist. I was so hard on myself. But I think when you get off. . . that hamster wheel, you see a whole different life. And you never want to get back on it because, it's like—ah—now you can really breathe. I feel like I can really have a great life, and I don't have to live like that.

I think [this philosophy] helps a lot in terms of not getting too consumed with the competition, with what other people are doing, and trying to be true to what we're about.

Today Kim focuses on creating a life that seamlessly incorporates all her passions. She revels in twisting the elements of her life together until they meld like her stuffed pretzels, which ooze with flavors like grilled cheese, mixed berry cobbler, spinach feta and (Kim's personal favorite) chocolate fudge crumb.

Appropriately enough, each of the Holstein children came at a pivotal time to the business: Sonia in 2000, not long after Kim & Scott's struck a deal to sell its pretzels at a national beverage chain; Daniella in 2003, after they'd just begun selling on QVC; and Aiden in 2005, a few hours (phew!) after a news conference to announce the opening of Kim & Scott's first pretzel café. As their family and business bloomed side by side, Kim and Scott learned to weave their work hours around their priorities as parents. Sometimes that meant taking a baby to a QVC appearance in Philadelphia—or even express shipping pumped breast milk home from a business trip. But because they own their business, Kim and Scott have the freedom to be present for the parenting moments that matter most in the Holstein family. Kim lives for walks to school and bedtime routines, and she schedules her day so those precious conversations ("What do you think will be great about your day today?") don't fall through the cracks.

But achieving this state of . . . *twistedness* doesn't always come easily. Kim and Scott work with a life coach who helps them navigate the ebb and flow of the entrepreneurial life. And it was essential for them to let go of perfectionism because their workdays don't end when they leave the office. Like many of the entrepreneurs we interviewed, Kim conceded that, without a plan, the business could easily consume her:

We've been really open to the idea that we're not the same generation as our parents, where everyone said, "Keep your work separate from your personal life." We don't believe that, for us. For us, having it all immersed together makes it possible. But the big challenge with that is, when I'm breast-feeding, I know I'm breast-feeding—and can I really be conscious and present to say, "I'm going to put those [work-related] thoughts here, and I'm going to visit them later." [Scott] and I both have been trying to meditate more, and do things that make us centered and present.

Sometimes I'll look at people who . . . go to work and then come home, [whose] work is not enveloped in their lives. Ours, it's here all the time, and we're always thinking about it. We're always thinking about ideas, and new flavors, and this and that—it could consume all of us, all the time. So I think the challenge is to say, "You know what? I'm with my kids right now, I'm not going to let that get in my mind. I'm going to put that aside." It really takes discipline.

But I'm still learning. That's my huge work right now. My mission is to be so present with them.

* * *

Despite that very real challenge, entrepreneurship among both genders has skyrocketed in recent years—the last decade saw the greatest number of new business launches in U.S. history.[8] And contrary to conventional wisdom, the typical entrepreneur is not a twentysomething hipster developing an online social networking company from a bachelor pad. A recent Kauffman Foundation study captured the surprising anatomy of today's typical entrepreneurs: most are married with children.

These entrepreneurs were motivated to build wealth outside the traditional corporate structure and eager to capitalize on business ideas. And perhaps not shocking for the generation taught (or forced) to be independent by their hard-charging Baby Boomer parents, more than 60 percent in the Kauffman study reported that "working for others did not appeal to them."[9]

Poring over these reports and statistics, we tried to get a handle on what caused the entrepreneurial explosion. The stats mirrored what we had heard anecdotally: The dot-com boom of the late 1990s made entrepreneurship mainstream, and the subsequent bust convinced many Gen Xers that they wanted to be the masters of their own fate. But consumer debt is often cited as the primary reason why this generation, as opposed to the previous one, is so markedly entrepreneurial. Gen Xers are the first generation to graduate from college with significant student loan debt—about 20 percent of adults in their thirties are still paying college loans.[10] And even as we try to whittle that down, financial planners remind us to set aside money for retirement and the kids' college funds (Have a headache yet?).

These factors, heaped on top of our generation's collective quest for personal satisfaction and life balance, have combined to push Xers toward entrepreneurism. Sylvia Ann Hewlett, the noted economist and founder of the Center for Work-Life Policy, nailed our generation's spirit in a *Harvard Business Review* piece about employees fleeing their workplaces:

> *In the twenty-first century, talented people of both sexes often feel sty-mied by a traditional vertical career path that follows a straight line up a narrow ladder. Rather, they're interested in and open to lateral moves and a variety of "work style" options, such as flex schedules and telecom-muting, as long as these options are intellectually challenging and/or satisfying personal obligations. If they don't know how to articulate those desires or think they won't be satisfied by their current employer, they'll look elsewhere.*

As we began exploring the "elsewhere" that these employees were seeking, we met (literally) dozens of moms who had started their own businesses. Their ideas ran the gamut, as different as the women and their dreams. It seemed like everywhere we turned, we found moms launching businesses, and lots of mentions of Ladies Who Launch—a resource for female entrepreneurs (the company offers live business seminars and online publicity and connections across the United States and Canada).

So Hollee called Ladies Who Launch founder Victoria Colligan to get the scoop. Like so many of the women who seek her company's resources (Ladies Who Launch has a community of more than 100,000 women and networking groups in more than twenty cities), Victoria told Hollee that it took some trial and error before she found the right career fit for her passion and skills. Victoria experimented with a series of professional positions—she worked as a lawyer, an investment banker, a residential real estate agent, and in online roles for two wedding companies—before she found her groove with Ladies Who Launch. It started small, with a weekly newsletter that Victoria developed in 2002 because she wanted to provide a hub for the women who "were starting businesses all around me" but "who maybe felt like misfits or freelancers, certainly not business owners" because they were working in isolation.

Eight years later, Victoria's company is an international success, with franchises in most large cities in the United States and Canada. The online part of her business provides vendor resources, publicity, webinars and a daily dose of inspiration through the "LaunchTips" that Victoria writes for her members. The on-the-ground portion offers live seminars for women who are looking for a new lifestyle through entrepreneurism. The current breakdown, Victoria told Hollee, is roughly 40 percent in consumer products (think custom jewelry and baby gifts), 40 percent in consumer services (massage therapy, life coaching), and 20 percent in some sort of business service or business product (designing websites for businesses).

Victoria works full-time—but according to her own rules ("I often schedule personal appointments during the middle of the day and then work all night," she told Hollee). She and her husband make their home in a picturesque Cleveland suburb (her daughters attend the same private girls' school that she did growing up), but she travels frequently, flying all over the country for speaking engagements and business meetings. An expert delegator (she does the "fun research" for trips, parties and camps—then leaves the logistics to others), Victoria says that much of her success stems from accepting that imperfection—and even failure—is part of the process.

"Our job is to anchor women with resources so if you fall down, you can get up again," she told Hollee. "Failure can be a good result because you ruled something out that didn't work. It's really about stamina. Just a slight shift can be the difference between success and failure."

OVERCOMING THE FAILURE PHENOMENON

With all the compelling motivations for choosing entrepreneurship, Victoria told Hollee that it's all too easy for women to dive in with everything they have—only to fizzle out because they didn't acquire skills or draw boundaries needed to make their businesses sustainable over the long haul. Entrepreneurship is not for the faint of heart; fewer than half of new businesses typically make it past the five-year mark.[11]

Self-employment is typically not as lucrative as working for a traditional employer,[12] and when you add the steep cost of health insurance for the self-employed, the notion gets even scarier. But it's still not stopping women from going for it—at twice the rate of men. In fact, mothers starting businesses have become so ubiquitous that they've earned their own moniker—"mompreneur." The mompreneur market is growing so quickly that there are now career coaches dedicated to their unique business needs, like certified business coach Lara Galloway. (Hollee first spotted Lara on Twitter, zinging out messages about entrepreneurial moms and the coaching service she offered them.)

For Lara, who believes her business has been successful because she represents her target "mompreneur" market, the decision to start a coaching business struck like a lightning bolt. Lara had ditched her high-paying IBM sales job after her first son was born in 2002, then turned her attention to "becoming Supermom with the cape flying and all." She tried to maintain a facade of contentedness, even through the frigid Michigan winters, after her second son was born two years later. But when she was diagnosed with postpartum depression, Lara decided that she needed to get back to work.

After a yearlong training program and a slow start plagued by the problems most new entrepreneurs face (more on that in a minute), Lara got her big break when she named herself "MomBizCoach" on Twitter in late 2008; almost immediately, she began getting coaching requests from mompreneurs all over the country. A year later, *Forbes Woman* named Lara one of the top thirty entrepreneurial women to follow on Twitter, which now generates almost all of Lara's client base—mostly moms who want to create rewarding at-home businesses that require only part-time hours.

Lara's clients face the same major stumbling blocks that she encountered when she launched: first, a lack of boundaries—when do we change clothes and become sophisticated business owners instead of moms in sweats smeared with mustard from packing lunches?; and second, a strong aversion to asking for help. When Lara interviews new clients and asks how they allocate their time and delegate responsibility, most say they do everything themselves, "trying to squeeze it all in while everyone else is sleeping, or locking themselves inside a closet so clients can't hear the kids screaming in the background." (This "hiding-from-the-kids-to-appear-professional" technique, by the way, was a common practice for almost every work-at-home mom we interviewed.) To create sustainable businesses, moms have to find a way to separate their kid time from their client time; otherwise, Lara says, "No one knows when they can count on you." And the moms who don't draw that line tend to burn out quickly.

Lara tackled the challenge by working with her own coach and setting strict limits. She devotes twenty hours a week to her coaching business, and the rest to her family. Three days a week she's in mom mode, although she admits to jumping on her laptop after the kids go to bed. But on Tuesdays and Thursdays, she's dedicated to her coaching job, heading into her home office after breakfast with a headset, water bottle and a bag of healthy snacks. From 10:00 a.m. to 3:00 p.m., she coaches nonstop, holding hourly telephone sessions with her clients and recording the Blog Talk Radio pieces that have helped garner her Twitter following. She's arranged child care for her daughter (her two sons are in school), her boundaries are set—and that combination really makes it work.

But not all of Lara's clients have found that balance. Many struggle because they lack a formal business education, yet resist asking for help. These moms have great ideas and the passion to start viable home-based ventures, but they lack business know-how and stumble. Mompreneurs are racing to pick up business-school basics—bookkeeping, sales, website and graphic design, networking, business plans. And many won't hire help because of the cost.

Then there's the added emotional challenge for moms: Guilt. Even Lara grappled with her conscience as she invested time away from her children to build something for herself.

Lara Galloway, 39
Certified Coach and Founder of MomBizCoach
Windsor, Ontario
Mother of Charlie, Paul and Ellie

You're gonna need a plan, you need a mentor, and you need market research. Without any one of those, you are probably setting yourself up for "not great" success, or maybe failure. Don't think you can be successful by yourself.

I struggled for a long time with the guilt that came with me wanting to do something away from my kids. Every single time I get near my business, [I think] I love this so much that I need to do it like I need to breathe. But I still stop and think sometimes that maybe I should stop all this and speak Spanish with the kids and make macaroni necklaces, that I should be homeschooling. I guess I once thought that I shouldn't want to be anything more than Mom because they're my top priority, and because they only will be little once.

But the big thing was accepting that part of my job as Mom is to take care of myself, and if I don't do that, I am absolutely doing my children a disservice. I grappled with that for years. And as the years go by, it's starting to feel so good. I'm getting more and more comfortable, knowing in my gut that I'm doing the right thing.

AN EXCITING BUT DIFFICULT ROAD—ESPECIALLY IF YOU GO IT ALONE

Because many new entrepreneurs work in isolation, under the raised eyebrows of family and friends who don't understand their sudden need for something more, Lara counsels her clients to build support networks of like-minded entrepreneurs. In Lara's circle of mom friends, some can't understand why she won't stop by for a cup of coffee on one of her scheduled "working days." She worked with a coach so she could make peace with her choices. And she recommends that her clients find local mentors—or, if that's not possible, network via the burgeoning online entrepreneurial community.[13]

Gena Gerard, the Minnesota mompreneur who created the Mother's Day studio, longed for support from women who would mentor her as the business went through growing pains, especially when the customers didn't flock as quickly as she had expected. But like many entrepreneurs, Gena didn't think she had the time to find a mentor, and she shot from the hip. She spent money on an expensive advertising campaign before learning that word-of-mouth marketing was her biggest draw. She started slow, offering classes only a few days a week, then realized that she would have brought in more customers if she had been open every day, simply canceling classes that didn't fill. Her initial price point was too high; some potential customers rejected her business based on that alone. And even though she had been warned repeatedly that it would take two or three years to break even, she had expected to break even in just six months.

In the early fall of 2009, Gena hit bottom with the business. The summer had been languid, and the crowds that she was hoping for once school was in session hadn't materialized. In the back of her mind, she worried that the end was near, that she'd have to get a "real job" and give up her dream.

Gena Gerard, 39
Entrepreneur, Owner of Mother's Day/Yoga Bella
Chanhassen, Minnesota
Mother of Claire and Joey

I still don't know what makes somebody an entrepreneur and think that they can take a new idea and have a dream and realize it. Maybe it's part insanity. It's certainly not rational to put yourself through it emotionally and financially, to the point of exhaustion. It's hard to justify why I did it.

After a winter of ups and downs, Gena eventually hit her groove in the spring of 2010. But it wasn't according to her original plan. Just as Victoria Colligan had told Hollee, sometimes entrepreneurs have to try something that doesn't quite work to find the idea that will stick. In April, Gena installed a new sign above the front door of the studio—it's now Yoga Bella, and the yoga, Pilates and dance classes she's offering are filling up.

* * *

In many ways, entrepreneurs and other working moms face the same basic challenge: They need to fit their jobs around the unique contours of their lives. But at some of the highest-stress stages in business building, entrepreneurs often find themselves taking on more than any one woman can handle—and just hoping that the boat doesn't sink.

Karen Jaworski, thirty-five, barely kept her head above water when she first tried to balance motherhood, entrepreneurship *and* a traditional job. After their first conversation, Hollee was immediately struck by how much Karen was doing at work and in her Seattle home.

Karen told Hollee that when she was pregnant with her first child, she began questioning her lifelong plan to become an at-home mom. Karen cherished her own childhood memories (nightly "from scratch" meals and the steaming heart-shaped muffins wrapped in festive linens every Valentine's Day morning), and she wanted to replicate that for her own family.

But when her doctors recommended bed rest just four months into her pregnancy, Karen struggled to sit still—that's when she launched an internet-based business from her bedroom.

A self-described "Martha Stewart type," Karen drafted a business plan for Swell Sweets in early 2005; she started with a basic website offering personalized gifts for special events. Karen had created "welcome gift bags" for guests at her own wedding and then for some friends, and thought the internet might bring paying customers.

After baby Maria arrived in June, Karen stayed home for six months, juggling the demands of her growing internet business against the demands of her newborn. She often thought back to her days in graduate school, when she'd spent afternoons walking the streets of Seattle's Queen Anne neighborhood overlooking Puget Sound, dodging stroller-pushing moms and imagining a similar path in her own future.

But when the new year arrived, Karen was surprised by her desire to return to her speech pathology career—*and* to grow her fledgling internet business into something more. "I wanted to have something just for me. I missed talking to my coworkers and interacting with my clients. I liked what I did so much and I missed it," she told Hollee.

Getting back to her speech therapy work while launching the business wasn't easy—child care was the first hurdle. Karen tried a nanny, then part-time day care, but found herself struggling to find the hours to keep up with motherhood and two time-consuming jobs. By the time Maria was a year old, she was in day care four days a week. For Karen, it didn't feel right—she lamented the dearth of quality time with her child, and felt like she was failing her family because she "wasn't doing as good of a job" as her own mom had.

She considered ditching the business.

"But I just liked the idea too much—I never had the heart to let it go," Karen said. "I thought it was a good-enough idea and no one else out there was doing the same thing. When I tell people about the business, they always say what a cool idea it is, and how they wish they had thought of it. And when I hear back from customers and they say how much they enjoyed my work, it's really fulfilling."

In the end, she just had to find a better balance. Karen sought the advice of a counselor, who helped her spot places to cut corners without straying from her core beliefs. First up: She joined a meal-planning club so that homemade dinners would be ready without the nightly scramble. She hired a monthly house cleaner. She then learned to protect her time, politely declining when clients asked her to schedule appointments late into the evening.

And through trial and error, she learned to squeeze more from her business with less time and effort. She adjusted her online advertising, turning off her pay-per-click ads in December so that a deluge of orders wouldn't keep her from creating the memories she wanted with her own daughter, like baking Russian tea cakes and decorating homemade sugar cookies for Christmas.

(Victoria Colligan explains that this sort of business "self-moderation" is a key to happiness for many entrepreneurial women.) But her biggest challenge was familiar: tearing herself away from the business to just hang out with her family.

JUST BECAUSE IT SOUNDS EASY, DOESN'T MEAN IT IS

No discussion of modern-day mompreneurs would be complete without taking a peek at the phenomenon known as "mommy blogging," which has drawn thousands of moms looking for a way to earn money while working from home. The idea seems simple: Create an interesting website that draws readers from the sought-after mom demographic, and earn money through sponsorship, ads or reviews aimed at those women. The catch? Though it's easy and relatively inexpensive to set up a site and start writing, it's difficult to make any money doing this. The majority of "mommy bloggers" never earn a dime from their online musings.

This, says Alli Worthington—who founded her own online media company and hosts a 500-mom blogger conference each year in Nashville—is blogging's "dirty secret." Even Alli, whose 2010 conference featured a private concert by Harry Connick, Jr., and had corporate sponsors like ConAgra Foods, spent nearly two years without turning a significant profit, despite being one of the better-known names in blogging. (Her blog's tagline: *We can't both look good. It's me or the house.*) Despite more than 10,000 Twitter followers and her well-read online magazine, *Blissfully Domestic,* it took a partnership with mom-friendly brands (and a second conference) to push Alli into the black.

Like Alli, a growing number of mom bloggers are finding their rhythm, either by leveraging their online presence to garner ad sales or corporate sponsorships, or by landing freelance writing gigs and paid speaking engagements. A 2009 study found that 23 million women are reading, writing, or commenting on blogs each week[14]—and the profit is starting to come as brands reach out to women who are influencing purchases via their blogging platforms.

For Amy Lupold Bair, who has been quoted in the *New York Times* and has flown around the country for various "brand ambassador" blogging events, the real financial success came when she ditched "pro blogging"—she blogged for companies and charged a fee—and created an online party concept in 2008.

Her idea: Host a "sitewarming" soiree for newly launched websites with a chat-room feel and lots of prizes. For her first online party, companies that wanted to tap into her mom market supplied about $2,000 in prizes—and she ended up finding a huge following on Twitter that night in September 2008. She immediately got three new party-hosting requests.

By the time Hollee and Amy met in person—at Alli's blogging conference in February 2010—Amy had hosted more than 150 online events. She was holding steady with about three parties per week (her service involves working with clients to pinpoint the party's theme and purpose, collecting prizes, strategizing for maximum participation, and then implementing the final event). She originally planned to return to the teaching career she had before motherhood. But now, with the experience she'd accumulated over the past eighteen months, she'd never need to return to a job with traditional hours.

And for Amy, that was better than perfect.

Amy Lupold Bair, 32
Entrepreneur, Founder of ResourcefulMommy Media
Olney, Maryland
Mother of Emma and Noah

I can't even imagine what my life would look like if I hadn't found a profession through social media. When my kids wake up, we curl up in bed together. I can walk my daughter to the bus stop, and I'm there when she gets off the bus.

Social media changes the game for moms entirely, and not just financially. The other piece was that I have these degrees and this experience and had traveled the world, and then suddenly my whole life was in my house. I had a hunger to do something professionally, but my desire to be home with my kids was bigger. Social media filled the gap.

I would hate to drop any aspect of my life right now—I would hate to suddenly have to work sixty hours a week and feel like I dropped a piece of parenting. But I think that's because I'm okay with good enough. I don't care about dishes in the sink—I'm feeding my children and sanitizing the bathroom. Good enough is why I have time to do what I can do. Anything more is not necessary and too confining for me. I just don't have time.

THINK LIKE AN ENTREPRENEUR

Like Amy, Becky cherished her time at home. She was calmer than she'd been in years, and she loved being with her children, seeing their eyes open wide with curiosity when she took them to a museum in the middle of the day. But something had been missing, and she'd felt a bit incompetent as a housewife. She'd never been able to shake the (admittedly hilarious) image of herself on Christmas Eve 2003, when she'd been barefoot and pregnant and covered in yet another cooking disaster. She wanted a professional outlet, but she was no longer willing to surrender to somebody else's schedule. It wasn't that she didn't want to work hard—in fact, she longed for a project that would inspire her passion—it was just that this time around, she wanted both control and a sense of purpose. Her worst fear was to find herself riding the mommy track, puttering away in some halfhearted version of her old life. She needed something new—but what?

So she started a business building a distribution network for a skin care and wellness company. What could be more outside her comfort zone than selling exfoliating masks and facial serum? The business was a good fit: The risk and investment were low, she wouldn't need to carry inventory, and she knew well-educated women who were finding success in the growing network marketing industry. The business model relied on the simple power of word-of-mouth marketing: All she had to do was build a base of loyal and enthusiastic clients, and train others to do the same. She wasn't keen on doing the home parties often associated with network marketing businesses, but an MBA-educated woman Becky knew had found reasonable success marketing her business one-on-one. Becky was sold. She wrote a plan and launched her business.

But it was harder than she'd imagined. At first, she loved meeting new people, and she got a rush from doing something that was completely outside her experience. She was mildly successful, building a base of regular clients and a small, international team of other business builders. The growing paycheck was nice, too; the dream that it might get even larger was also enticing. She loved the idea of taking the pressure off Pete without having to give up what they'd gained by having her at home.

But Becky never learned to love selling—or, for that matter, to truly believe that she could do it well. And aspects of the business that came naturally to other people completely overwhelmed her. Despite her ability to manage large writing projects, she seemed to lack time-management skills when it came to sales. Often, she found herself shifting gears too quickly or spinning her wheels. Others in the business had found their success by following a system, but Becky felt the constant need to "do things her own way." She knew she was overthinking everything, and talking about it too much, but she couldn't seem to redirect herself. Her perfectionist tendencies took over: Anytime she felt less than "the best," she began to lose steam.

By contrast, Julianne Lagerstrom, a mother of three working from the suburbs of Kansas City, had found rapid success with the same company. Within just seven months of launching her business, she'd been able to quit her corporate job with a pharmaceutical company because she'd nearly replaced her six-figure income. Within several years, she was earning double what she'd earned as a pharmaceutical rep—and was working fewer than half the hours.

The difference between the two women? Julianne had learned to think like an entrepreneur. She later told Becky: "Starting something of your own— it just seems like a leap off a cliff. No matter what, in any kind of business, you know there are people around you saying, 'That's not going to work.' That mental toughness in the beginning is critical."

Becky didn't have it—not for something as far outside her comfort zone as sales—but in the end, her venture into entrepreneurism served a broader purpose: It helped her figure out exactly what she wanted to do. It stretched her ideas of what was possible—and it led her to reconnect with Hollee. The two almost immediately started talking about how very difficult it was to find the right balance between motherhood and career, and how important it was do something that they loved. Hollee even briefly considered joining Becky in the skin-care business.

Then she had a better idea:

From: Hollee Temple
To: Rebecca Beaupre Gillespie
Thursday, August 30, 2007 8:22 AM

Hey, Becky, I thought you might be interested in this [article on women seeking work/life balance]. I am actually thinking about developing a book proposal on this topic ... might be looking for a coauthor ... any possible interest?

At 4:23 p.m., Becky wrote back:

Extremely interested.

8

REDEFINING THE SUMMIT IN HIGH-STAKES CAREERS

- Even in the most demanding fields, moms are finding success by creating their own paths.

- Many moms have sacrificed income and a quicker path to the corner office in exchange for time with their small children.

- If your current workplace isn't working for you, explore alternative careers. Even demanding professions offer balanced options if you look hard and make strategic choices.

- Moms (and moms-to-be) need to think long term. Are you choosing a field and specialty area that will allow you to be the kind of mother you want to be?

Libby Windsor didn't always dream of becoming a lawyer—it was more of a logical next step, a path of least resistance. In fact, when she was winning awards as a top art history student at Kenyon College, her professors urged her to make a career of that.

She'd pondered an artistic life, imagining herself in graduate school for interior design—then opening her own business, bringing her deep knowledge of art history to residential design. Libby had grown up with parents who adored the visual arts and took her to the National Gallery in Washington, D.C., for all the latest openings. Vermeer and Matisse were a part of her vocabulary before she started college; she interned at the Barnes Foundation in Philadelphia and at Pittsburgh's renowned Warhol Museum during her undergraduate summers. She became so well-schooled that she developed categories of favorites: an affinity for "those seedy Montmartre artists working in post–World War I Paris" like Modigliani, Toulouse-Lautrec and Bonnard; a favorites-to-study group—Rothko, Pollock, Frankenthaler and Kline; and, her list-toppers for overall "most intriguing" artists—Duchamp and Picasso.

But Libby, a pragmatist at heart, worried that she wouldn't be able to support herself, or her eventual family, if she followed her passion. So she went with plan B: Law school.

* * *

We're not a generation of women intent on *marrying* doctors and lawyers. We *are* doctors and lawyers—and industrial engineers, dentists, airline pilots, financial analysts and corporate CEOs. In just two generations, women have gone from dreaming about jobs they'd never land (like the legal career that Becky's grandmother yearned for) to filling nearly half the seats in demanding professional school classes. And our work/life choices have evolved, too— we're beyond the heartrending decisions that plagued Baby Boomer women, who came of age at a time when pursuing a challenging career often meant remaining childless.

The Boomers' daughters were determined to do things differently, and after excelling in school for many years, we hustled to join the exalted ranks in the revered professions dominated by men. We coveted those advanced degrees, the titles, the money, the respect. After all, we wanted to believe Marlo Thomas when she sang that mommies could be *almost* anything we wanted to be, and she made it look so effortless, strutting the streets of New York with her shiny dark hair and her (not visible) baby in the pram.

But there wasn't a chorus singing to us about the challenges. The song didn't tell us that even if we collectively managed to crack the glass ceiling, we'd run up against a "maternal wall" of workplace bias, with employers assuming that motherhood would automatically make us less committed workers.[1] It also failed to mention (probably a good thing) that some of us would build our careers alongside spouses who also wanted top-dog positions, a phenomenon that professors Karine Moe and Dianna Shandy discuss in their recent book, *Glass Ceilings and 100-Hour Couples.* In a section titled "Inside the Hectic Household," they describe the conundrum of the high-powered couple with children. In a nutshell: How can two (mortal) parents stay afloat when one is on a business trip, one has a deposition in fifteen minutes, two kids need to be dropped off at different locations, and the babysitter is running late?

When we started interviewing mothers for this book, we found ourselves drawn to the stories of women in pressure-filled careers, particularly those that had traditionally been dominated by men. The story didn't feel complete without a hard look at this tough question: How, exactly, does a modern mother define her own success in fields with predetermined markers? How does she create her own New Perfect when her employer expects complete dedication, when ascending the ranks means aiming for...*perfection?* And how can she do it with a spouse who is also striving to be an ideal employee?

EXPECTATIONS FOR WOMEN IN MALE-DOMINATED FIELDS

We can't sugarcoat what we found: It's not easy to be a mom (whether the Good Enough or Never Enough variety) in a pressure-cooker field. For starters, the expectations for near-constant availability and insane hours can feel like a gag. Yet moms in these professions invest a considerable number of years—and many incur significant debt—before they see a financial return on their educational investments. By the time they become mothers, it often doesn't make financial or professional sense for them to seek a more flexible or reduced-hours schedule. (Several of the women we interviewed outearned their husbands; their family budgets relied on the mothers' full-time salaries to make ends meet.)

What's more, some of these hard-charging careers were built around the premise that those who survived the rigorous training would be defined, pretty much forever, by the job. That's how Hollee remembered her dad's medical career—he was "Doc" everywhere they went, making house calls for friends and regularly being "beeped" away from family activities. In the fall of 2009, about a year after her father retired from his thirty-one-year career as an ear, nose and throat surgeon, Hollee asked him about the sacrifices.

"Becoming a doctor was about joining a profession rather than assuming an occupation," Joel answered. "It required effort and integrity far beyond any other field. I couldn't tell people who were sick that I wouldn't see them so I could go to my child's ball game or school play. I couldn't tell a patient that I would do a lesser operation so that I would be on time to go out to dinner. I couldn't tell people that I wouldn't care for them because they couldn't pay."

Joel entered medicine—arguably the field where perfect matters the most—under a punishing work model that essentially required one at-home parent (almost always the mom) to handle the house, kids and everything else while the physician father worked a dizzying schedule. When Hollee's dad started medical school in 1969, only 9 percent of entering students nation- wide were female. It was a time when laws didn't limit the numbers of hours that resident physicians could work. (They were originally called residents because they were supposed to "reside" at the hospital.) When Hollee's mom called to say that she was in labor in the summer of 1974, her father, then a sur- gical resident, was in the middle of an appendectomy; he had to finish before swooping down to the obstetrics unit—at the last minute—right before Hollee was born.

As Hollee was growing up, middle-of-the-night phone calls, followed by the whir of the garage door opening as her dad rushed to the hospital, were the norm. For years, her father shared a call schedule with a single partner—there were few days off, let alone vacations. Before she even got out of bed, Hollee's dad was usually gone, "making rounds" at the hospital to see his patients.

Libby Windsor remembers a similar childhood; she grew up with a father who was a high-powered litigator. Her dad would often come home for dinner to spend a little time with the family; she'd watch *Who's the Boss?* or *The Cosby Show* on the couch with her mother while her father, wingback chair turned away from the TV, curled over a legal pad before his nightly return trip to the office.

Libby's father told Hollee that even in the mid-1970s, though computers weren't yet pumping out daily reports of the hours he billed or the fees he generated, an attorney who wanted to make partner still needed to charge clients for about 2,000 hours of work per year. When he started practicing law in 1975, women filled just more than a quarter of the seats in starting law school classes. Part-time work was rare, and just like their physician counterparts, most attorneys were men who relied on their wives to manage the home front. An "immersion" in the culture of law was the norm.

IS THERE A WAY TO MESH MOTHERHOOD AND A TOP-DOG CAREER?

When Baby Boomer women dipped their painted toes into these male bastions in the 1970s, they were true pioneers. But when their Gen-X daughters started pursuing advanced professional degrees in historic numbers in the 1990s, the stage was set for an inevitable duel between motherhood and work. These women were determined to find high-flying careers *and* satisfying family lives, and they wanted to do it in fields where the stakes were high.

When Jen Canter started medical school in 1993, the percentage of women in the average medical school class had swelled to 42 percent. By the time Libby Windsor started law school in the fall of 2000, women took nearly half the seats.[2] Women are continuing to flock to hard-charging professions today, comprising almost half the recent classes entering medical school, dental school and law school.[3] For the 2007–2008 school year, women received 42 percent of the MBA diplomas, and even in engineering, seemingly the last male holdout, women earned almost 20 percent of bachelor's degrees.

But how are these women coping as they weave motherhood into the mix? Is it possible to stay true to Good Enough ideals in careers where perfect matters? We wanted the inside story, and we got it from women who had chosen two particularly large, and notoriously demanding, professions: law and medicine. Many view these careers as the epitome of professional accomplishment, and there are at least half a million female doctors and lawyers practicing in this country.[4] In both these professions, family-friendly policies have been slow to come—and that's why law and medicine make an ideal prism for examining some of the toughest challenges of working motherhood.

When we asked our blog readers about the unique challenge of meshing motherhood and competitive careers, the comments poured in from across the country:

MELISSA FROM MORGANTOWN, WEST VIRGINIA:
Lawyer moms can be thrown in jail for contempt of court if you are expected in court and don't show up for work!

TRACY FROM LAUREL, MARYLAND:
As a doctor mom, the biggest challenge I face is the "unexpected absence." For most other professions in the world, when you or your child is sick, you call out sick and the world goes on without you for a little while. As a doctor, when I call out sick, that means that twenty-five sick people don't get taken care of. My colleagues have to pick up my slack in addition to their busy schedules. Talk about guilt! Every working mom has coworkers and customers who rely on them, but not every working mom runs the risk of *really bad things* if she calls out sick.

SARA FROM PHOENIX:
One of the more significant challenges I've found as a lawyer mom is that I can't talk about what I do. I think many professions have high degrees of confidentiality, but doctor and lawyer moms are faced with significant repercussions for talking about what we do. We get overwhelmed and frustrated and we often don't have a release.

That toxic combination—the fear of really bad things happening heaped on top of frustration, isolation and guilt—may be why many women seem to be petering out in the middle of the race. In a nationwide study of large law firms, women comprised 46 percent of the starting associate classes, but in the end, they accounted for only 16 percent of equity partners at large firms and 15 percent of general counsels at Fortune 500 companies.[5] Similarly, women start out strong in medicine (45 percent of the resident physicians),[6] but are far less likely to choose the most prestigious (and lucrative) surgical fields. In a 2009 study of surgical residents, less than 13 percent pursued orthopedic and thoracic surgery, and only 12 percent specialized in neurological surgery.[7]

There's more than one way of interpreting these statistics. Some posit that women aren't making it to the summit in these professions because they still can't break into the boys' club, or because they charge in without much consideration for how they will eventually blend their professions and family life, throwing in the towel when the going gets tough.

But there's another possibility, one that came up in interview after interview in our research. In many instances, women are choosing to redefine success in these fields; they're trading money and prestige for lifestyles that allow them to cull all they want from motherhood. For many moms we interviewed, these changes were not concessions or "mommy tracks"; they'd found ways to protect the parts that brought them the most passion and pride, even if they didn't take the fastest possible route to *traditional* success. The experiences of these women offer insight into the challenges faced by all working mothers, and show how it is possible to find a New Perfect in spite of competitive career choices.

THE JD JUGGLE: FINDING BALANCE WHEN TIME IS THE VALUED COMMODITY

When Libby Windsor took our survey, she described her approach to juggling work and family this way: "I try to be a superstar at work and at home, even if it kills me." She had been a superstar at Boston University Law School, too, even though she was prepared to hate the experience. Her dad had made practicing law look easy ("like all good parents do," she added), but Libby would never forget the stories about his three years in law school at the University of Pittsburgh. Serving in the Navy during Vietnam was better, he often joked.

But when Libby started law school, she quickly fell in love with the competitive teaching methods—and especially with the satisfaction she got from excelling in such an objective way. In fact, even a decade later, Libby remembered the triumph she felt after opening the heavy black binders in the law school registrar's office and finding herself at the top of the curve.

Her love of problem-solving, of mastering new sets of facts and applying the law to her clients' evolving legal situations, led to a fairly seamless transition into her sophisticated practice in employment law. Libby never wanted a rote job that would get boring over time—she wanted to engage her mind every day and, in employment law at a prestigious international law firm, things were always changing. She liked the "human story" behind her class action suits; she could pore over Family and Medical Leave regulations without getting the least bit bored because she viewed the study as an investment in her arsenal of legal expertise.

But that's not to say that Libby's transition was easy. Early on, she struggled to transfer her academic knowledge to a practical setting—a problem that's all too common, according to Susan Cartier Liebel, an attorney and expert on solo law practice who has worked with new practitioners for more than a decade. Susan believes that until law schools offer more practical skills training, the problem will linger. ("Can you imagine going to medical school and never working on a cadaver? Law schools need to provide that equivalent," she told Hollee.) It's little wonder that there are so many dissatisfied lawyers; a 2008 study found that 72 percent had left their entry-level positions within five years.[8]

When you add motherhood to this less-than-auspicious starting point (and the timing of law school graduation—average age twenty-six—makes that likely), it's no surprise that although nearly half of all students at law schools are now women, only a sliver makes it to the profession's highest echelons.[9] The proportion of women reaching law firm partnership status has increased *only 4 percentage points* over the past decade—and women still haven't topped the

20 percent hurdle.[10] If the pattern continues, it will be 2086 before men and women share equally in law firm partnerships.[11]

Not the most heartening prediction.

That's why Deborah Epstein Henry, forty-two, has spent more than a decade trying to change the hidebound culture of the law—and when Hollee first interviewed her in March 2009, it was clear that Debbie had no plans to slow down. A leading advocate for the promotion and retention of women in the legal profession, Debbie started Flex-Time Lawyers in 1999 as a support group for working lawyer moms. As the years passed, Debbie's organization evolved, ultimately giving voice to a growing yet often disenfranchised segment—working mothers who couldn't find a way to manage the JD juggle. In the fall of 2010, the American Bar Association published Debbie's first book, *LAW & REORDER: Legal Industry Solutions for Work/Life Balance, Retention, Promotion & Restructure.*

From Debbie's vantage point, there is some good news: Today's working parents have demanded flexible options, earning notice as the first generation to circumvent the "dead-end career track" that used to be the only option for lawyers who wanted less than full-time schedules.[12] That observation was made in a Flex-Time Lawyers/*Working Mother* survey of best law firms for women, where almost all the winning firms said they allowed their attorneys to progress to equity partner (the top rung) while working reduced hours. This was a big step forward; the phenomenon was unheard of when Hollee began her law career in the late 1990s.

But here's the problem: The numbers tell a different story. When Debbie looked at the winning firms and their promotion rates from 2004 to 2008, the average number of women who had made equity partner while working reduced hours during that period was troubling: *two women per firm*—and these were the "Best Law Firms for Women."

So why is it so hard for large law firms to appreciate that they're losing some terrific talent by sticking with their traditional ways? First and foremost, reduced hours simply don't mesh with the current reality of large firm practice—given the billing rates for these attorneys (most *start* at more than

$200/hour), clients expect them to be available around the clock (or at least that's the perception). And that's why so many lawyers don't consider part-time work to be a real option. In 2009, fewer than 6 percent of lawyers nationally were working reduced hours and, not surprisingly, the vast majority (about 73 percent) were women.[13] What's more, female attorneys repeatedly told us that scaling back carried great risk; they feared they would not be taken seriously because so few men were making similar requests.

Next, the legal profession is about as traditional as they come. Lawyers venerate tradition—after all, the easiest way to win a case is to convince a judge that scores of other judges have ruled the same way on an issue. Further, the current mechanism for assessing value in most legal settings—the almighty billable hour that has been entrenched for the past sixty years—discourages efficiency and puts a premium on the one thing moms don't have enough of: Time. (Did you know that law firms often refer to their attorneys as "timekeepers"?)

On top of that, internet and smartphone technology that keeps lawyers "on call" around the clock is thwarting family time; several female lawyers we interviewed referred to the "'CrackBerry' leash" and lamented computer networks that showed which attorneys were virtually connected after hours.

Jodi Cleesattle, 42
Deputy Attorney General, California Department of Justice
San Diego, California
Mother of Annika and Josie

As a lawyer, the balance is tough because of the heavy workload and crisis-management nature of litigation. Strangely, it's somewhat easier now that I'm a divorced single mom because, for a couple nights a week, my daughters are at their dad's house. On those nights, I can stay late at the office for marathon work sessions if I need to.

I think the hardest challenge for professional women in settings like law firms, though, is that they're working with professional men who—for the most part—do not have the same outside responsibilities. Even in "progressive" law firms, it's not uncommon for nearly all of the male partners and a surprisingly large number of the male associates to have wives who stay at home or work part-time. That means that the standard work expectation is set by and for people who can devote all of their waking hours to the firm. Worse, even if a woman with children puts in as many hours as the men, she still is perpetually viewed as not as committed to the firm because she's a mother. And, believe me, the men will tell you this right out loud. It's just not a level playing field, and, mentally, that's very draining.

* * *

So where is that good news for female lawyers? While the biggest law firms may not be the best landing spot for long-term quality of life, Debbie Epstein Henry has unearthed some new trends that do bode well for the future.

First, there is a ray of hope in the large law firms, as some move away from the billable-hour model and substitute alternative fee structures that do reward efficiency. While none of the large firms have entirely abandoned the billable hour, some are negotiating deals that don't rely exclusively on that method.[14] Debbie says those firms are a better bet for mothers, "who have never been as successful competing [with men] over time."

An even more promising newcomer is the home-based virtual law firm. With little overhead, these firms reward quality work done in a timely manner—a win for the client *and* the efficient lawyer mom. "What's really nice about the virtual firm is that it takes away the stigma of working from home," Debbie told Hollee. "It's part of the business model—there's no issue about whether this lawyer is committed. Everyone is doing the same thing."

Debbie notes that some of the more traditional "alternative" arenas—government, in-house counsel, nonprofits and academia—are still popular for moms, offering women a chance to utilize their degrees without giving their entire lives over to their work.

Finally, there is the entrepreneurial solo route—the one that Danielle G. Van Ess (the lawyer we met in chapter 4 who struggled with whether she should shed her maiden name) chose. Danielle, a mother of three, works exclusively from her home-based office in the Boston suburbs. When her youngest was a baby, she often drafted estate planning documents with her daughter asleep in a sling on her chest. While building her own practice has been far from easy, it's been the right path for Danielle.

"I went solo to fit my life," she told Hollee in the spring of 2010. "It's hard as hell, I'm not going to lie there, but I think ultimately the sacrifices (for instance, late-night meetings, no dinner, exhaustion) are worth it to spend the time with my babies while they're still so little!"

And that's really what it comes down to—choosing the path that creates the most happiness at this time in women's lives—as mothers *and* professionals.

Susan Cartier Liebel, 50
Attorney and Founder of Solo Practice University
New Haven County, Connecticut
Mother of one son

What these women have to do is look down the road, five, ten, fifteen years, and create markers for deciding what success means to them. They have to start stepping back, personally and professionally, to see what steps they have to take to get there. There is no right or wrong; it's whatever they want, and then they need to fashion a game plan that's in sync with those values.

You have to lay out your personal and professional goals side by side, push them together and see how the time lines mesh. Once your career starts mirroring and complementing your personal goals, the tension starts to disappear.

MOMS ON CALL: FINDING GOOD ENOUGH WHEN LIVES ARE ON THE LINE

Our research showed sharp differences between doctors and lawyers—in work arrangements, accommodations made for motherhood and overall satisfaction. The biggest difference was the ability to work reduced hours: Lawyers repeatedly said they felt they wouldn't be taken seriously if they worked part-time; the doctors, for the most part, didn't have that worry. (National statistics show that lawyers are far less likely than other professionals, including physicians, to work part-time.)[15]

Based on survey responses and interviews, we concluded that medicine offered more balance because the profession had evolved to a point where reduced hours were no longer stigmatized. In the New Perfect survey, nearly 65 percent of the lawyer moms surveyed worked full-time; several asserted that it was the only arrangement that made it possible to advance in law. By contrast, only a little more than half the doctors described their work arrangement as full-time, and, those who did were more likely than their attorney counterparts to describe their work as "flexible."

But that's not to say it's an easy life. When we started a discussion on our blog about the challenges of working in high-pressure fields, doctor moms didn't hold back:

JAIME FROM DOUGLAS, GEORGIA:
In today's society, I have found that people think their doctor (especially their children's doctor) is supposed to be available immediately—at all times! I have actually had patients leave my practice because I was out of the office with my own sick child!

MICHELLE FROM LEXINGTON, KENTUCKY:
This afternoon, my two-year-old daughter has been sick with vomiting, diarrhea and fever. She feels miserable and looks pitiful, but I called to check my schedule at work, and I am booked almost solid with checkups from 8:15 a.m. to 4:30 p.m.

There is just no way to reschedule that many patients—some of whom I'm sure have parents who have rearranged their own work schedules for their appointments with me. I love being a pediatrician, but you know what? I love my children more. If I had it to do over again, I would choose a different profession. I have no doubt I could make the same amount of money doing something that allowed me more flexibility. This is what I will teach my own children someday when it comes time for them to choose their own career pathway.

Of Hollee's five closest friends from high school, four are doctors, so she's spent the last decade watching them jump through the MD hurdles. All four are now doctor moms (with a combined nine children among them), and while their stories have slightly different plot points than lawyers and other high-powered professionals, they share many of the same work/life challenges. The first hurdle: Women physicians have invested so many years in their training that the timing of motherhood is problematic. Even those who leap straight from college to medical school often reach their mid-thirties before finishing advanced residencies; the desire to start a family coincides with the career point when many are just taking off. (Only one of Hollee's friends had a child before she started her residency; the others were all in their thirties before they became moms.)

The work demands are also a stressor—perhaps that's why so many women are opting out of the most prestigious, and most inflexible, specialties, like surgery. A recent analysis of medical residents found that slightly less than a third are women—and that's the highest number ever reported. Even though Hollee's friends had never settled for anything less than "the best" in their previous pursuits (all were academic standouts), impending motherhood seemed to change the game. Even though surgical specialties offered the most prestige and money, only one of Hollee's friends, Jenny, chose that route—and then, because she knew how unpredictable life as an obstetrician would be, Jenny opted for more advanced training in reproductive endocrinology so that she would eventually have a more family-friendly lifestyle. The others chose practice areas that they could moderate a bit more—pediatrics, family practice and academic medicine.

Los Angeles–based psychologist Ricki Bander, who has been counseling female doctors and other professional women for more than twenty years, told Hollee about another challenge in medicine: "the doctor's God complex." While physicians come to medicine to heal and console others, they are often seen as heroes or saviors. And this noble aspiration has a flip side for women seeking balanced lives—if you're the hero, then you're the one and only person who can accomplish the work that needs to be done.

"While expectations are high and lives may be at stake, the bottom line is that doctors aren't gods, but people—and parents—who need to learn to ask for what they need," Ricki told Hollee. She finds it curious that the women she counsels, typically assertive go-getters, are often hesitant to seek the flexibility and support they need to make life work for their families.

That said, the culture of medicine has been changing over the past two decades, and Ricki believes it has become more hospitable to mothers; women are better able to define their expectations and reset the boundaries. While particularly innovative doctors make themselves indispensable by honing specialized skills or taking an entrepreneurial path (Jen Canter, the child abuse pediatrician, somehow does *both*), many are choosing the relatively new field of "hospitalist" work or selecting traditional specialties that are more amenable to part-time practice.

* * *

The hospital medicine movement—which refers to doctors who work solely in hospital environments—is a relative newcomer that has given doctors the opportunity to lead more balance lives. There are two primary tracks: the "community hospitalist" option, where staff doctors take care of inpatients on a fixed schedule, or the "academic track," where the doctors serve on an in-hospital team with fewer clinical hours and more flexible academic work.

Predictable hours drove Stephanie Walsh, an Atlanta pediatrician and mother of three, to choose the community hospitalist path. Stephanie works at Children's Healthcare of Atlanta Pediatric Hospital, treating inpatients on a 75-percent schedule—three days a week plus nine weekends a year. The work is intense and fuels her passion for medicine; she works with very sick children. But because her shifts are scheduled, she can work around her own kids' activities. "If I know Conor has a field trip on October 15, I just take October 15 off," she says.

Arpana Vidyarthi, forty, an academic hospitalist in San Francisco, believes the field provides a "phenomenally welcoming career" for women because it offers so many options. When Arpana, a mom of two young daughters, joined her hospital medicine group in 2002, women made up about a quarter of the team. Now, about 60 percent of new hires are women ("mostly of childbearing age," she adds), and many choose this specialty because of the flexibility it offers. Arpana notes several other advances during her tenure: The team now plans for at least one doctor to be on maternity leave each year so the remaining doctors don't have to take extra shifts while the new doctor mom recovers. (Before the formal policy, an "informal mommy brigade" pitched in as needed.) And the women in the group are actively mentoring their new recruits with advice that sometimes contradicts the "be efficient so I can get home" attitude of working mothers.

Arpana Vidyarthi, 40
Academic "Hospitalist" Physician
San Francisco, California
Mother of Anaiya and Nika

I had a leadership coach who taught me something I had never thought about. He talked about [how] women who have kids are some of the most efficient workers out there—they get the job done beyond belief. But we as women sometimes focus so much on protecting our time that we don't want to "waste time" doing chitchat and lingering over lunch. But that can hurt you if you're trying to become a visible leader in the organization. He encouraged me to take the time to have a "networking lunch" every once in a while; he said that the water cooler conversations can make a difference and should be given some importance.

Arpana keeps this advice in mind as she works long hours—she estimates spending fifty hours per week in the hospital, and starts her day on the computer before the kids get up. She often stays up through the night writing papers or answering emails. But the flexibility means a lot. She makes it to her daughters' preschool to participate in folk dancing and story time, and has never missed a pediatrician visit, even though she has a full-time nanny. Still, she struggles with knowing when to pull back.

"I have to remind myself that I can take my career in steps," Arpana told Hollee. "It's like each woman just has to find her true North and make that touchstone constant and really think about how to get there. You don't necessarily need to get off the path—the path is wide and you can find other ways to continue on that path and still be fulfilled."

HOW THE GOOD ENOUGHS ARE TAKING CONTROL

But that's not to say that the path to happiness comes without sacrifice. Alison Gaudet, a pediatrician in suburban Philadelphia, deliberately chose to focus on her young daughters early in her medical career—even though that wasn't a painless choice. Her oldest daughter was born during her final year of residency, when "you pretty much belong to the hospital," and with no family in town, full-time day care seemed like the only option. Alison found it heartbreaking to wake her newborn in the darkness, and as a pediatrician, she couldn't swallow some of the practices other working moms had suggested. ("I wasn't going to keep her up late to adjust to my schedule; I knew it wasn't good for her.") So shortly after she completed her residency, Alison sacrificed salary and a quick path to partnership.

Alison considered surgical fields, but distinctly remembered the weary look of a female surgeon she encountered during a hospital rotation. That attending physician was frank: "If you want a family, don't go into surgery," she advised.

Alison listened. When Hollee first interviewed her, she was working for an all-women's pediatric practice that scheduled her patients two days each week (she hired a nanny to watch the kids and keep up with the housework while she was gone).

"For the past five years, I've been home five of seven days," she said. "I call myself a part-time stay-at-home mom, part-time pediatrician."

The career sacrifices—less money, less continuity of patient care, and less prestige than if she had plunged into a full-time practice—seemed worth it most days. But because she worked part-time and her husband worked longer hours in the insurance industry, Alison assumed almost all of the home- and child-related tasks. It stung, she said, when her contributions outside the home felt undervalued.

"Even though I have playdates at the pool, I'm still a pediatrician, and I feel like I don't always get credit for that," she said. "Sometimes being part-time is hard because you have this career that you're trying to grow but at the same time you have so many responsibilities at home. Of course I feel torn between the two, but in the end I decided that while it would have been easier to focus on my career full-time, it wouldn't have been as gratifying. They're only going to be this little once."

By the fall of 2009, Alison had bumped up her schedule to three full days a week, with two afternoons reserved for her girls. Though she had hoped to maintain a reduced schedule indefinitely, she recognized that she wouldn't gain partnership without putting in more hours. But now that sacrifice feels different because her daughters are more independent.

"When both girls are in school all day and with the hours our office operates, I'll be missing only about an hour a day with them," she says.

And with plans to keep her nanny on at least part-time, to handle the chores that she'd be doing at home if she weren't working, Alison feels good— but not perfect—about the balance she's striking.

* * *

In the fall of 2009, as Libby Windsor shared her career goals with Hollee, she explained that despite the hefty billable-hour requirements at her top-rung firm, she was firmly committed to returning to a full-time law career after her second son was born. Even in her early twenties, she knew she wanted to be a mom with a big-time career; she just didn't know how to do it. When she became pregnant with her first child (three years into her career, as suggested by a female mentor), her crisis became acute. Should she ask for a reduced-hours schedule? Her father, the former managing partner of a major international law firm, advised her to return full-time after his grandson was born; it would prove her commitment to the work.

So she took the standard four months off after Will was born in 2006, and was surprised to find herself itching to get back to work even before her leave was up. One reason? When she traveled with the baby and tried to explain her "nonworking" situation, new acquaintances didn't ask another question about her job. For years she had been building her credentials as a go-to litigator, and because she had a baby in her lap, she felt a sudden identity loss. She longed to get back to the professional world, where she felt productive and proud of her growing employment law expertise.

With a full-time nanny at home, Libby found it easier than she'd expected to return to full-time work after Will was born. And after baby Andrew made his appearance in March 2009, she told Hollee again—with a clear determination—about why she planned to return to full-time work as soon as her maternity leave with her second son was complete.

But that's when the trouble that had strained Libby's marriage had appeared, when Will's anxiety and the stress of two young children had worn her down and convinced her to opt for an 80-percent schedule.

"I felt like I was cheating Andrew out of something he couldn't get back," she told Hollee.

She'd coped by reminding herself that it was "just for now," though she conceded that she'd needed to give herself *permission* to scale back, a carry-over from her Never Enough mind-set. So much of Libby's self-identity and self-worth had come from her accomplishments at work; the decision brought pain, angst—and, surprisingly, a sense of relief.

"It's a weird sense of loss, like I'm throwing up my hands in defeat," she'd told Hollee shortly after she made the decision to scale back. "But in my heart I know that it's right even though I'm surprised to have so much sadness over it. But there is that mental benefit—it's like I feel a pressure valve release."

Several months later, Libby had gotten used to the idea. The 20-percent pay cut wasn't easy—she needed to think hard about luxuries that she'd never worried about before (weekly cleaning help, buying her boys $25 turtlenecks from the Hanna Andersson catalog). But the newfound freedom meant a lot.

She found that she enjoyed dropping her son off at preschool every morning, and with less pressure to bill, she could put more emphasis on herself and her marriage. Libby now spends Friday afternoons focusing on herself instead of on the number of hours she bills. She'll pick up groceries (which were often missing in her home before her schedule change), take an extra-long run, get a haircut . . . and it feels, in her words, "luxurious."

"I think it is worth it. In my heart I know that it is. I'm giving up so much money that if I wasn't getting some trade-off I think I'd be angry about it. And I'm not. The release of pressure has been good in that way."

"The truth is, deep down, women in high-pressure jobs share a lot with all the other moms out there," said Ricki Bander, the California psychologist who told Hollee about the two decades she spent working with resident physicians. From Ricki's perspective, it comes down to recognizing that your choices have risks and consequences, and then moving forward on that path to happiness.

Ricki Bander, PhD, 57
Licensed Psychologist and Coach to Executives and
Medical Professionals
Los Angeles, California

I was at a breakfast recently with two women executives and they were talking about how there was always too much to do, how they were on the edge of burnout—some of the same things I hear from doctors.

And I said, "Look, you keep saying that what you're doing isn't enough, yet you don't feel like you can do any more. So what you're saying is that you're not willing to accept that at some point, enough is enough, that there is always more you can do on your plate." Until you can get to "What I am doing is good enough," it's hard to feel okay.

And that's true no matter what profession you're blending with motherhood. To get to your own New Perfect, you need to plant the seeds, pull out the weeds that get in the way and create the garden that's beautiful to you.

EVEN THE BEST-LAID PLANS

- **When faced with a crisis, try to accept help. You need it, and it makes people feel better to be able to do *something*.**

- **When things go wrong, priorities come into focus. But it's better not to wait for the crisis to discover what really matters in your life.**

- **Moms are stronger than they think they are; they have to be.**

John wasn't feeling great when he set off for North Carolina in the spring of 2005, but he wasn't the type to let a little cold keep him from his work. Hollee didn't think much of it. She just bought him some decongestant, drove him to the airport and then hunkered down with a *Blue's Clues*–obsessed Gideon and chubby, six-month-old Henry.

John made it to Durham, conducted some interviews for his latest book, and then copied boxes of legal documents to lug home. His cold got worse, so he took more pills. During a layover at Dulles Airport on his way home, John argued with his boss over his cell phone. When he hung up, the room began to close in, his field of vision narrowing to a pinhole. John realized that his heart was hammering.

What the hell is happening to me? he wondered.

But then, just as suddenly as it had started, the odd sensation passed, and he could see again. The crew began boarding his flight to Pittsburgh. John forced himself to stand up. His shirt was soaked with cold sweat, but he didn't want to end up in a hospital bed far from home.

John tried to forget; he didn't even mention the incident to Hollee as they chatted on their drive home to Morgantown.

Over the next year, the heart issue that no one could explain came and went. The first emergency room trip happened less than a week after the Dulles incident; doctors declared an unexplainable case of atrial fibrillation—nothing life-threatening, nothing to *really* worry about. They put John on some mild medication, and the summer was quiet. In January, when John started feeling strange again, he spent thirty days connected to a portable monitor. When Hollee saw the monitor's leads attached to John's chest, she felt a sense of doom. The monitor recorded beats of more serious ventricular tachycardia, but given John's otherwise normal health, it went untreated. When spring came, Hollee and John went to Pittsburgh for a high-tech heart scan; she wept with joy when the radiologist said everything looked great.

It wasn't great, though. Sometimes the palpitations were so intense that John sweated through his clothes. Sometimes his teeth hurt. Right before Gideon's fourth birthday party in July, John went out to mow the lawn and kept having to stop to sit down.

He called out to Hollee. "What is this?" John asked with a fear she had never seen in his pale blue eyes.

"You're just under the weather, and it's hot out here," she answered confidently, stroking his hand. "Remember how all the doctors have said this isn't life-threatening?"

The next month, however, those words were proven wrong. To this day, Hollee can't shake the image from her mind; it was the most awful moment of her life. First, John was laughing, chasing the boys around the inside of a racquetball court at the WVU Student Recreation Center. She looked away for a moment, and then, through the glass doors, she saw John reaching toward her, calling her name. Then, he collapsed and his lips turned blue.

Her thirty-six-year-old husband's heart had stopped beating.

Hollee screamed for help and then grabbed her babies, got them out of the room. A doctor who happened to be standing right outside the court took over; Hollee, on autopilot, ushered the kids to the gym's child-care center, then threw up in a garbage can. By the time she got back, emergency workers had arrived, the paddles were out; medics were trying to shock John's heart back to life. After multiple tries, they succeeded.

The next six weeks were a nightmarish blur, filled with 911 calls, two life flights, hospitalizations in three cities. John was alive, but Hollee was at—no, *beyond*—her emotional edge.

Alone in a hospital chapel, she prayed for one thing: Strength.

* * *

Hollee couldn't have planned for this, not back when her life was consumed with racking up gold stars, when she was so busy trying to do everything right. Until John's health crisis, Hollee had been able to conquer any obstacle if she pushed herself hard enough. She had even successfully maneuvered around the work/family dilemma that had confounded so many of her friends and colleagues. She'd crafted her escape from the law firm, sacrificed salary in exchange for time with her children and a more satisfying job, and had found her place in academia. She was regularly flooded with gratitude when she stopped and realized that things had worked out *even better* than she'd hoped. It was amazing, really: She and John had both secured university teaching jobs with sane hours in the same town. She was happier than ever. She looked forward to going to work (a first!) and was grateful that her babies were cared for by adoring college students, in her own home, when she was teaching or conducting conferences with her law students.

A part of her had never quite trusted the good fortune. In the back of her mind, she worried that the scales were tipped too far in her favor, that life was somehow too good. But it never occurred to her that something like this could possibly happen. Not to John. Not to her.

Hollee had never stared down something that couldn't be fixed or explained. But Lord knows she tried during the early days of John's health crisis, spending her sleepless nights on the internet so that she'd know what to ask when the cardiologists made their quick rounds the next morning.

But Hollee couldn't figure out why something had invaded John's heart and caused his cardiac rhythm to go so out of whack—and as it turned out, neither could the country's most experienced heart doctors at the Cleveland Clinic.

Life had obliterated her best-laid plans.

For almost two months, Hollee turned over everything—the care of her children, her house, her pets, her career—to family, friends and colleagues. Perfection was no longer an option—and, frankly, neither was good enough.

At first, she felt as if she'd been singled out for suffering. But many months later, after seeing a therapist who specialized in post-traumatic stress disorder, Hollee began to accept that everyone endures challenges, albeit of varying degrees. Her high school classmate Alicia had three kids when she was diagnosed with breast cancer at thirty-two. Two of Hollee's best friends, despite trying everything, couldn't seem to get pregnant. Another friend, the mother of a preschooler and a toddler, learned that her husband of ten years had been having affairs—and had contemplated leaving his wife and daughters behind.

This was the ugly truth: No matter how much we plan, life sometimes takes us in an entirely different direction.

When that happens, it changes the whole conversation about finding "balance." Hell, it sometimes *wipes it off the radar entirely.* Who has time to Have It All when we're worried about just holding it together? It was evident from our interviews, and personal experience, that very few things challenge women's ideas about success like the unanticipated tremors and quakes of life. The discussion of work/family fit simply isn't complete without acknowledging the things that make that goal feel temporarily impossible.

Not every woman faces a crisis of great magnitude, of course. And sometimes things that unravel us at first turn out to be great gifts later. (Although not always.) Our generation, like the others before it, has its signature stresses. We've wrestled with infertility. We have endured sharp increases in autism rates and life-threatening food allergies. We have found ourselves sandwiched between the competing needs of young children and aging parents.

In our survey, 10 percent of respondents said they faced "special circumstances," such as an illness or a special-needs child that made it harder to juggle work and motherhood. For some of us, these trials have given new meaning to words like Good Enough. After all, some of us have watched Perfect topple from its lofty perch. And for some moms, these unexpected bumps have shaped our vision in a way that no amount of ambition or expert advice ever could have.

* * *

Cathy Calhoun's big whammy was motherhood itself. More specifically: An unplanned pregnancy when she was thirty-six and in a relatively new relationship. It seems only fair to acknowledge right away that this particular curveball turned out to be a blessing. But that doesn't mean it was easy.

On one hand, Cathy had never really been the type to "color inside the lines" (her words). But, on the other, she was a "good Midwestern girl" (also her words). Cathy remembers having to tell her parents and her boss; they were all, to her relief, very supportive.

Cathy knew she wanted this baby, and she was reasonably confident about taking on single motherhood. (She never married Sophie's dad, but he lives nearby and plays an integral part in his daughter's life.) Cathy thought she'd master parenthood by attacking it the same way she'd managed her high-flying career: She'd get the baby to do things her way and keep everything under control. And why not? This strategy had worked in other areas of her life.

But then Sophie came along, and she hadn't quite gotten the "We'll-Do-It-Mommy's-Way" memo. She didn't sleep when Cathy wanted her to sleep. She didn't eat when Cathy wanted to feed her. Cathy couldn't make things happen at home the way she made them happen at work; even her track record as a "super-aunt" didn't confer the advantages she'd expected. Being a mom was different, and harder, than any of the other roles she'd ever played.

Cathy Calhoun, 48
Public Relations Executive and President of
Weber Shandwick North America
Chicago, Illinois
Mother of Sophie

I always thought that I'd be a mom, but I was also raised to be fairly ambitious [in my career]. I figured both would happen, but I don't think I ever had the sequence figured out. I've never been married, so I wasn't one of those women who said, "I'm going to get married in my twenties, and then I'm going to work for ten years . . ." It's funny, on a day-to-day, tactical level, I sort of need to have a game plan—especially now, to keep track of everything. But in my life, I never had a real game plan. It just worked out okay for me.

I think, deep down, I thought—and my father taught me this—You get a job, you work really hard, you exceed expectations, you do something you love, you get ahead. That was the extent of my game plan.

And, of course, my story unfolded in a way that was completely unplanned. Sophie was a wonderful surprise. I was thirty-six . . . I'd had a series of good relationships, but . . . I ended up getting pregnant when I was in a relationship with someone I hadn't been with terribly long. And, immediately, I thought, "I'm doing this." I was emotionally ready. I was financially able to support her.

I felt like I had accomplished a lot, and I thought, "What's this? This is motherhood. The labor and delivery will be the hard part." [She laughs.] *Not!*

It was always hard. Honestly, I was always trying to figure out [how to balance work and motherhood]. I think the reason it was hard is that I wanted that to be perfect, I wanted this to be perfect. I like to have control over my life. I'm a typical overachiever. And I really wasn't that good at it, especially the baby thing. I didn't know what she wanted. [I was used to things working out the way I pictured] and that stopped with her.

But it's been the greatest lesson ever. I am a better boss because of her. It's so much easier for me to be more go-with-the-flow, to not sweat the small stuff, to have a big-picture vision.

She's the best thing that ever happened [to me].

* * *

What's not new: Our children bring us joy and pain. They teach us important lessons, even ones we hadn't planned on learning.

What is new: In the information age, worry compounds the equation. When Hollee's mom was pregnant, she didn't have the option of signing up for weekly emails detailing her baby's development—or warning of potential risks and harbingers of bad news. She wasn't like her daughter's generation, where many of us jump online to debate whether to vaccinate our children. (Who can blame us? One study said that immunizations might be behind the startling rise in autism. And even though this link has been largely discounted as lacking scientific evidence, it hasn't stopped some from forgoing vaccinations.)

Today's moms are on the lookout for disaster. We're cautioned to undergo chromosomal screenings before we even get pregnant, and after that, it's test after test—all looking for problems. It's hard to find a woman who doesn't know someone who's experienced a false positive on an early pregnancy screening, then had to weigh whether to let doctors perform tests that might deliver critical news—and might (and it is, admittedly, a small *might*) harm the baby.

Of course, all this information, and how much of it we choose to consume, has little effect on which moms will actually weather the crisis.

Ellen Seidman hadn't worried much during her pregnancy. In fact, she remembers her premotherhood life as "perfectish." She reveled in her job as deputy editor of *Glamour* magazine, her husband of two years, and her 1910 colonial in the New Jersey suburbs. In December 2002, that fairy tale seemed to take its next logical step when all 7.11 pounds of her son, Max, came out pink and perfect, not the slightest bit E.T.-like or even wrinkly, thanks to a cesarean delivery.

But a few hours later, Max stopped breathing when Ellen was feeding him—the first sign that something was wrong. It happened again a few hours later, and Max was whisked to the neonatal intensive care unit, where doctors realized that Max was having seizures.

In that moment, the "perfectish" period of Ellen's life came to an end.

In the following weeks—really, for the whole first year of Max's life—nothing went as Ellen had planned.

She learned that, at some point during birth, Max had suffered a stroke. It caused brain damage and seizures, and eventually resulted in cerebral palsy. As Ellen later wrote on her widely read special-needs parenting blog, it wasn't just one nightmare scenario—it was all of them. Doctors said Max might have mental retardation, might not walk, might not talk, might not be able to see or hear.

"I don't want a handicapped child," she blurted out in the raw panic of the moment.

The first year was a dark time Ellen barely remembers; she spent her days trying to come to terms with the reality that she wouldn't have the child she'd expected. She was depressed and immersed in a frenzy of treatments—she tried anything that had a chance of helping Max. During the first two years of Max's life, he received speech, occupational and physical therapy, along with alternative treatments such as hyperbaric oxygen treatment and craniosacral therapy. Ellen fed him a special omega-3 supplement that was supposedly good for the brain. While Max slept, Ellen was glued to her computer screen, devouring, in her words, "too much information" about the frightening possibilities.

She subsisted on the help of friends and family who realized how physically and emotionally drained she had become—Ellen occasionally let her mother and sister take care of Max so she could have some time for herself, to begin to heal from the trauma of the unexpected. Sometimes she would just crash into a deep sleep; other times she'd drive aimlessly around her neighborhood or walk the aisles of her local CVS store because being someplace "normal" brought relief. She sought comfort in an online community of moms created by the Pediatric Stroke Network, sharing her grief with mothers who had been there (they typically knew more about her emotional state, Ellen confessed, than her closest friends).

The passage of time helped—a lot. And so did Max's progress. Over the next few years, Max learned to walk. He also began speaking some words, succeeding in a way that none of the early doctors had imagined, and Ellen adjusted. In 2008, she started her blog, and found it inspiring to help other mothers who were struggling with their own grief.

Ellen Seidman, 42
Creator of LoveThatMax Blog
Freelance Editor/Writer
Suburban New Jersey
Mother of Max and Sabrina

I think that it's really important to stop viewing children through a lens of perfection because that will do neither of you any good. Your child will always be deficient in your eyes, and you will always feel that you are deficient as a parent, that you lost out.

So you just have to kick that word out of your vocabulary and accept your child for who he or she is, and adore her for that, and work with her challenges and not compare her to other kids. Is there such a thing as a perfect kid anyway? I'm not so sure. It's a good word to erase—for any parent, whether she has a kid with special needs or not.

* * *

A flying intensive care unit delivered John to the Cleveland Clinic, where he endured an excruciating ten-hour ablation procedure that failed to completely cure his arrhythmia but seemed to calm his heart. Hollee spent twelve days by his side, shuffling back and forth between his room and the hotel that was connected to the sprawling medical complex. When John's parents arrived to relieve her and Hollee's brother, Matt, came to take her home to Gideon and Henry, she realized that she hadn't breathed fresh air, hadn't stepped outside, for the entire stay.

They drove home mostly in silence, Matt encouraging her to eat something, Hollee forcing down a few cashews and popping Xanax. She fell asleep, and woke up as Matt pulled into the driveway.

When she looked out at the acre of grass that she didn't know how to mow and at the burnt-out lightbulbs that she couldn't reach—and at the four-year-old son who had told his aunt that he wanted to "smash all of the houses in Pittsburgh" so he could go home to Morgantown—Hollee railed against her misfortune. She cried. She hyperventilated whenever she saw an ambulance. And she did all of this privately, of course.

In public, she nodded when well-meaning acquaintances said how lucky she was that John was still alive. And how fortunate they were that he had "gone down" ten feet from a defibrillator with a physician trained in cardiology standing a few feet from the racquetball court. She looked in the eyes of the women who brought dinners to her house, night after night, and she thanked them—and then realized that their names hadn't even registered.

A few days later, John's parents delivered her emaciated husband home, a bulging defibrillator implanted under the skin of his left collarbone. John retreated to their bedroom, sedated from his new drug cocktail and afraid to move too quickly for fear that he would set off the device. A few weeks earlier, during a brief stint at home, that very thing had happened: John had been shocked seventeen times—literally jolted into the air while clinging to the arms of the recliner in his home office when his heart started racing and his defibrillator had to shock it back to a normal rate. John said the lifesaving electrical jolts felt like being slugged in the chest with a baseball bat, and they'd had to call 911. Now Hollee wouldn't even enter the room. There was a bloodstain on the carpet, the result of the EMT's scurry to find a vein that would accept an antiarrhythmic needle, and she couldn't face the memory. She remained on red alert all the time, listening for the pained cry. If John found the strength to move from the bed to the couch, she made sure a phone was within reach. When she took a shower, Hollee left a phone on the bath mat.

She almost cracked: It was just too much to be in panic mode all the time, to live life in a perpetual crash position. As she sank deeper into a depression,

Hollee secretly began planning to run away. It was pure fantasy: With a new cell phone and credit card that no one could track, she would pack up the kids while John slept (which he did most of the time). In a scene that she later realized she had stolen right out of Anne Tyler's *Ladder of Years,* she decided she'd drive and drive until she was far away, where no one could find her and she could start a new life.

She knew there were huge flaws in her reasoning (the biggest being that deep down, she knew she wouldn't just leave John, her soul mate, no matter how un-John-like he was acting), but she indulged her imagination. She almost admitted her evolving plans to her friend Carrie, who emailed her every morning with kind words and messages of strength. Hollee willed herself to hold it together, even if only for the next hour.

And the hours and days passed, and no new crisis came. Ten days without a shock, then two weeks, then one month. John came downstairs one October morning and decided he wanted to walk around the block. Hollee grabbed his hand and her cell phone—and they went.

* * *

Jen Canter was better prepared than Hollee when life tried to swallow her whole. As a doctor, Jen spent years training to remain calm in emergencies— and she tends to look life's imperfections right in the eye. Her mother, a kind and funny woman who raised her three children alone after a divorce, showed her the meaning of strength through her daily example. Despite their family's own struggles, she took Jen and her two brothers to feed the homeless and work at camps for children with disabilities; she taught her children that they were *lucky.* And Jen knew it was true: She was loved in a way that made her feel secure and confident. When she entered adulthood, she had the tools she needed, and she had perspective.

In 2009, those tools came in handy. That was the year that brought a seemingly endless parade of pressures and disasters; it was the year that could have undone Jen, had she been a different person.

When it started, Jen was barreling ahead with her already-full life: a job as a child abuse pediatrician, four children, plans for her new company set to launch in the fall. She'd taken on overnight hours at the hospital, in part to pay for the investment she'd made in Play This Way Every Day. But she had all this (mostly) under control; little problems, it seemed, couldn't sap her characteristic stockpile of energy.

But that spring, her backyard barbecue grill exploded in her face, setting her hair on fire and searing off her eyebrows. The accident was made all the more bizarre by the fact that she'd only recently regrown her left brow after losing it to a freak waxing disaster the year before. Friends sent eyebrow pencils and fake eyebrows; Jen kept her sense of humor and tried to focus on the positive. Her children were happy and healthy. She had a job, a loving husband—and friends who knew just what she needed. She was lucky.

But the next month, severe pain from a back-joint issue slowed her down—sometimes confining her to bed—and shortly after that, her husband's behavior began to shift. Suddenly, Wade was sluggish and tired and just not himself. The timing was bad: Jen was already feeling stretched too thin, and having Wade pull back was more than she wanted to bear.

Jen Canter, 38
Child Abuse Pediatrician and Owner of Educational Toy Company,
Play This Way Every Day
Westchester County, New York
Mother of two sets of twins

I thought that what was going on must have been depression. . . . But he kept saying, "Jen, I'm not depressed. I'm just tired. I love my life, I love you, I love the kids. I'm a happy person—I'm just tired."

We had a pretty bad argument about how lazy he was. He had slept an entire weekend when my mother-in-law was visiting. I was like, "Dude, I can't do this. You cannot sleep all weekend and expect me to do all this." We had cut down on child care because of the economy . . . and I was doing overnights at the hospital, and it was just like, "Oh my God, I cannot be alone with all these kids all day and you sleep. This a point of no return for me."

And then, one morning, he woke up with a rash. And he said, "Jen, I think there's something wrong."

As soon as Jen looked, she knew what it was—and she felt horrible for having been so upset at him. Wade had contracted Lyme disease, a tick-borne illness that had invaded his heart. Jen, still unable to stand for long periods because of her own back pain, cobbled together child care so she could be with Wade in the hospital for several days.

It was a rough summer. After his short hospital stay, it took about a month for Wade to return to normal, and he was on intravenous medication until the end of the summer.

As he recovered, life in the Canter house continued its frantic pace. Jen still had her job and the new business. Meanwhile, her medical specialty was being certified for the first time, and in the months leading up to the November exam, she had no choice but to spend hours studying. (She passed and became one of a handful of doctors nationwide certified in child abuse pediatrics.)

But that fall, the chaos reached a peak, and Jen began to stress about the level of drama in her life. She worried about how others saw her: frenetic and overwhelmed, always in the midst of a storm. "I was a little embarrassed by how much had happened," she told Becky. The worrying stole even more of her energy.

By the end of the year, sheer exhaustion had triumphed, and she was almost too tired to care. And that's when she began to reassess her desire to worry about, and fix, every problem that came along. She began to draw even more on the gifts her mother had given her as a child. It was good enough, she decided, to simply solve the problems that actually needed solving. She didn't need anyone to see her as perfect. In December 2009, she told Becky:

This year gave me much more confidence. I used to become paralyzed with worrying that I'd offended somebody or hurt somebody's feelings or that one of my actions or omissions might have gotten somebody angry or upset. I just couldn't

handle it. I've always had a lot of people-pleasing in me, and I don't anymore. . . .
I have given up trying to be everything to everybody.

I think I've really realized that I take on too much. There were certain
points in this year, especially right before my exam, when I said, "This is
a breaking point."

This [next] year is going to be about doing less.

And it was.

* * *

Throughout that difficult year, Jen Canter learned that the setbacks not only made her stronger, but they edged her closer to finding her true priorities. Not right away, of course. After a crisis strikes, many of us find it hard not to wish we could go back to a time when life felt easier, to receive the gift of an ordinary day. The kind of ordinary day that we hadn't quite appreciated before facing the shocking realization that we weren't *really* directing and controlling our own lives.

There is a loss of innocence and a loss of expectation that comes with these setbacks—and then a constant concession and acceptance that the lives we'd planned simply weren't meant to be.

On Ellen Seidman's blog on January 8, 2009, she offered her hard-earned wisdom on making it through the darkest days:

If you need therapy, get it. I did. If you need to cry, do it. I did. In the car when I drove Max to therapy appointments, in the shower, as I lay in bed at night. You've been through a trauma. You have to get the grief out of your system.

Accept help. I am a pretty independent person who likes to do things myself. But after Max was born, and I was feeling overwhelmed by all the doctor and therapy appointments while adjusting to having a baby, I let my sister do the housework. I let my friends look up information for me. I let Dave spoon-feed me dinner as I breast-fed Max. They got me through that first year.

Try hard, try so very hard, to enjoy your child. Look at how delicious Max was. I knew it, but I didn't enjoy him as thoroughly as I could have because I was so consumed with fear about what he would "be" like. All of you have beautiful children. Stop peering so hard into their future, and enjoy them in the here and now.

Of course, not all our crises are related to health or babies. Sometimes our ambition takes us in the wrong direction, and work winds up being the thing that tears us apart. That's what happened to Nikki Adcock Williams when she began her career as a lawyer.

* * *

Nikki didn't realize what was happening at first. But, somehow, she found herself working for years at a job that made her utterly miserable.

She'd wanted to enjoy the good fortune of landing at a prestigious big-city firm right out of law school at the University of Kentucky—really, she did. She had been planning to become a lawyer since the seventh grade, when a classmate in Mr. Lowery's history class said she couldn't because she was a girl.

I'll show him, she vowed.

But the honeymoon ended before the job even began—the firm called to say that even though Nikki had planned to practice intellectual property law, there wasn't enough of that kind of work to keep her busy. So she was assigned to the bankruptcy group, just to start.

From her very first assignment—working on the Enron bankruptcy—Nikki knew it was the wrong fit. And though she asked repeatedly, in her sweet, unassuming way, for a transfer to the practice area that actually excited her, no one seemed to care. She was labeled a bankruptcy attorney, and stuck in an area she knew she wouldn't enjoy.

Her husband, Tom, thought the firm was trying to "break her in" that first year. He figured they wanted to weed out associates who didn't share the ruthless mentality needed to make partner. But despite her kind heart and warm smile, Nikki was determined to succeed; she'd prove them wrong, just as she'd shown that boy in seventh grade.

But the unpredictability of big-firm life—the price she paid for starting off with a six-figure salary—soon began to exact its toll. For their first Christmas as a married couple (also Nikki's first at the firm), she and Tom were planning to visit his family in Ohio and then head to her home in Kentucky for New Year's. But, on December 23, a partner knocked on her office door.

"Nikki, I hate to do this to you, but you can't leave tomorrow. We're going to need you to be here all day," he said.

Nikki turned to her go-to solution: She decided she'd just work harder and get it done efficiently so they could leave on time. She researched, wrote, and edited her memo, leaving the office at 9:00 p.m. and praying that the partner would read it and give her the green light to head off to Ohio.

But he never called.

The next day, when the firm was officially closed, Nikki sat by herself on the thirty-eighth floor, waiting for the call that would set her free. Hours passed. Around 4:00 p.m., after she had left several voice mails and emails, she got a message from the partner, who was at an airport in Connecticut. He had read everything and it was fine—he just hadn't bothered to tell Nikki that her family vacation could begin.

And so it went, for the next four-and-a-half years. Tom bought tickets to the opera; Nikki was drafted for a project at the last minute and couldn't go. They planned vacations; they canceled them. Before she knew it, Nikki had fallen into a deep depression, crying before, during and after work at least several days a week. On really rough mornings, she'd throw up before heading into the office. It got to the point where her husband, Tom, just didn't want to hear about it anymore.

"It became like a routine, like, 'Oh Nikki's crying again,'" she said.

Looking back, Nikki knows she was depressed. (Several of the moms we interviewed experienced depression of varying degrees, which isn't that surprising considering that major depressive disorder is the leading cause of disability in Americans aged fifteen to forty-four.[1] The disorder, which is more prevalent among women, has a median onset age of thirty-two.)[2]

Nikki, a naturally extroverted woman who had always liked meeting new people and taken pleasure in the camaraderie of groups, felt herself turning inward. Her confidence was shattered; she felt as if she could never measure up and everyone was looking down on her because she wasn't satisfied with a life that required her to be tethered to her BlackBerry. She started second-guessing her every move.

She looked for an escape, but ended up turning down two jobs that, looking back, she thinks she would have loved. One, with Atlanta Legal Aid, would have required her to sell the dream house that she and Tom had built together, and she wasn't yet ready to part with that symbol of her sacrifice.

Then an Atlanta judge offered her a job, without even interviewing her, based on the strength of her resume and writing sample.

At that point, Nikki had become emotionally paralyzed. She needed to be ready to start in three weeks, but the child-care center she'd selected for her daughter wouldn't have an opening for six weeks. The old Nikki would have worked out a solution to cover those three weeks; the new Nikki, overcome by inertia and fear, couldn't muster the energy.

Nikki Adcock Williams, 33
Attorney
McDonough, Georgia
Mother of Anna and Liam

I lost all confidence. Before I was a fairly confident person—I had been very outgoing and I liked to talk to people and go out and do things. But the firm life, working the long hours, I felt like I was prevented from doing things that made me happy. It really made me a quiet, reserved person. I felt like I was always being looked down upon and that I didn't measure up to expectations. I guess I felt like something was wrong with me because I wasn't happy working around the clock.

I never sought counseling, and I really should have. I felt like I should have been able to fix it myself, like if I did this or that, it would get better.

In Nikki's case—as she later learned—it would take more than simply "working harder" to find a way out of the dark and move forward to a brighter place.

* * *

Enjoying the present, looking for that silver lining—those were not Hollee's strengths during her darkest period. She found it impossible to become accustomed to her new reality when the future felt so uncertain. She was grateful for the lifesaving device implanted in John's chest, but infuriated that it had completely debilitated her family. John was in a catch-22; he needed to test his limits to heal psychologically and physically, yet because doctors never pinpointed the cause of his arrhythmia, he had to do it with the terrifying knowledge that his next step forward might land him back in a dreaded hospital bed.

But they forged ahead—they had two little boys who were relying on them, so they didn't really have another choice. Generous colleagues filled in for the entire fall semester and, as a couple, they focused on recovering. An acquaintance told Hollee that she was a strong person, and Hollee returned to that thought when her faith wavered. She began regular therapy sessions, which helped her see that she had indeed survived her worst nightmare.

Hollee replaced their bedding because she associated it with curling up on it in the fetal position, trembling, while the team of EMTs were tending to John. She told John she also wanted to throw out the home-office recliner where John had been sitting during his terrifying seventeen-shocks episode.

John said no. He was starting to heal, to see that he just might be able to get back to where he'd been before the crisis. All the things that John thought he'd never be able to do again—to write books, to roughhouse with his boys, to make love to his wife, to take care of his family—he tried. Gradually, as his body and mind healed, and every day became a step toward something better (despite his still "being scared witless" about most physical activity), his old personality resurfaced; the hilarious John crept back.

He told Hollee that he wasn't going to get rid of the chair; instead, he named it "Old Sparky" in what became an ongoing joke that they used to get past the pain.

They went back to the gym, and John joked with the front desk workers that they should alert emergency services, just in case. He renamed the spot where his heart had stopped beating the "John Temple Memorial Racquetball Court." To friends who were brave enough to ask what Hollee would feel if the device went off while they were having sex, they quoted the defibrillator manual that featured a seventy-something couple on the cover: "Just a gentle tingle."

They got a new dog and started going on their weekly date nights again. And Hollee reemerged, but in a new incarnation of herself. John had always been her rock, the optimistic and steadfast part of their duo, while she was prone to negative thoughts and worry. She vowed to change. Slowly, she did.

She got into yoga (really into it), and signed her boys up for Kids Yoga so that they would learn to love it, too. She sang onstage for the first time in years, filling her heart with a joy that she couldn't get from any other source. And she decided that it was time to write the book that had been rattling around in her brain for the past several years—there wasn't any time to waste.

When all was said and done, John's crisis prompted Hollee to reexamine her priorities and move further along toward the New Perfect. She had seen with horrifying clarity that life was too short for Never Enough, and she renewed her commitment to spending her precious moments on the things that mattered most.

At night, she kept singing her babies the lullaby she had created for them when they were infants, which ended with a silly version of "Ooh Child." When John was lying in hospital beds, her voice cracked when she sang the "Things are gonna get easier" line to Gideon and Henry.

Just as the song promised, they did.

10

REENTRY AND REINVENTION ON THE PATH TO THE NEW PERFECT

- You can start over. You're not "throwing away" the past by seeking happiness in a new career.

- Take stock of your strengths and get comfortable telling others about how you excel. Men don't feel as if they're bragging when they do this.

- Get out there and talk to people. Start networking with the people around you, get ideas, and find out who they know.

- Don't to be afraid to ask for help.

- Don't limit yourself. There probably are more options than you are considering.

On an unseasonably cool January afternoon (by Atlanta standards, anyway), Nikki Williams sent the email she had been composing in her head for nearly five years:

From: Nikki Williams
To: All Attorneys
Wednesday, January 31, 2007 4:10 PM

It is now my turn to write those familiar words . . . today is my last day here. After five years of being a bankruptcy attorney, the time has come for me to take some time to decide what it is that I really want to do "when I grow up."

> I will be taking the next year off to stay home with our two-year-old daughter, Anna, and Baby No. 2 due in August. I hope to spend some time figuring out in what way I want to contribute to the profession of law.

Nikki had spent hours crafting the perfect send-off; the "goodbye email" was a tradition for departing associates. In fact, Nikki was so consumed with editing those paragraphs, tidying her files and returning her laptop and despised BlackBerry to the technology department that she was the last to arrive at her own farewell party. It was already dark when she walked through the doors of Front Page News, a favorite midtown restaurant where she had been "wined and dined" as a summer intern, back when the firm was trying to convince Nikki to accept its offer.

This time, though, the focus was on Nikki's future, and she celebrated her "escape" with fellow associate attorneys and friends from the library staff. (She would have indulged in an extra-large glass of pinot noir had she not been pregnant, Nikki later told Hollee, recalling the night that was still so vivid in her mind.) The colleagues who joined her had been through the rough times with Nikki, had seen her struggle to manage big-firm life and motherhood.

Nikki's first child, Anna, had arrived in 2004, and, after a four-month maternity leave, Nikki had returned to work full-time because "it felt like it was the only option."

But as her anxiety over work had mounted, she'd begun questioning whether her six-figure paycheck was worth it. It was hard not to appreciate the privileges her salary provided: She adored the three-story Craftsman bungalow that she and Tom had custom-built in Atlanta's Edgewood neighborhood; it was the dream home where she'd envisioned her children growing up, where the family would sit on the sprawling front porch and "watch the world go by." She'd painted flowers by hand on the pink walls of Anna's nursery and luxuriated in their master bath Jacuzzi tub.

Nikki had always assumed that hard work, by itself, would get her where she needed to go. But, gradually, she realized that she needed more—in order to make peace with her sacrifices, she needed to be motivated by her *own* ambitions.

The realization had hit one day in 2005. Nikki had called in sick to work that day; Baby Anna had woken up with a high fever and was too ill to attend day care. But later that morning, a partner had called: He "didn't care" and insisted that Nikki come in and help with a research project. Her husband, Tom, was busy with a court hearing, and the couple had no family in town to pitch in. So within thirty minutes of receiving that call, Nikki packed up and headed to the firm library with a feverish Anna, who slept by her feet on the scratchy waffle-weave carpet while Nikki frantically conducted her research. The firm's kindly librarians watched over her baby when Nikki had to get up from the long cherrywood table to retrieve a book.

That moment proved to be a turning point; as she watched Anna struggle to sleep in the brightly lit, fortieth-floor law library, she knew her career would not end at a large law firm. She could almost rationalize the drudgery of the work and the relentless hours as a means to an end—but now her job was keeping her from being the kind of mother she wanted to be. And that was too much too swallow.

So, a little more than a year later, when Nikki left the firm for good, it was true cause for celebration. Her husband, Tom, was there, of course, hoping that the relief on Nikki's face meant she'd turned a corner toward happiness.

But soon after the celebration died down, Nikki and Tom faced an unsettling financial reality. Nikki had been earning three-quarters of the family income, and as a government attorney, Tom was prohibited from seeking additional clients. They studied their budget and slowly came to accept that they'd have to sell their beloved house, move out of the city and downsize their lifestyle. It seemed like the right move. The law firm, Tom felt, had sucked the life out of Nikki; she wasn't the same ambitious woman he had married five years before.

And he wanted that woman back. Tom hoped Nikki could find a place for her talents to shine—where a terrific writer who described herself as "actually a nice lawyer" could find work that felt meaningful.

But there was no panacea on the horizon. After Nikki resigned, she spent the next year and a half caring for Anna, and then her newborn brother, while picking up some part-time work with a juvenile court judge.

Nikki hadn't planned to stay home for so long; even with the profit from their house and the move to the less-expensive southern suburbs, they needed her income. But she didn't know where to start looking. She'd felt like an outsider at the law firm, and now she was "lost" in her new world of at-home mothers—women who didn't understand how she could contemplate leaving her children in someone else's care.

An afternoon at a local park left a scar: As she pushed Anna on a swing, another mother approached and asked for her business card.

"You're the most attentive nanny I've ever seen," she said.

Nikki explained that while she was biracial and didn't look a bit like her flaxen-haired baby, she was Anna's *mother*. The other mom quickly changed the subject to motherhood—justifying her own stay-at-home decision with statistics and urging Nikki to stay home permanently, or at least to ask her husband to make the sacrifice.

"My husband loves his job and I would never ask him to do that," Nikki said. "And I want my daughter…to see me get up and go to work so she can have that hope that she can be whatever she wants."

The woman stared at her blankly; Nikki packed up her diaper bag.

In her new neighborhood, she tried to make friends, but she felt a division between the moms who planned to stay home indefinitely, and those who wanted to return to work. She was confused—weren't all the women in the group *mothers,* members of the same sleep-deprived team? Why did everyone seem so focused on how she was different? "It was a big eye-opener when I realized that everyone didn't just automatically get to be a member of the Mommy Club," she recalled.

Stuck in a netherworld—first the law firm didn't fit and now her house felt like a prison (in fact, Tom remembers that if he wasn't home by 5:15 on the dot, Nikki would start calling, desperate for a break from the around-the-clock demands of a toddler and newborn)—Nikki felt frightened, stranded and alone.

* * *

But she wasn't. Most of the women we surveyed made changes to their professional lives to accommodate motherhood—nearly 75 percent.

This is the final piece of the puzzle for the women of our generation. Once we've come to understand all the challenges that confront us as modern mothers—our bevy of choices, our tussles with identity, the realities of workplace fit, marriage, technology (and even the whims of fate)—we have one thing left to do: *Take action.*

Here's how it broke down for the women who answered our survey: Nearly a quarter took advantage of flexible scheduling with the same employer, almost a fifth switched to part-time work with the same employer, 15 percent took a new full-time job with more flexibility, 10 percent went part-time with a new employer, 10 percent started freelancing, and 11 percent started their own businesses.

Only 8 percent classified themselves as having "quit" their jobs to stay home (although, keep in mind, the survey targeted working mothers; women who had made long-term plans to stay home were not included).

The survey comments revealed a dizzying array of decisions:

My husband "retired" to be a stay-at-home dad.

I'm not taking the aggressive jobs that would propel me forward because the hours can't fit with my needs for my family.

I'm telecommuting.

I'm reducing the number of wedding cakes I will make.

I'm leaving work on time!

I'm refusing matters that involve travel or trial commitments.

I'm bringing the baby to work.

I moved to where my mother could help me.

I paused my tenure clock three times.

I changed careers before I had my child in anticipation.

No wonder Nikki felt so confused. Where was that manual again—the one that tells us what to do when our jobs don't fit and at-home motherhood isn't the solution? Nikki was caught between worlds, and she wasn't sure how to segue into something that matched her personal and professional goals. To use the buzzwords that experts coined to describe career transformations, Nikki didn't know how to reenter, relaunch or reinvent—so she simply retreated.

GETTING YOUR ATTITUDE BACK

Debby Stone, a lawyer–turned–certified career coach, says Nikki's loss of confidence is not at all uncommon. Since starting her coaching practice in 2002, Debby has counseled hundreds of women, and has found that two groups consistently report diminished self-image: (1) women with conflicted feelings about work/life choices, and (2) women who were dissatisfied by their previous work environment. Many of the women we interviewed fell into one, or both, of those categories, and some desperately needed to rebuild their self-esteem before they could even broach the "What comes next?" dilemma.

That can be a very difficult process for women who feel defeated by the past, but it's essential to quell the critical inner voice. As a starting point, Debby suggests that women list ten strengths and how they've applied them in real-world examples. Then it's time to reveal those triumphs to a friend or spouse. While many women struggle because their self-perception has been clouded, most will become more comfortable touting their selling points as a result of the exercise.

Next it's time to identify passions and priorities. In Debby's experience, most women approach the career transformation process feeling the way Nikki did, "stuck in a pink box and thinking only of other pink boxes as possibilities." To clear this hurdle, women need to get past the myth that they're throwing away what they've done before—even though that's just the kind of thing many hear from friends and family when they announce that they're considering a career makeover. Instead, they need to focus on the skills and strengths that can be transferred to a new setting.

While it's very difficult to let go of a professional identity, Debby believes that most of us don't have a single career calling, and lots of women will develop new ideas about what they want to be over time. What's more, many moms made these pivotal career decisions at young ages and sometimes based on a childish whim—like Nikki's wanting to be a lawyer because her middle-school classmate said she couldn't.

Most women begin the journey filled with panic, or at least some level of fear, but as these women identify their passions and transferable skills, they clear away their doubts and start getting excited about the endless possibilities. Debby has witnessed some radical transformations. Her favorite? A woman lawyer who now prepares dog handlers for canine obstacle competitions in her new life as a dog agility trainer. Other makeovers include a pharmaceutical sales representative who became a career coach, a corporate employee who became an interior designer and an attorney who became a corporate event planner.

But no one can make the leap without preparing, psychologically, for a major life change. Carol Fishman Cohen, an internationally recognized expert on career reentry, agrees with Debby that lost confidence is widespread among female employees, especially those looking to reenter the workforce after a career break. Carol, a Harvard Business School graduate, cowrote a popular guide for moms looking to reenter the workforce, and has spoken to thousands of women on the topic of career transformation.[1] Interestingly, she finds no correlation between the prestige of a woman's previous job and her sense of confidence about returning to the workforce. It's Carol's job to get these women "unstuck" and moving forward psychologically.

While many fear that they won't be remembered and lament their failures to keep up with contacts (Nikki Williams expressed serious regret about severing her ties when she "ran away without looking back" from her law firm job), Carol offers a much more positive take. "What career relaunchers don't understand," Carol said, "is that their former colleagues remember them as images frozen in time. So while the women have experienced turmoil and doubt, their former employers often haven't seen any of that. They're likely to be enthusiastic about connecting with a stellar former employee or colleague."

After Nikki and Hollee met in person in January of 2010, they scheduled a follow-up interview to discuss Nikki's plans for reinventing her career. At that point, Nikki was working full-time as a judicial staff attorney, and while she liked her boss and tolerated the work, it certainly didn't inspire her. Nikki frequently cried when she talked about her career and how she longed for something more fulfilling.

Later, she told Hollee that maybe she needed to start from scratch.

Nikki Adcock Williams, 33
Attorney
McDonough, Georgia
Mother of Anna and Liam

Honestly, I'm just not sure this is the profession for me. I've witnessed a lot of bad parts of the law. I used to feel guilty that I left the law firm behind, and I'm starting to feel like I'm not even sure what I want to be when I grow up. I sacrificed so much income potential when I left the firm and most of the time I feel okay with it because my family is pretty happy. Still, there are a lot of tears, lots of prayer. I'm really not sure where I'll be in a year or two. I just try to keep my family happy and hope that when the right employment opportunity presents itself, I'll be ready to realize it.

In the spring of 2010, Hollee caught up with Nikki's husband, Tom, who said he felt that a change was brewing. Nikki seemed more energetic and positive than she had in months—being included in the group of moms from *Good Enough Is the New Perfect* gave Nikki a new view of herself and her worth. Tom wondered if this would be another turning point.

Later that night, Hollee emailed Nikki with career coach Debby Stone's contact information—and, the next day, Nikki called her.

NOW WHAT?

Once the confidence piece is under control, it's time to start exploring the possibilities.

There are numerous ways to evaluate career options; for women who can't afford to hire a coach, there are hundreds of books that include assessment tools for determining what types of jobs suit a candidate's experience, interests and strengths.

While some women fear the outcome, Debby Stone believes these tools often explain why their current jobs don't fit. (As Hollee grew increasingly unhappy at the law firm, she completed an assessment with a career coach and learned that only a tiny percentage of lawyers shared her personality type. Teaching was her most natural strength, and that was a huge relief.)

While career experts offer varied approaches for tackling the assessment piece, most agree on the major considerations. In her book, Carol Cohen focuses on the "Three C's" of a Career Relaunch: Control, Content and Compensation.

Control over time is a hot button for moms, and Carol shared this great tip: Be very careful about how you're describing the kind of work you'd like to do. While many use *part-time* to describe the ideal job, what many moms really crave, according to our survey, are flexible schedules with some element of control. They often don't mind working forty hours a week or more if it's on their own terms.

Turning to content, it's all about finding appealing prospects that accommodate a mother's current life situation. Carol told Hollee that most career relaunchers take one of three paths: A woman returns to the same sort of job she had before her break; she tries a permutation of her former professional life; or she switches gears completely. Moms who have been home for an extended stay may feel as if they're stuck in a time warp when they get serious about returning to the workplace. They'll wonder when open-toed shoes and bare legs replaced business suits, and worry that their experience ("Do I really need to know Excel *and* Twitter?") has become outdated. A skills update can boost a candidate's resume *and* confidence. For example, Carol told the story of a former city planner who had worked on volunteer fund-raising projects while on her career break. When the woman decided to return to the paid workforce, she enrolled in a fund-raising certificate program to enhance her resume. She excelled in the classroom (in part due to her volunteer experience), and began exuding the confidence needed to complete her relaunch.

Another option? For women who want to ease their way back in—or those who want to make sure the job's content is really as advertised—Carol suggests testing the waters with a consulting, freelance or contract gig.

Next, there's the compensation issue. According to oft-cited Center for Work-Life Policy statistics, skilled women who drop out of the workforce for three or more years suffer a 37 percent income hit.[2] But Carol pointed out that the survey pinpointed women at the moment of reentry and did not track them as the years passed.

"Sometimes," she explained, "relaunchers are intentionally choosing to earn a lower salary in exchange for a more flexible or less stressful job; a new mother, for example, might choose to work reduced hours temporarily. And those moving into completely new fields might expect to take a temporary pay cut as an investment toward a more prosperous future. The bigger lesson," Carol said, "is to focus on combined household income—current and projected—with the knowledge that the early years might not be profitable."

Finally, Debby Stone recommends that moms looking for career makeovers forge connections with women who are working in careers that seem exciting.

"Very often, they'll hear these inspiring stories and think, 'Wow, I never would have thought that you could go from there to here,'" Debby said.

PASSION AS THE FUEL OF REINVENTION

Hollee was inspired by a duo of relaunchers she met at a mom blogger conference last winter: Emily McKhann and Cooper Munroe's story energized her.

Emily and Cooper are a job-sharing pair with more than twenty years of shared professional history. They harnessed their extensive public relations experience and corporate contacts to build a successful web-based business that they run virtually from their homes in New York and Pennsylvania. Their product, TheMotherhood.com, is an online community that currently serves 10,000 registered moms and thousands more visitors. (Because they're PR pros, their site's taglines constantly change, but here are a few favorites: *We are your neighborhood of friends; We are stronger than you know; We are tired of being the good girls.*)

Emily and Cooper met while, in their words, "doing time" in a windowless Washington, D.C., public relations firm, and then worked together in a New York City firm ("with plenty of windows") that Emily founded in the mid-1990s. Life happened. The short version: Emily cowrote *Living with the End in Mind* with her best friend, Erin, who succumbed to breast cancer not long after they shared their story on *Oprah*.

After years of fertility treatments, Emily became a mother in 2000, and then had her second child in 2002. Meanwhile, her longtime friend Cooper moved back to her hometown of Pittsburgh, became the mom of four kids, wrote for the local newspaper, and started talking to Emily about writing a parenting book together.

Instead, they fell in love with the idea of creating a community of moms on the internet. They made their first big dent in 2005, when they created a clearinghouse for readers to donate to Hurricane Katrina evacuees. After screaming "Why isn't anyone helping these people?" at their televisions for two straight days, they did what none of the relief organizations seemed to be able to manage, converting their blog into an online clearinghouse for donations earmarked for displaced evacuees. Their idea went viral on the internet—overnight, tens of thousands of people visited their site with offers of everything from a mobile home to an 18-wheeler full of diapers and other supplies.

It was a turning point for Cooper, who days earlier had been weeping in her kitchen, frustrated by the demands of raising four children under seven while her husband traveled each week for his job. The Katrina project gave her an outlet for making a difference outside the walls of her suburban home, and jolted her from a postpartum depression.

Cooper and Emily spent the next three years working on motherhood issues via prominent websites MomsRising.org and BlogHer.com (making connections and revising their own business plan in the meantime). In 2008, they officially launched TheMotherhood.com as an online community providing moms with support and advice on all the major motherhood topics—and on top of that, they started a sister site that helps brands like Sea World, Kellogg's, Verizon and Tropicana connect with the online mom community. One cool example: When Hebrew National wanted to kick off the 2009 and 2010 grilling seasons, Cooper and Emily crafted the "Picnics with a Purpose" campaign, which resulted in picnics and accompanying service projects in nine American cities.

Emily McKhann, 48
Cofounder of TheMotherhood.com and TheMotherhoodCreative.com
Owned Public Relations Firm, Author, Director of International
Business and Acting Commissioner to the United Nations and
Consular Corps for New York City
Larchmont, New York
Mother of Erin and Ellie

After having my kids and writing this book about living with the end in mind, I've really learned to live life out of a sense of priorities, from an emotional, mental, physical and spiritual standpoint. I go through my busy life and ask myself about the connections I want to make and where I want to leave my mark.

It was really an eye-opener to notice how hard it was to put my interests first—I was such a hard worker and so used to having everyone else's interests come first.

And then I realized that my life is important, and it's not just about showing up as a professional all the time. It was eye-opening to step back and slow down a bit and breathe.

And then I was able to find where I needed to be, what spoke to me and deeply interested me, and I realized that I was always on this track to where I was meant to be. With this mom blogger community, I feel like I can change the world by having a place where moms are taking care of each other. It's completely the right path for me. Looking back, it's almost like somebody had planned it, but I just had to be ready to recognize it.

Cooper Munroe, 43
Cofounder of TheMotherhood.com and TheMotherhoodCreative.com
Worked for Two Decades in Public Relations, Freelance Writer
Pittsburgh, Pennsylvania
Mother of Clyde, Willis, Grady and Finn

There really is no right way to go about your life as a mom and as a professional—it's got to be your own definition. Really and truly, good enough has to be your own interpretation and not anybody else's. I felt it my whole life—you have to do this, there's only one way to have success, and I've come to know that this is absolutely not true.

I deeply believe that if you find yourself a group of people to support you in whatever you want to become, it will go a lot better. So to a mom out there who wants to make a change, I would ask: What is it that you're so afraid of? What would happen if you jumped—and what would happen if you didn't? I have this quote on my office wall that says, "Leave everything a bit better than you found it." That applies to us, too. If you are unhappy or if your work is not working, your unhappiness is palpable to the people around you. It's up to you to make it better.

PREPARING THE WORLD FOR YOUR COMEBACK

More good news for women who are ready to make a change (and according to Carol Cohen's research, nearly 2 million college-educated mothers would like to make a leap back into the workforce):[3] Now is an ideal time to dive back in.

When Carol started researching formal career reentry programs for her book in 2004, she found that only a handful existed worldwide. Flash-forward six years, and Carol could document more than sixty-five reentry programs that had been offered across a wide swath of work environments; she located programs sponsored by corporations, universities, professional associations, foundations and government entities.

The explosion of reentry programs, including those run by prominent universities, gives employers great models to emulate, and a pipeline of graduates to tap. Employers are starting to discover what Carol knows from personal experience (she landed a full-time job at a prestigious investment firm after taking eleven years out of the full-time workforce to care for her four children): The relauncher demographic is a gem from the employer's perspective. The core group, mostly thirty-five to fifty-year-old women, are at a life stage that makes them ideal employees—they're mature, settled and very loyal to employers who give them a ticket back into the game.

* * *

Sometimes the comeback is all about being open to the possibilities—and being willing to make an unexpected leap when the right opportunity comes along. That's how it happened for Becky's friend Debra Fanning, a teacher whose two children attend the same small Lutheran school as Becky's. In the spring of 2008, when Maggie was in her first year of preschool and Tim was in kindergarten, Debra was an at-home mom and only beginning to contemplate a return to work. She hadn't even started looking when a teaching position became available at their school, and someone casually mentioned this to Debra one Thursday at swim lessons. It couldn't have been more ideal: The job was for the age group Debra had taught when she'd worked in the Chicago public schools, she'd be near Tim and Maggie all day—and Pilgrim Lutheran School was three-quarters of a block from her home. They wouldn't need a second car; Debra and the kids could make it to school on foot in less than two minutes.

Debra updated her resume and took it to Pilgrim's principal the next morning. With her experience, master's degree and belief in the school's mission, Debra was a strong candidate. She interviewed with the hiring team on Monday; by Wednesday, less than a week after applying, Debra had the job. Shortly after accepting, Debra was grocery shopping by herself and just started crying: "I was in mourning," she told Becky. "It was a good thing but it was, you know, changing my whole life."

Debra started work at Pilgrim the following fall—the new routine was exhausting for everyone at first, especially four-year-old Maggie—but it turned out to be exactly the right move. In 2010, the Chicago Public Schools faced massive budget cuts; had Debra returned to that district, she might have lost her job.

* * *

When Jennifer Pate returned to work, she started right where she was standing at that moment in her life, by mining her experiences as a mother. And, of course, not all of those experiences were easy.

In those early months after her web series, *Jen and Barb: Mom Life,* launched in November 2008, Jennifer experienced a certain amount of bedlam—much of which she made part of her show. In fact, as she recounted some of the absurd moments to Becky over the phone, she laughed. These, after all, were the very realities of motherhood she'd set out to share.

Jennifer Pate, 43
Co-Executive Producer and Cohost of *Jen and Barb: Mom Life*
Los Angeles, California
Mother of Cooper and Lilah

This show could not be a more perfect fit—but I am working my ass off.

My kids are mostly good [with the change], but they are going from a mom who was stay-at-home and president of the PTA to now I'm working and I'm a little worried because Lilah has ballet and we're shooting [an episode]. My hope is this is just an adjustment period.

On shoot days, [the crew] starts showing up at 6:30 in the morning. I'm in the makeup chair and my kids are getting ready for school—it's cuckoo. We shot this morning, and it was a disaster. The cat had peed, Lilah refused to get dressed and was naked . . .

But the feedback we've been getting is that people are appreciative that we're sharing this real part of our lives. How do we expect people to share if we don't? I want people to [watch us and] say, "Oh my God, it's not just me."

But Jennifer took it step by step and addressed issues as they arose. When she felt overwhelmed, she added extra help at home or asked her husband to take on more. She adjusted her expectations as she went along, and she kept her eyes locked on her priorities:

I take my kids to school, and I pick them up, and I'm home for dinner with them, and I'm with them on the weekends—and I still work. Now, talk to me in a year, I don't know if that's going to continue. But, right now, I'm sort of like a stay-at-home-working mom.

By pursuing her passion on her own terms, Jennifer found a purpose *in addition* to motherhood, crafting a New Perfect career that met many of the criteria the moms we interviewed were imagining for themselves. They longed for fulfilling lives, at work and at home, where they could essentially rewrite the definition of "working mom" to match their personal priorities. Some had to wipe the slate clean, to start again to end up in the place where they truly belonged. Others made less drastic shifts, but simply by realizing that they had some say in how their days should play out, their lives took a turn for the better. And with planning, courage and a little bit of luck, some of the moms we interviewed found that by choosing what was good enough for them, they didn't need perfect anymore.

And what a relief that was.

11

MARTINIS ON THE FRONT PORCH

- Defining success on your own terms is a key to happiness.

- If you love what you do, it won't feel like work.

- Find a group of supportive moms and discuss your work/life challenges and successes with them. Trust us—you really are not alone.

- Never give up. Attitude makes a difference in finding happiness and success.

How we work, how we mother, how we define success—all of it, in the end, boils down to a single question.

Are we happy?

Becky found herself contemplating this on her porch late one afternoon, a little more than seven years after she had left the formal workplace to seek out...well, more happiness. Isn't that what custom-fitting motherhood and work is really all about? Finding the mix that makes us feel most alive, most fulfilled, most proud, most satisfied that we're living our best possible life?

It was the aching dawn of spring in Chicago, and the tulips, daffodils and hyacinths were poking through the dirt, finally freed from the last remnants of snow. The lilac tree and the hydrangea had sprouted their first buds. And, on this day, Becky had willingly abandoned her writing, even though the manuscript was due to her editor in eight weeks. But it was a nice day, and that's the lovely thing about defining your own New Perfect: Becky could decide to pick her kids up early from aftercare, take them outside to ride scooters with the other kids on the street, and enjoy a cocktail with the neighbors. It was *her* time, *her* choice.

Becky had spent most of the fall, the entire winter and the first part of spring writing. She was working far more hours than she had during that time when she'd struggled to understand why being a newspaper reporter didn't fit her life the way it once had. Now, oddly, she was happy working this much, sinking into a project and wrapping it around her life in a way that didn't dull the luster of accomplishment.

Her life wasn't perfect, and for this she was deeply grateful. Her insane era of overparenting was long over, and she had a litany of violations to the Supermom code to prove it: She'd forgotten a preschool parent/teacher conference, run out of gas in the middle of the road with the kids in the backseat and loaded her iPhone with kids' movies to keep herself from going crazy on the way to Australia.

She wasn't proud of these things, but she'd reached a point in parenthood where she'd made peace, more or less, with the inevitable mistakes and concessions. She'd (almost) learned to stop comparing herself to other moms, and she finally believed, *really believed,* that loosening the reins on "perfect" made for happier, better-adjusted children. She wanted her children to be themselves, to persevere even in the face of disappointment or failure, to take control of their own success (rather than having it micromanaged by their parents) and to enjoy the world around them. What a relief it had been to realize that letting her children see her make mistakes *could actually be good for them*. Plus, she'd discovered that accepting imperfection, rather than trying to orchestrate it away, actually felt good.

Other points of gratitude: Pete was home more than he'd ever been, and the girls were finally old enough for family soccer games, rounds of Uno and long walks in the city. She and Beth, now eight, had recently agreed, while reading *Little Women* aloud together, that independent and outspoken Jo was the most fascinating of the March sisters. And Katie, who turned six that spring, started every morning by climbing into her parents' bed and curling up in a hug.

Evenings on the porch were, in many ways, like those morning snuggles: A blissful slowdown in a busy life. An exercise in purposeful loitering. These gatherings had taken root a few years before and grown into something of a tradition. The kids would play—emptying houses, apartments and garages of every toy imaginable—and the adults would pour wine or mix martinis and sometimes cobble together a shared potluck so nobody would have to go inside and cook.

Although the majority of parents on the block worked, the moms were an eclectic mix of work/life fits: a full-time doctor, a part-time social worker, a graphic designer working from home, a couple of therapists, an at-home mom and an executive/event producer/entrepreneur with three daughters, multiple careers and an impressive ability to negotiate her way to anything. This group, together and in various segments, had mourned major losses, celebrated numerous victories and taught their children to dance to "Thriller" while gathered on Becky's front porch. Becky's friend Michelle had told Becky about Cathy Calhoun on this porch ("You should interview her for your book. I'll introduce you"); and her friend Elsa had often made her laugh so hard that she'd struggled to catch her breath. This stoop, with its greenish paint and white columns, had become a good enough place for pretty much anything.

So, on this evening, Becky willingly chose it over her work because she believed that a full life would make her a better writer and a better mother.

Either way, these little moments were the ones she'd remember.

* * *

On a similarly warm spring day in Morgantown, Hollee lounged in her scarlet-red backyard Adirondack chair watching her boys play baseball on the grass that John had freshly mowed. Gideon was hitting; Henry was fielding, and then—squeals of glee!

"I caught it! I caught it!" cried Henry. His first successfully fielded pop fly.

Hollee cheered and caught John's attention; he was heading toward the front yard, wearing his favorite straw cowboy hat as he hauled the weed whacker around their property. John looked strong, confident and happy as he cleared his land of the winter debris, roping the evergreens that the snow had pushed toward the earth and tilting them back toward the sun.

Later that night, they headed out for their sacred weekly date, where they sat outside on the front porch of Café Bacchus, enjoying a decadent goat cheese appetizer and soaking in the early-evening sun. Hollee talked about her book; John talked about his new book idea, the one he wanted to plunge into as soon as Hollee was done. They laughed over Henry's constant joke-telling (Favorite recent zinger: After Hollee announced that they'd be having a challah baking party at their house, Henry replied, "Challah *and* bacon? Awesome!"), and discussed how proud they were that Gideon had started his own blog and was posting almost every day.

Hollee was practicing one of the personal commandments she'd learned from her new favorite book, Gretchen Rubin's *The Happiness Project* ("Act the way I want to feel"), but as she was sitting with her husband, enjoying the food and the warmth, she realized that she didn't need to force it. Hollee felt happiness, pure and unadulterated, and the feeling remained as they ended that glorious night hand in hand listening to the Pittsburgh Symphony play a concert, aptly titled "The Human Spirit."

* * *

Some funny things about happiness: Money can't buy it (unless it is pulling someone out of poverty)—and having children actually *lessens* it.[1] Researchers reported in 2009 that women are less happy than they were in 1970s, despite—and maybe even because of—all the opportunity we've inherited in the meantime.[2] So, collectively, we're getting less happy—and making money, having children and mulling over an unprecedented array of options aren't improving the situation.

Not the happiest news for overachieving working mothers.

On the other hand, good marriages and sex can make us happier. Same with socializing after work and having dinner with friends[3]—meaning Becky's affinity for loitering with the neighbors serves a very real purpose. (More good news for her: Having cheery neighbors also has been linked to happiness.)[4] In fact, interpersonal relationships, in general, have a big impact on personal satisfaction and well-being. And although a higher salary doesn't necessarily lead to greater happiness, work can make us happy—especially work that we love.

Which means that the Good Enoughs in our study were actively doing things that tend to make people happy. The women in this group felt better about their relationships with their spouses, and they seemed to find more time for friends and family, and more time for themselves. They were just as likely as the Never Enoughs to say they worked because they loved their jobs.

And they also may have had a leg up in combating an expectations gap that researchers debated in the much-discussed 2009 study called "The Paradox of Declining Female Happiness." The study's authors, two economists from the University of Pennsylvania's Wharton School of Business, wrote:

> *The changes brought about through the women's movement may have decreased women's happiness. The increased opportunity to succeed in many dimensions may have led to an increased likelihood of believing one's life is not measuring up ... Or women may simply find the complexity and increased pressure in their modern lives to have come at the cost of happiness.*[5]

By defining success on their own terms, the Good Enoughs in our survey, as well as the most satisfied women we interviewed, had essentially rejected the belief that they "weren't measuring up." They had learned that their own expectations were the ones that mattered. And by deliberately *choosing* their priorities, they had reduced some of the complexity and pressure in their lives.

In fact, the Good Enoughs were more likely to feel that their sacrifices reflected their priorities—the closest measure of happiness from our survey.

But were their kids making them less happy? On one hand, any parent knows that tantrums and toilet training and the constant clutter of toys aren't exactly exhilarating. But . . . an overall reduction in life satisfaction? Really?

Everyone who took our survey or participated in interviews was a mother, so they started on equal ground. However, the Never Enoughs were more likely to have only one child—one-third compared to just more than a quarter of Good Enoughs. Hard to know why, but it may have reflected an evolution we observed: The Good Enoughs were much more adept at tolerating imperfection—a necessity for mothering small children.

But that troubling news on kids and happiness was still lurking, cropping up in multiple studies: Married couples tend to start out pretty satisfied, see a big dip when they have kids—and don't return to their original happiness levels until their kids leave home.[6]

Yikes.

But—wait—maybe it's all in how we look at it. We like Gretchen Rubin's spin on the topic; and her bestselling book *The Happiness Project* has made her a bit of an authority on the subject. Gretchen rejects the whole kids-as-killjoys argument by pointing out that maybe parental happiness isn't always an every-moment kind of thing, but something far more profound and harder to label. She wrote:

> In many ways, the happiness of having children falls into the kind of happiness that could be called fog happiness. Fog is elusive. Fog surrounds you and transforms the atmosphere, but when you try to examine it, it vanishes. Fog happiness is the kind of happiness you get from activities that, closely examined, don't really seem to bring much happiness at all—yet somehow they do.

Gretchen has several Secrets of Adulthood, and one of them is this: Happiness doesn't always make you feel happy. Rebecca Molloy, the counterterrorism researcher, hit on this as she assessed her own level of happiness (which she placed as pretty high).

"Motherhood has got to be—more than being in counterterrorism—the most empowering thing I've ever experienced," Rebecca told Becky. "I think being able to give life is just—it's just awesome. It's really, really awesome."

Which didn't mean that she always feels awesome. There are also "those moments of parenthood when only the loud sound of one's own voice offers temporary calm," Rebecca said, acknowledging what most of us feel from time to time. "My kids are wonderful, but sometimes they're wonderfully irritating. But if I wanted 'perfect' kids, I would have gotten mannequins."

This is the simple truth we learn along the way: Motherhood is a million unbelievably frustrating moments that somehow add up to . . . empowerment and joy. And a happiness that we can't always see.

Except, perhaps, in some of the other little moments, the ones when we stop and that happiness shimmers into focus, clear as day.

Rebecca feels it when she turns on the music, and she and her four children just dance.

* * *

And that brings us back to the great lesson the women we interviewed taught us: There are many ways to look at something, and many ways to find happiness. We just have to know where to look. We have to know ourselves.

It was tempting, at the beginning of the project, to stick neat little labels on each of the women we interviewed. Even the labels that worked so well in aggregate (Good Enough and Never Enough), and offered so much insight into the broad trends, didn't fit perfectly on individual women. But that was as big a part of the story as any: Not everything can be tied up with a neat little bow. The 905 women we surveyed and more than 100 women we interviewed—and the dozen or so we followed closely—couldn't have been more different.

Or had more in common. Rebecca Molloy—whose background and profession make her unusually aware of what can result from focusing too heavily on differences—tends to gravitate to the similarities. ("We're all looking for the same things," she told Becky.)

The most satisfied women we interviewed were linked in one big way that should be pretty clear by now: They'd pinpointed their priorities and they were doing their best to live by them. Some had found their way naturally. Some had undertaken a lot of soul-searching to find the right path. A few had sought outside help, consulting therapists or life coaches who had hammered these themes home: Take control. Define your own success. Be *you*.

Kimberly Fulcher, 39
Life and Business Coaching Expert
Founder, President and CEO of Compass Life and Business Designs
Stepmother of four

We need to give ourselves permission to step off that treadmill.

When I stepped off, it wasn't like angels started singing . . . I began using a very simple set of tools to ask and answer some basic questions. Start by looking at how you are using your energy, how you manage those mental things that are running around in your head. You need to take control of taking care of you. We don't nurture ourselves very well. I think nobody ever told us it was okay to do this.

What I've heard is, "I don't have enough time." Yes, you do, you just don't know how to manage it.

In the two years we spent researching and writing this book, we witnessed a few transformations, including our own. We experienced some exhilarating highs and some unexpected lows; a couple of times, one or the other was brought to her knees by a rough patch that required perseverance, faith or some kind of medication. As is always the case, life happened while we were trying to fit all the pieces of life into the same puzzle. Our lives, in that respect, were no different from those of the women we interviewed.

Some of the changes we witnessed in other women taught us the most about happiness; it gave us a chance to see courage, grace, self-reflection and determination in action. Between the first interview and the last, all our subjects experienced the ebbs and flows of life. Some found themselves surprised by their desires or strength; a few had to reevaluate the true goals of their ambition. Some discovered how invigorating it can be to try something new—and how much they were able to achieve when they felt inspired.

As it happened, many of the women we had interviewed were in particularly good places that spring:

Molly Morse Limmer, the Christie's art expert, got a promotion at work. "I'm working hard, but I'm enjoying it and I'm feeling appreciated, which is good," she told Becky. "My kids are thriving and seeing them thrive is just wonderful. Spring is always great. This time of year…it's still light when you get home, so it feels like you have more time with the family."

Kim Holstein opened a new pretzel café in Chicago's Lincoln Park neighborhood. And she was among fourteen women honored by the Women's Business Enterprise National Council for their leadership and ability to inspire other women business owners. It was a time of personal and professional milestones: Her business celebrated its fifteenth anniversary, and, in the fall, she'd send her eldest to middle school and her youngest to kindergarten. The café opening made for an intensely busy spring, but Kim was as enthusiastic as always: "My plate is so loaded, but I am loving what I'm doing," she told Becky. "I love my life."

Cathy Calhoun spent a week and a half in Italy with her daughter and came back confident that Sophie was, well, truly happy. "We talked about everything without the noise of everyday life," Cathy said.

And Jennifer Pate, Libby Windsor, Jen Canter and Nikki Williams—they, too, had a thing or two to say about success and happiness.

REACHING NEW HEIGHTS: JENNIFER PATE

That spring, *Jen and Barb: Mom Life* had just won the Webby Award (the online version of an Emmy) for best reality/variety hosts. Their second season was under way and was drawing about 1.6 million views per episode, and Jen and Barb had appeared as guests on the cooking shows hosted by Rachael Ray and Paula Deen.

It was an exciting time, but the women were moving carefully, making sure each step reflected their goals and priorities. Jennifer had even turned down an opportunity involving a well-known talk show host because the offer didn't involve Barb.

"I didn't get into this to become famous," Jennifer told Becky. "So I'm trying to make my choices very wisely. . . . I'm trying to create a really good web show and create a community online. The key for Barb and me is really going to be to stick to what our vision is—and to have a clear vision. There are definitely people circling right now, and talking to us. But what does that look like? I don't want to be on TV just to say I'm on TV."

Jennifer and her husband had adjusted to the new dynamics as a dual-career couple: Jonas was doing more around the house, and Jennifer had plugged the other gaps by hiring additional household help. That need to adjust initially had caught her off guard—mostly because it just hadn't occurred to her that she and Jonas would need to rethink their roles when she went back to work.

"We're in a better place, always moving forward," she told Becky. "Our communication has gotten better, it's gotten softer, it's gotten kinder. Now we have a healthier line of communication."

And this was even clearer to Jennifer: "You can't do it all yourself. You can make it all happen, but you have to know who is going to take what part."

Jennifer was also reveling in this aspect of her success: She finally could make a solid financial contribution to her family—and that felt really good.

Jennifer Pate, 43
Co-Executive Producer and Cohost of *Jen and Barb: Mom Life*
Los Angeles, California
Mother of Cooper and Lilah

I'm enjoying being able to provide for my family.

My initial [goal] wasn't "How much money can I make?" It was "Hey, I want to do this, and if I make some money, that's great." But now that I am,

I actually am ... enjoying being a real participant with my husband. There's a definite stress that's been lifted from him in providing for the family. It's so much better for both of us. He's definitely more involved in the domestic [scene], so much more. And I love that.

I have an additional purpose other than just being a mom. Being a mom is amazing and wonderful, and I feel so blessed. But I feel even more complete having something that is my own purpose. It's outside of just taking care of my children. And my children are watching me as a role model ... seeing that I'm working, I'm doing something I'm passionate about.

What I love is there's so much hope and potential. It's very exciting. The future feels very full of opportunity.

FINDING POWER IN NUMBERS: LIBBY WINDSOR

Libby Windsor, the employment litigator who once envisioned a career in interior design, often felt alone in her journey, even though so many of the ambitious moms we interviewed could relate to her story.

Libby just needed to find a place to hash it out, to feel validated—and then her stepsister called in the fall of 2009, proposing a women's empowerment group. It started with eight Pittsburgh-area moms who wanted to talk about their challenges and successes, and who wanted to be accountable for making some progress.

They drafted a mission statement and found the best format: Socialize for half an hour, then gather around a table to discuss how the women can support each other in their goals. Libby's husband, Ben, jokingly calls it "The Jerry Maguire Group" because no men are allowed.

Hollee was invited to join the group for their May 2010 meeting. It was a warm night, and the ladies gathered on Libby's secluded side porch, sinking into the cushioned Restoration Hardware wicker while Ben snuck in to light a few candles. Hollee couldn't help but smile as Libby, surrounded by supportive friends who nibbled on baklava while sipping chardonnay, spoke about her progress since the last meeting.

"The last time we met, I was feeling sort of lackluster about my work, and my six-month goal was to be more reengaged," Libby shared. "And it's a really wonderful feeling, because I am getting charged up over my work again. I think it's partly because Andrew isn't a baby anymore, and partly because the economy is getting better and my clients are coming to me with more diverse projects. I'm back to solving problems, and I'm back to a good pace."

"Tell me what you mean by that," one of the group members, a life coach, chimed in.

"For me," Libby said, "a happy pace at work is when I have a little too much to accomplish; it keeps me sharp and efficient, but it's not like, 'Oh my God, I'm going to have to work all weekend.' I'm getting it done at work, I'm keeping up with the kids. I guess I'm just kicking ass."

The group broke into applause.

REDISCOVERING HER CENTER: JEN CANTER

Jen Canter was, finally, doing less.

During two years of interviews, Becky had seen the passionate doctor steam forward full throttle, launch a business, find herself overwhelmed by the business and recalibrate to get herself back on track. Jen, it seemed, was always reflecting, choosing and solving. Always circling back to her core, reminding herself of what was important and what truly made her feel happy. It made it easier to take risks—she knew she had the strength and savvy to readjust if she overshot her mark. In the spring of 2010, Jen was back at her center. She had cut back on the things that weren't meeting her personal definition of success—she was delegating better in all areas of her life, she was making time to go to the gym and do things for herself, she was worrying less.

Her children were good, her marriage was good, her medical career was as fulfilling and stable as always.

And, perhaps most exciting: Jen licensed the U-Play Mat and the "Dr. Jen" brand to Sassy Inc., a global infant and toddler products company.

Jen Canter, 38
Child Abuse Pediatrician and Owner of Educational Toy Company,
Play This Way Every Day
Westchester County, New York
Mother of two sets of twins

I am actually really proud of how it's been going the past few months. I have hired more people to do things with pieces of the business that I don't have to [personally] be dealing with—invoicing, customer service, dealing with pieces of the internet.... And that's been liberating.

At home, I've gotten better about [delegating]. The other morning, I needed to get to work early to handle something with a patient, and I asked Wade to take the kids to nursery school, and he just did it. It was like, okay, I just asked him and it was over and it was no big deal. I think in the past I was like, Oh, I feel bad asking him—he has such a busy day. But, you know what? I have a busy day, too.

I enjoy our kids so much. They're at such a cute age, and they're so [much] fun. And now's the time to figure out how the other pieces of my life can still go on, but in a more compact and organized way, so I can maximize the time I have with them.

I'm still striving for the same things: stability and security and happiness. I think it's never changed. The kids have been happy and thriving. That's really been the measure. This may sound corny but, who can really say you're a failure if your kids are thriving?

I think I'm more confident that I can speak up for myself, and say no to things, and say how I feel in a more appropriate way. And that's just getting better and better. I'm starting to look at things and say, "I'm not doing this, and I'm not doing this"—and it's really okay.

Jen's story particularly touched us, perhaps because her honesty and plain-spoken demeanor made her so likable and real. Maybe because she was running a business and raising four kids and working full-time as a doctor and was still so . . . normal. Jen sometimes found herself exhausted by her vision—but she neither abandoned it nor allowed it to take over her life. She just kept reflecting, choosing and solving.

In the first interview, Jen had talked about being motivated by wanting to avoid the stressors that had defined her mother's life. She still didn't want those stressors, but she'd deepened in her awe and appreciation of all her mother had overcome. The lessons and the love she'd absorbed as a child had helped make her the success she'd become.

"Over the time I've been talking to you, I've gained so much more respect for my mother," Jen told Becky. "I don't know how she did it. It was always kind of crazy in our house . . . but there was always this knowledge that [my mother] loved us amazingly and passionately. And there was always a way to solve a problem."

It had been, Jen felt, an abundant inheritance.

THE FAIRY-TALE ENDING: NIKKI ADCOCK WILLIAMS

Throughout the time she interviewed her, Hollee felt a special kinship with Nikki: They both had spent too many years in jobs that had threatened to steal something from their souls; they were both "nice lawyers," and as Hollee had gotten to know Nikki over the course of their interviews, she was struck by how much they had in common.

Hollee hoped that Nikki would get the jolt she needed by connecting with career coach Debby Stone, but in February, Nikki told Hollee she'd decided against working with a career counselor. She and her husband, Tom, had looked at the budget and decided that it didn't fit.

But being part of *Good Enough Is the New Perfect* had stirred something in Nikki. The months of interviews, capped off by the time she spent with the other moms at the roundtable in New York City, prompted Nikki to seriously consider a change for the better.

For too long, she told Hollee, she'd viewed herself as a victim. She wasn't moving forward: She'd just accepted that she had a job she didn't love, and she wasn't putting any energy into finding something else.

Slowly, as she told Hollee her story over months of interviews, Nikki began to believe that she deserved more. That to be the kind of mother and wife that she wanted to be, she had to find a job that made her happy, too.

Nikki started with baby steps that made her feel more in control at work, like asking for comp time from the judge she worked for if she worked late. She began talking to her husband, Tom, about possibilities in juvenile law, an area that inspired her passion.

And then, in April, Nikki called Hollee to say that she had just heard about an opening for a legal writing professor at Georgia State University, just thirty-five minutes from her home. Immediately, Hollee knew it would be an ideal fit.

"You *have* to go for it," Hollee answered when Nikki wondered out loud whether she had a reasonable shot of landing the job.

Hollee was in the process of hiring a new professor for her own department; she knew that Nikki had the exact skill set that Georgia State would be seeking. She just wasn't sure whether Nikki could see that in herself.

So Hollee stepped out from her role as interviewer and gave her some friendly advice. She reviewed Nikki's cover letter and resume, reassured her that the application looked great. When Nikki called to say she had been invited to interview, Hollee offered to help her prepare. They spent several hours on the telephone the weekend before Nikki's interview, running through potential questions, tweaking Nikki's answers.

Nikki dug deep for the confidence that she knew was still inside, and she nailed the interview. On May 19, the law school called with the news: Nine of the ninety applicants had been invited to interview—but they wanted to hire *Nikki*. She was still in her high heels and work clothes, playing on the church playground with Anna and Liam, but she literally jumped in the air, celebrating her victory.

The "old" Nikki, the one her husband, Tom, remembered from their law school days—the energetic, ambitious, loving woman who could stare down any challenge—was back.

She called Hollee, who was making her near-nightly trek to the baseball field.

"So what do I need to pack for the legal writing conference next month?" Nikki almost sang.

Hollee cheered, and then Gideon and Henry (with just a little prompting) yelled into the phone: "Congratulations, Professor Williams!"

Nikki Adcock Williams, 33
Legal Writing Professor, Georgia State University School of Law
McDonough, Georgia
Mother of Anna and Liam

While I was reflecting on my professional journey, I realized I had been playing the role of the victim for too long. I just got tired of it, and I realized that until I changed my outlook, good things weren't going to come to me.

This job is the absolute perfect fit for me at this point in my life. I know I still have a lot of self-examination to do, but I think with this move, I have created space and time to really find myself.

This process of being able to talk about my feelings, of getting it out there and making that decision to be in New York with the other moms, that helped me find the confidence I had lost. And because of that, I was able to change my frame of mind, and to attract the good things I wanted to happen.

And now I feel an excitement about work that I haven't had in a very, very long time.

The feeling is just pure joy.

No matter how it's defined, that's what the New Perfect is all about—protecting the parts of life that give us pure, unadulterated joy. Those things can be as complicated as finally finding the right career, as profound as realizing that our mistakes can make us better mothers and, sometimes, as ridiculously simple as allowing ourselves an evening to sit on the porch with our friends, sipping a martini.

THE NEW PERFECT SURVEY

In May 2009, we surveyed 905 working mothers, born between 1965 and 1980, who were living in the United States and had at least one child under eighteen living at home. *Work* was defined as full-time or part-time jobs, including regular freelance or consulting work or running a business. Unpaid work qualified if it was consistent work on a project intended to generate, or help generate, future income (for instance, launching a business or spending more than twenty hours a week working toward a degree).

The survey, designed with the help of a research specialist at West Virginia University, was conducted online over a period of ten days, using email and social media to draw participants. More than 1,000 responded, but we analyzed only the 905 responses that met the criteria described above.

Our respondents were, for the most part, married, well-educated, professional women.

Almost all respondents attended college, and the vast majority (more than 92 percent) had a college degree. Nearly two-thirds had a graduate degree—27 percent reported a master's as their highest degree, 28 percent reported a professional degree (such as an MD or JD), and 5 percent reported a doctorate.

Eighty-five percent of respondents said their jobs required at least a bachelor's degree. Nearly half said their jobs required an advanced degree.

More than half the respondents earned more than $60,000 a year from their own jobs. More than half had family incomes exceeding $125,000 per year.

Ages were distributed evenly: Nearly 28 percent of respondents were born between 1965 and 1969; just over 47 percent were born between 1970 and 1974; and nearly 25 percent were born between 1975 and 1980.

Respondents represented forty-four states and the District of Columbia.

Every racial group was represented, but the vast majority of respondents were white. Some 2.5 percent were African-American, 3.4 percent were Asian and 2.6 percent were Hispanic or Latino. Fewer than 1 percent described themselves as Native American, or as Native Hawaiian/Pacific Islander.

Nearly 38 percent of respondents had worked for ten years or more before having children. Nearly 13 percent worked for fifteen years or more before having children. More than a quarter, however, had worked five years or fewer before becoming mothers.

THE SURVEY

1. Are you a working mother, born between 1965 and 1980, who lives in the United States and has at least one child under 18 living at home?

   ○ Yes
   ○ No

2. How many children do you have?

   _____

3. What is the highest degree you have attained? (Choices were provided.)

4. What is your current profession (besides being a mom)?

   _____

5. What is the annual income from YOUR job alone? (Ranges were provided.)

6. What is the combined annual income of everyone in your household? (Ranges were provided.)

7. What changes did you make to your work to better accommodate motherhood? (Check ALL that apply.)

   ○ Switched to part-time work with same employer.
   ○ Began job share.

O Took advantage of flexible scheduling with same employer.

O Took part-time job with different employer.

O Took full-time, but more flexible, job with different employer.

O Started own business.

O Quit work as employee but secured work as independent contractor/freelancer with former employer.

O Quit work as employee but secured work as independent contractor/freelancer with new employer.

O Quit work to stay home.

O Work arrangement did not change.

O Other

Questions 8 and 9 apply only to women who said they "quit work to stay home."

8. **How long were you out of the workforce? (Ranges were provided.)**

9. **When you returned to the workforce, did you return to the same profession?**

   O Yes, same job or type of job.

   O Yes, but a different type of job.

   O No

10. **Which best describes your current work arrangement?**

   O Full-time hours as an employee, not flexible.

   O Full-time hours as an employee, flexible.

   O Part-time work as an employee.

   O Own my own business/work as independent contractor or freelance—and work PART-TIME.

○ Own my own business/work as independent contractor or freelance—and work FULL-TIME.

○ Other (please describe)

11. **Why do you work? (Please rate each answer as Strongly Agree, Agree, Neutral/Unsure, Disagree or Strongly Disagree.)**

	Strongly Agree	Agree	Neutral/ Unsure	Disagree	Strongly Disagree
Financial necessity	○	○	○	○	○
Desire for financial independence (I don't want to depend on my husband/partner for money)	○	○	○	○	○
I love my job too much to give it up	○	○	○	○	○
I need a sense of accomplishment outside the home	○	○	○	○	○
I am worried about what people will think if I quit	○	○	○	○	○
I feel obligated because I worked so hard to get to where I am	○	○	○	○	○
I feel obligated because previous generations of women had to work so hard for the opportunity to work and advance in my field	○	○	○	○	○
I need a break from being a mom	○	○	○	○	○

12. **Which best describes your career BEFORE having children? (Note: Career advancement can include promotions, salary increases, increases in responsibility, improved assignments— anything that is viewed as "moving up" in your field.)**

   O I advanced to top position in my company/organization.

   O I advanced to an impressive position, earning clout and respect, but could have gone higher.

   O I advanced somewhat in my career.

   O I did not advance at all.

   O I didn't have an opportunity to advance before having kids because I switched jobs or did not work long enough.

13. **Which best describes your career position NOW?**

   O I am still in the top position in my company/ organization.

   O I stayed in the same profession and continued to MOVE UP.

   O I stayed in the same job or MOVED LATERALLY (equivalent position at same company or elsewhere).

   O I stayed in the same profession but MOVED DOWN.

   O I switched professions and MOVED DOWN to a less demanding and/or prestigious position.

   O I switched professions and am in an EQUALLY demanding and prestigious position.

   O I switched professions and have MOVED UP to a more demanding and/or prestigious position.

   O I MOVED DOWN but it was unrelated to motherhood (laid off because of the economy, for example).

14. **Which best describes the amount of time you spend at your job?**

   O I work MORE HOURS at my job than I did before having kids.

O I work the SAME NUMBER OF HOURS at my job as I did before having kids.

O I work FEWER HOURS at my job than I did before having kids.

15. **Aside from what your employer does for you, which of the following factors contribute to your ability to juggle work and motherhood? (Please rate each option as Strongly Agree, Agree, Neutral/Unsure, Disagree or Strongly Disagree.)**

	Strongly Agree	Agree	Neutral/ Unsure	Disagree	Strongly Disagree
I have an efficient and organized work style	O	O	O	O	O
I regularly pay for help at home (nanny, cook, cleaning service)	O	O	O	O	O
Husband/partner helps at home	O	O	O	O	O
Technology (PDA, email, mobile phone, etc.)	O	O	O	O	O
I am willing to make sacrifices at work and/ or at home	O	O	O	O	O
I have realistic expectations for myself	O	O	O	O	O
I am willing to delegate	O	O	O	O	O
I know when to say "no"	O	O	O	O	O
Other (please specify)					

16. What sacrifices or concessions have you made in order to accommodate both your career and motherhood? (Open-ended response.)

_____

_____

_____

17. Did any of the "sacrifices" you made to better juggle work and family lead to any surprise successes? If so, please describe. (Open-ended response.)

_____

_____

_____

18. In which area did you make your GREATEST sacrifices?

- O Career.
- O Motherhood.
- O Personal (hobbies, exercise, reading, relaxing).
- O My relationship with my husband/partner.
- O I haven't made any sacrifices.

19. How do you feel about your sacrifices?

- O I feel I sacrificed too much either at home or at work— but feel it is too late to change course.
- O I feel I sacrificed too much either at home or at work— and am actively trying to change that.
- O My sacrifices reflect my priorities.
- O I haven't made any sacrifices.

20. Which factors make it HARDER for you to juggle work and motherhood? (Please rate each option as Strongly Agree, Agree, Neutral/Unsure, Disagree or Strongly Disagree.)

	Strongly Agree	Agree	Neutral/ Unsure	Disagree	Strongly Disagree
Financial pressures require me to work more than desired	O	O	O	O	O
My job is not flexible enough	O	O	O	O	O
I constantly feel like I need to be "the best" at everything	O	O	O	O	O
I am not good at delegating responsibility	O	O	O	O	O
My husband/partner doesn't help enough at home	O	O	O	O	O
We have special circumstances at home (e.g. illness, special-needs child) that require extra attention	O	O	O	O	O
I can't afford extra help with cleaning and/or cooking	O	O	O	O	O
I do not have access to adequate child care	O	O	O	O	O
Other (please specify)					

21. How would you HONESTLY rate your performance in the following areas? (Please rate each option as Disaster, Not Very Good, So-So, Good Enough, Supermom/Superstar or Not Applicable.)

	Disaster	Not Very Good	So-So	Good Enough	Super-mom/ Superstar	Not Applicable
Routine parenting (meals, bedtime, getting to school)	O	O	O	O	O	O
Connecting with my children on a regular basis	O	O	O	O	O	O
Finding time to volunteer at school/kids' activities	O	O	O	O	O	O
Connecting with husband/ partner	O	O	O	O	O	O
Keeping the house clean	O	O	O	O	O	O
Taking time for myself	O	O	O	O	O	O
Finding time to spend with friends and extended family	O	O	O	O	O	O
Performance in my job	O	O	O	O	O	O
Keeping my boss happy	O	O	O	O	O	O

22. Which BEST describes your approach to juggling work and family?

○ Family needs FAR outweigh work and almost always come first; I only work out of necessity.

○ Although my children are very important to me, my job must come first—I need to be a superstar at work in order to provide for my family.

○ I try to be a superstar at work AND at home, even if it kills me.

○ Both family and work are important, and I try to do a relatively decent job at both and accept that I am not perfect.

○ Both family and work are important, but I constantly feel as though I am not doing a good job at either.

23. How much do you agree with the following statements? (Please rate each option as Strongly Agree, Agree, Neutral/Unsure, Disagree, Strongly Disagree.)

	Strongly Agree	Agree	Neutral/ Unsure	Disagree	Strongly Disagree
Most of the pressure I feel is pressure I put on myself	○	○	○	○	○
Most of the pressure I feel is pressure from external sources (e.g. work, my spouse, society)	○	○	○	○	○
A WOMAN who makes lateral career moves or downshifts to less demanding positions while raising children can still be viewed as serious about her career	○	○	○	○	○

	Strongly Agree	Agree	Neutral/ Unsure	Disagree	Strongly Disagree
A MAN who makes lateral career moves or downshifts to less demanding positions while raising children can still be viewed as serious about his career	O	O	O	O	O
The key to "balancing" career and family is to RAISE our expectations: We need to work even harder to do well in both areas	O	O	O	O	O
The key to "balancing" career and family is to LOWER our expectations: We need to do less and stop trying to be perfect	O	O	O	O	O

24. Which best describes your style as a working mom?

O The key to juggling a busy life is to be organized, orderly and goal-oriented. We stick to a schedule and, most of the time, the house is picked up and organized. I know where we need to be and when—and I make it happen. Things rarely fall through the cracks.

O My children's achievement is my top priority. We spend a lot of time on schoolwork and extracurricular activities, sometimes at the expense of other things.

O I have a lot of balls in the air and do an okay job of keeping them there. The house is sometimes a little messy and things occasionally fall through the cracks, especially when we have a lot going on—or we decide to spontaneously veer off schedule. I am not as organized as I'd like, but the important things get done.

○ We are very laid-back and spontaneous. Things are unstructured in our house—and we like it that way.

25. **Which bests describes your overall attitude?**

○ I feel a strong need to be "the best" at everything.

○ I want to be "the best" mom but am happy to simply be "good enough" at work.

○ I want to be "the best" at work but am happy to be a "good enough" mom.

○ Being "the best" is not important; I try to be "good enough" and happy, both at home and at work.

○ I just live my life and don't worry about how well I'm doing.

26. **How has your definition of success changed since having children? (Open-ended response.)**

_____

_____

_____

_____

_____

27. **What is your current state of residence?**

_____

28. **What year were you born? (Choices were provided.)**

29. **What is your marital status? (Choices were provided.)**

30. **Which categories describe your race or ethnicity? (Check all that apply.)**

   O   American Indian or Alaska Native
   O   Asian
   O   Black or African American
   O   Hispanic or Latino
   O   Native Hawaiian or Pacific Islander
   O   White

31. **How many years did you work before having children? (Choices were provided.)**

32. **What are the birth years of your children?**

   _____

33. **Does your current job require at least a bachelor's degree?**

   O Yes
   O No

34. **Does your current job require an advanced degree?**

   O Yes
   O No

THE ROUNDTABLE:
A LIVE DISCUSSION ON WORKING MOTHERHOOD
JANUARY 21, 2010, NEW YORK CITY

On a brisk January afternoon, we found ourselves running through midtown Manhattan in heels, carrying several large boxes of pastel-frosted cupcakes from the Magnolia Bakery. The confections were for the twelve women who had promised to join us that evening to discuss the trials and triumphs of working motherhood.

As we checked in at security, we wondered whether the women we'd invited would open up, whether they'd focus on their differences or what they had in common. The panelists were all smart, accomplished and articulate. Many were leaders, and all had been interviewed for the book. As working mothers, they shared many of the same concerns—but they also differed in countless ways: their careers, their definitions of success, the ways they'd chosen to blend motherhood and work, the things that made them feel guilty. These dozen women didn't even agree on the title we had chosen for the book: Some loved it, some ... didn't.

So we decided that to get to the heart of the matter, we needed to hear these women *talk to each other.*

The group represented an array of professions: There were executives and lawyers, a pediatrician, a counterterrorism researcher, a web series host and an auctioneer with a specialty in antique art. Most of the women had young children at home; two were grandmothers who had helped break down barriers as working mothers in the 1970s and 1980s. Several were from New York, but others came from Chicago, Atlanta, Pittsburgh and Philadelphia. Two of the women, Kim Holstein and Jennifer Pate, participated remotely by speakerphone and Skype.

The conversation, which we moderated, was energetic and honest and probably could have gone on for hours. (It didn't; it was ninety minutes, as planned.) The women didn't always agree and, at one point, some of us cried.

But by the end, one thing was clear: No matter how different we are, we have a lot to gain by listening to each other's perspectives, sharing our own stories and identifying the common ground that brings us together as women and mothers.

What follows is a transcript, edited for clarity and length. In a few instances, women asked to address questions that had been posed earlier in the discussion; their responses were added under that question heading. When the women were speaking directly to each other, the order of their comments was preserved to ensure the integrity of the dialogue.

The panelists were:

Cathy Calhoun, president of Weber Shandwick North America; mother of one

Jen Canter, child abuse pediatrician; founder of Play This Way Every Day, an educational toy company; mother of two sets of twins

Deborah Epstein Henry, lawyer; work/life flexibility strategist; founder and president of Flex-Time Lawyers; mother of three

Kimberly Oster Holstein, president, CEO and "chief inspiration officer" for Kim & Scott's Gourmet Pretzels; mother of three

Molly Morse Limmer, vice president and head of Department for Antiquities, Christie's; mother of two

Manini Madia, executive director of Global Makeup Marketing at the Estée Lauder Companies; mother of two

Rebecca Molloy, expert in Arabic linguistics, Mideast affairs and counterterrorism research; mother of four

Susan Fleming Morgans, public relations officer and editor of *Mt. Lebanon* magazine in Pittsburgh; mother of panelist Libby Windsor

Linda Morse, owner of an upscale knitting boutique, called String; former technology executive; mother of two grown children, including panelist Molly Morse Limmer

Jennifer Pate, cocreator, co-executive producer and cohost (with Barbara Machen) of online reality/talk show, *Jen and Barb: Mom Life;* mother of two

Nikki Adcock Williams, legal writing professor, Georgia State University College of Law; former judicial staff attorney and bankruptcy attorney who worked on the Enron case; mother of two

Elizabeth "Libby" Windsor, employment attorney; mother of two

ON EXPECTATIONS, PRIORITIES AND PERFECTIONISM

BECKY: *Let's start by talking about this whole idea of "Supermom" for a minute.... Do you think these expectations are realistic—and how do you think they affect working moms?*

JEN CANTER: *I think there are a lot of pressures out there for us to do a lot of things, and, personally, I just make priorities based on what I can handle with the kids. I did not make their baby food. I did as much mommy-and-me stuff as I could. If my kids are happy, and they're laughing, and they're loved—that's enough. Everything else, which is always a lot, comes after.*

REBECCA MOLLOY: *If you don't take it in as an expectation, it's not. So to say, "Oh, I can't live up to it ..." You don't have to because it's not [an expectation]. You know, as we say in Israel, "It's not written in stone, it's not one of the Ten Commandments." So it's okay. Chill.*

JENNIFER PATE [TO REBECCA MOLLOY]: *You're absolutely right with the idea of these expectations. Who's putting these expectations on us? We're putting them on ourselves, so, you know, we have to own our own life and say, "Well, this works for me, or this doesn't work for me." But there is no perfect, and I think that the word is getting out there. I think more and more people realize that.*

DEBBIE HENRY: *But that being said, I think that there's an inordinate amount of pressure on working moms.... At work, there's an expectation of 24/7 availability to colleagues and clients. And that—complemented by the expectation of involvement in our kids' lives, in our community, in our kids' schools, for example—is so disproportionate. I mean, I remember my mother baking brownies once a year for the annual bake sale, and now it's the weekly fund-raiser for this and that.... The expectation is everywhere. Being at every basketball game or every dance recital.... I think that really creates a lot of pressure for the women I interact with, as well.*

BECKY: *Do you think it affects the choices they make about how they're going to structure their careers?*

DEBBIE HENRY: *I think it does. And when it doesn't affect the choices, I think the result is that the women are so much more squeezed and so much more pressured and stress-ridden or guilt-ridden about the choices that they have to otherwise make.*

MOLLY MORSE LIMMER: *And I want to comment on that a second because I think the fact is, we are all multitaskers—we're all working women, and by definition I think we know how to analyze what is necessary versus what might not be quite as necessary. And it doesn't mean that it's always easy to sleep at night or easy to be socially involved in our communities or whatever. But I think most of us probably have a better way of sort of cutting through the bull than a lot of our friends who stay at home. So, you know, I wanted to say that.*

But the other thing... is I've worked really hard and prided myself on how to never seem at work any different than I was before I had kids—to make sure there's no perception that I've done anything that's less than I did before. I've worked very hard to be more efficient during the day, and I figured out when I don't need to be there—I mean, sort of the same way you don't need to be at every mommy-and-me class, you don't need to be at every meeting to be as good at what you do.

KIM HOLSTEIN: *I really relate [to that]—really being selective about what meetings you attend and not having to be at every mommy-and-me class. And I kind of see that as being good enough. I can go to the things that I need to be at, and I can go to certain events or occasions at the school that really mean something to me. It's [about] checking in with myself. I look at it from my heart versus feeling what [everyone expects out of me]. Also, not being too hard on myself— you've got to be good enough in it all.*

MOLLY MORSE LIMMER: *See, I didn't say it from a perspective of feeling "good enough." I mean, I want to be clear about that ... Figuring out what's 100 percent necessary, versus what's not, doesn't make me less of a perfectionist. It just is my own prioritizing and my analyzing of a situation to make myself more successful.*

DEBBIE HENRY: *Maybe this is rationalization, but what about the fact that it's actually a good thing for our kids [when we're not] hovering all the time? For us to enable them to have other relationships with maybe babysitters or grandparents or aunts or friends, or relying on a community to support them, and not always having a parent at everything.*

MOLLY MORSE LIMMER: *Promoting independence.*

DEBBIE HENRY: *Exactly, exactly.*

KIM HOLSTEIN: *I love that. That's great.*

NIKKI WILLIAMS: *There's a psychologist ... he had the idea that, and— again it's the phrase you don't like—but that "the good enough mother" is actually more healthy for our children. And "the good enough mother," the model he talks about, it's about lessening your adaptation to your children. When you have a baby, you totally adapt to your child. You take care of all of her basic needs, you answer her cry 24/7, and as she gets older you do that less often.*

You don't answer your child right away, and your child becomes more able to deal with frustrations. You're not there all the time, and your child learns how to interact with other people. So that's very interesting what you said because I think it is helpful when you're not always constantly there taking care of absolutely every need—not introducing them to . . . all of the arts, all at once, all of the time. It's okay.

ON CREATING OUR OWN DEFINITIONS OF SUCCESS

LIBBY WINDSOR: *I have always really thrived on competition. It was one of the things that drove me in school and, you know, throughout my life. And [defining my own success has been about] finding an internal compass and what makes me happy. [It's been figuring out] if I'm being my best in terms of being a good mom and being a good wife and doing a great job at work and all of those things. And that's been, I think, an adjustment for me. Not that motherhood has slowed me down in my job, but it's changed my focus and how I define excellence and success in my work and at home. It's not so much anymore about being the best in relation to others. It's more about finding my best, I guess.*

LINDA MORSE: *It's interesting to me to listen to this . . . because I think our generation didn't really define it that way. We thought about it more in terms of accomplishments and outputs, not about process . . . We had specific goals for our career, and success was that you met those goals or [it was] the degree [to] which you met them. We had specific goals for our children and for our marriages, and success was meeting those goals. It wasn't about what we did, it wasn't about how we did it. It was about what the outcomes were. I think that's very different from what I'm hearing.*

MANINI MADIA: *That's actually a really interesting point. I feel that process is such an important part of everything we do. Like, yes, my child is happy—but how did we get her there? That just starts the . . . questions in my head: Am I* doing the right thing having her in school all day and having my infant with the nanny all day? *And those are things that my mother—*

LINDA MORSE: *Those are things we never ever thought about.*

LIBBY WINDSOR [MOTIONS TO HER MOTHER, SUSAN]: *She tells me the same thing.*

SUSAN FLEMING MORGANS: *You know, I think honestly the access that you young women have to the internet can be confusing and complicating in terms of raising a child.*

LIBBY WINDSOR: *We overthink* everything.

SUSAN FLEMING MORGANS: *Ultimately I find that [Libby] still comes to me and says, "Mom, I've read this and this and this on the internet. What do you think?" So, personally, I still think if a working mom or a stay-at-home mom can find friends her own age, friends with children a little older, her own mom, an aunt, whatever, to bounce things off . . . that's better than just staying on that computer all day long driving yourself crazy.*

MANINI MADIA: *That's so true. We've lost so much of that human touch, and lost so much of that common sense that I feel like my mother has but I just don't— like I'm missing that. So I need my computer.*

LIBBY WINDSOR: *It's so much of* Am I doing the right thing? *And so often, when I feel like I'm torn between choices, I ask my mother. And she tells me exactly what you said: "We never thought about that, and you all turned out fine. So whatever you do is fine."*

ON FACING DOWN STRESS AND DISAPPOINTMENT

BECKY: *One of the interesting things as I've interviewed Molly is—Molly has always been extremely good at articulating what her goals are and how she meets them and what her priorities are.*

MOLLY MORSE LIMMER: *Even though they might change from conversation to conversation.*

BECKY: *But, Molly, where do you find that compass that helps you define success?*

MOLLY MORSE LIMMER: *I don't know. I mean, I think I must inherently be centered in some way that I think about these things ... to make sure that I'm able to get where I want to go.*

CATHY CALHOUN: *Does it stress you out trying to get there?*

MOLLY MORSE LIMMER: *All the time. All the time. And wondering if they're the right decisions or the right directions. You know, I applied for a different job this year, which was a huge thing to do because I've always done the same thing sort of in a linear, goal-oriented way. But I've had the same job for thirteen years, and an opportunity presented itself. [I asked] my mother's advice first because I didn't feel 100 percent comfortable about it. And I went for it, and I spent the two weeks of the interview process convincing myself why I wanted it so badly—and then I didn't get it. And it was really the first time—pretty much in my life—I didn't get something. I was rejected, and it sort of turned my life upside down briefly. It was like, "What do you mean 'No'? What do you mean I was the runner-up?" But it was the best thing that happened because I would've hated the job. (Looks at her mom, Linda.) Right?*

LINDA MORSE: *Right, right.*

SUSAN FLEMING MORGANS: *But don't you think that it makes you a stronger person knowing that you had a disappointment ... and it didn't crush you and you moved on, and you became stronger?*

MOLLY MORSE LIMMER: *Yeah, at age thirty-seven. Yeah. But had I been seventeen and applying to college, I don't know if I would've been mature enough to take it the way I can now.*

SUSAN FLEMING MORGANS: *I think, in a way, we parents in our generation did a disservice to our daughters by trying to make their worlds so* *perfect and protect them from failure. I think sometimes a little hit at seventeen or eighteen is not necessarily a bad thing—but we didn't want any of you to experience that.*

LINDA MORSE: *That's true.*

JEN CANTER: *I feel like I'm on another planet when I hear these things, to be honest with you. And I'll tell you why. I grew up in a house where my mother was a single mother with three kids who had various odd jobs, and I had to do so many things for myself. I did my homework myself. I'm convinced that if I don't do homework with my kids they will be just as successful, if not more successful . . . because they're going to problem-solve. And none of this happened to me as a kid, and I don't do any of this for my kids—partly because I don't have the energy and time, but partly because I just don't believe that that's the style of parenting that's going to be effective in our house. It's just not going to fly. I don't worry about any of these things. I don't really think about any of these things. I don't think,* Am I doing the right thing? *You know, sometimes I'll hit a point where I say, "Oh, are they in the right program?" But I don't really think about it that much. I just kind of do it. I think I'm more impulsive. But it's worked so far. They're okay. They're nice kids.*

ON FINDING FLEXIBILITY AT WORK

NIKKI WILLIAMS: *I am a lawyer, and [when I worked for a big law firm], I was supposed to be a lawyer twenty-four hours a day, seven days a week. And it didn't matter if my kid was sick. And I've told this story to Hollee. When my daughter was about ten months old, she had a very high fever and was very sick and couldn't go to day care. I stayed home with her, and I called in and I said, "I'm staying home. Anna's sick today." I got a call an hour later, saying, "You need to come in. We need you to do some research." I said, "Fine. I'm bringing the baby. I have to." So my daughter and I went to the library, which was the quietest place because nobody goes and uses the books anymore. We were in* *the library, and my daughter slept on the floor next to me. And, of course, I felt awful the entire time. But the partner expected that of me, and to me, that was insane. I could have done it at home, but I was expected to be in the office. And just because I was a mother [who] had a sick child, there was no changing that expectation of face time. So I think we can talk about all these great things, and people can say that there's flexibility, but I found that the expectations and the requirement to be "perfect" in my field—it meant that you were there all the time, and you had no flexibility to take care of personal things, family concerns.*

HOLLEE: *Why don't you [talk] a little bit about what you chose to do as a result?*

NIKKI WILLIAMS: *Well, that very incident of Anna sleeping on the floor next to me in the library, that's when I knew:* I'm not going to last. I don't want to. I don't want to be a partner here. I don't want to work here. *And so, about two and a half years later, I got pregnant with my son, and I quit. I had no plan, but I was miserable and I knew that there was no way that I would be happy there, and I quit. And we sold our house, and we lost a lot of income because my husband is a government attorney, and we moved out of the city. And I went back to work eventually, and now I work for a judge. And he's a state court judge, not a federal judge—but for me it's fine because I'm happy. I'm happy with what I do, and I know that if I need to take care of something, if I need to go to the doctor, no one's going to look at me when I walk out the door and frown.*

It's okay to take care of myself, and it's okay, too, because now I'm able to sit and think: What is it that I really want to do? *I have some time to focus on me and try and figure out:* What is it that I really want out of life for me? *And I'm also able to be there for my kids, so I like the title because for me—*

HOLLEE: *I'm crying listening to you. I love it.*

NIKKI WILLIAMS: *—you know, I realize that—I'm going to cry, too!*

HOLLEE: *I'll get you a "Becky and Hollee" water bottle.*

NIKKI WILLIAMS: *—you know, that that perfect path wasn't going to work* *for me. I wasn't going to be a partner. I had no joy in my job anymore, and now, you know, I have a job that's not prestigious, but it works. And for me, that's why I like the title because it's good enough for me for right now. And that's all I'm going to say.*

JEN CANTER: *I think the legal profession's really hard for women—medicine is very different. And I hear—I interface with lawyers every day as a child abuse pediatrician, and it's a much different environment in law. I brought my kids to a child abuse evaluation in the middle of the night and had them play in the playroom ... I know it's not a choice. I'm the doctor, and my kid's sick, and my husband's traveling, and I had to go in, and I wasn't upset or anything about it. It is what it is. I didn't have a babysitter that night, but nobody's saying it to me, and nobody's putting that pressure on me. I think it's different in law as a rule.*

SUSAN FLEMING MORGANS: *You know I am a woman boss. I don't have hundreds of people working for me. I have ten. But I have had women who have worked other places come in to me and say, "Thank you, thank you for hiring me," because I do offer that sort of flexibility that I think is important for women with children. And I've had not only sick kids in the office, but I've had a dog the dog sitter couldn't take in the office. And I do let people work from home, so I think, getting back to what you said, maybe law, even though there are more women lawyers graduating ... today, I think that men are still in charge for the most part.*

NIKKI WILLIAMS: *Yeah. Billable hours make it rough.*

REBECCA MOLLOY: *We have to have a system in place that makes everybody comfortable. And it's not insane to be flexible. You need the flexibility which other countries have come to.... I mean, the discussions in this country drive me nuts sometimes because, I mean, we're all humans, and why aren't we taking care of each other? It's heartbreaking.*

ON GENERATIONAL DIFFERENCES AND EQUALITY

LINDA MORSE: *One of the differences, from our generation and now, is we faced all these problems, and there were no laws then. They hadn't been defined and what we did when we faced those problems is [that] we made a big deal about them, and we went to management. We got in trouble a whole lot of the time. You know, people were sick of us. We did all sorts of things, but we really worked for change, and I think that now what I hear from so many people is they accept the status quo. I mean, there were times—I worked for a technology company, and technology companies in those days were 24/7 and we had to travel all the time, and we had to do this, that and the other thing. But, you know, I said, "No." And I said, "Go ahead. Fire me." Well, they didn't . . . I think that one of the reasons why [there are still issues] is because* people stopped being activists about it.

DEBBIE HENRY: *Can I make a comment to that? I think these are a different set of issues. I think that in your generation the issue was entry...*

LINDA MORSE: *No. It wasn't just entry.*

DEBBIE HENRY: *But, that was—*

LINDA MORSE: *It was every step of the way.*

DEBBIE HENRY: *Right. But one huge issue was entry. Whereas in our generation, except for women of color...there isn't an entry issue anymore.*

LINDA MORSE: *That's true.*

DEBBIE HENRY: *So for the legal profession, women have comprised 40, 50 percent of graduating classes for nearly twenty-five years, but we're only 16 percent of equity partners at law firms nationally. So it's an issue of retention and promotion, which is a different issue. [There is another] thing I just want to come back to, because I think it's not just a workplace issue: There was a really great letter to the editor that was written years ago . . . in response to Lisa*

Belkin's "Opt-Out Revolution" article, where the writer said we can't have equity in the workplace until we have equity at home. And I think that's the other big picture here . . . we don't have the same equity and roles in our households. [Linda], you mentioned in your introduction about how supportive your husband was. That was, I'm sure, very instrumental to your success.

LINDA MORSE: *Couldn't have happened without him.*

DEBBIE HENRY: *But it's not always the case, and that's an impediment for a lot of women working in the first place, or working successfully as mothers.*

LIBBY WINDSOR: *I work for a man who plays a huge role in his family. His wife has a big job, and he is always running around for his kids. And he is wonderful to work for because you can tell he is part of a household where there is more equal parenting. So when I need to run out to do something with my kids, he's not looking at me like, "Uh, woman lawyer." You know, it's just a person next to me with a child.*

NIKKI WILLIAMS: *I was able to work with some of the male attorneys in my firm, and female attorneys, too . . . partners who were active not just in their kids' lives but were active in the community, who had outside things, who felt like it was okay to have life outside of work. They were more responsive to me when I needed things. It makes such a difference when you have someone who's already been there and done that and chooses to do it. It's not always the case.*

ON MARRIAGE

BECKY: *One of the interesting things that came up in interviews when we were talking about marriage and division of labor at home is many of the women I interviewed described relatively egalitarian marriages or at least the hope of relatively egalitarian marriage. But the interesting thing was that quite a number of women . . . [also] described retaining this emotional responsibility for the home and for child care. The domestic buck essentially stopped with them. Why is this?*

REBECCA MOLLOY: *We're queens.*

BECKY: *Because it certainly affects the decisions we make about work and about our ability to juggle work. Why do we still retain emotional responsibility for the home?*

JEN CANTER: *I don't think we all do.*

MOLLY MORSE LIMMER: *It's like, I don't see that aspect of myself at all. You know, other than playdates and stuff like that with the kids, which I'm responsible for... none of my brain power is used on anything having to do with my home. Zero.*

BECKY: *Was that a decision you made or is that how you're wired?*

MOLLY MORSE LIMMER: *That's how I'm wired.*

JENNIFER PATE: *As far as moms taking care of the home, I mean ... you guys are clearly all type A working moms, maybe not all of you ... but I'm not. I believe that women are nurturers. I believe that it shows our love [for] our family. I mean, I have people come over, and I do bake cookies and I do put out fresh flowers, and I think that that is very important—I think ... that's a beautiful thing about [women]. I mean, we can still be the earners, and we can still make an impact in the business, but, for me, God, the beauty of being a woman—that nurturing, that caretaking. And listen, I don't clean my own house. Don't get me wrong. But I love making a homemade dinner for my family. I love doing that for my husband. I love doing that for my children, so that softness of womanhood, I think, is a beautiful thing. There. I've spoken.*

MOLLY MORSE LIMMER: *But I want to take that somewhere else. You know, I love cooking also, and sometimes I have time to do it. But I love cooking with my husband.*

JENNIFER PATE: *That's fine. I'm glad that works for you. I love to cook for my husband.*

MOLLY MORSE LIMMER: *Right.*

JENNIFER PATE: *You know what, though? To me, I think if it works for you, then ... that's awesome. My husband ... I know, for him, that being cared for and cooked for makes him feel loved, and so I do it lovingly. But, once again, that works for me. If it doesn't work for you, that's all good, too....*

ON GUILT

HOLLEE: *So here's something that's come up a lot in our conversations: Guilt. What makes you feel most guilty as a mom and as a professional? Do you have guilt?*

JEN CANTER: *Yeah. Like tonight I feel horrible because I didn't see my kids all day. I left really early this morning—not trying to make you feel bad—but I left really early this morning, and I, personally, I made a decision to never be more than ten minutes from my kids, and that's why we moved to Westchester.... So days when I don't see my kids are really hard for me, and I feel guilty. That's my guilt. It's different for other moms.*

LIBBY WINDSOR: *Well, Hollee knows I feel very little guilt. And you asked me, "Why do you feel so little?" And I don't know the answer. But I feel very little guilt. I'm more inclined to feel—if I stop and think about it—I feel bad. My kids are with their nanny all day, and my husband was working late, so the babysitter had to come relieve the nanny. But I really didn't think about it until right now, and [now] I feel sort of bad, but they're fine.*

SUSAN FLEMING MORGANS: *You never felt very guilty about anything when you were growing up, either.*

LIBBY WINDSOR: *I know. Every once in a while—*

SUSAN FLEMING MORGANS: *She's very hard to punish.*

HOLLEE: *Does anyone struggle [with guilt]?*

MOLLY MORSE LIMMER: *Yeah. I found the first year of motherhood very difficult because I couldn't come to terms with my feelings of guilt everywhere. I* *felt that I was not doing anything well. And I guess that goes back to the perfect thing, and I felt that I couldn't leave work when I wanted to leave work. And I felt that I wasn't at work as much as I should be. I wasn't at home as much as I should be. I wasn't getting anything done. And I had an incredible sort of boss-of-my-boss who I sat down with at one point, and he said, "You have to stop feeling the eyes on your back." Which was just an incredible piece of advice. It took a while to stop feeling the eyes on my back when I walked out the door—both at home and at work.*

BECKY: *Are the eyes still there?*

MOLLY MORSE LIMMER: *I have no idea.*

JEN CANTER: *Were they there or did you think they were there?*

MOLLY MORSE LIMMER: *I don't know.*

JEN CANTER: *Are your kids really feeling bad, and is work really looking at you?*

MOLLY MORSE LIMMER: *I mean sometimes they say, "Mommy, don't go. Mommy, don't go."*

JEN CANTER: *Yeah. I feel that.*

MOLLY MORSE LIMMER: *And part of it is to hear themselves say it. I understand that.... They don't notice two seconds later. They're onto the next thing. But I don't know if the eyes were really on my back or not. I perceived them to be everywhere.*

HOLLEE: *I think a lot of women have that experience, at least that's what we've heard.*

DEBBIE HENRY: *I'm driven by guilt. I used to be a litigator at a law firm, and I had tremendous guilt. And I designed my consulting practice when I started almost eleven years ago around a lifestyle that I wanted because I didn't want to miss out. And it's evolved over time as my kids have grown. But I have tried* to mirror their schedule because I don't want to miss out, and I don't care about certain things . . . household things and things like that.

But I do want to drive carpool because I get my best information when they think I'm not listening, and I've got my back to them. And I do want to be in the schools because I feel like there's more accountability. So I actually feel like I design my work around that. And, on the home front, when I do miss things—because we all do, and I travel for work—I definitely rationalize. You know, I work it through my mind. Is this something I can miss and that kind of thing. Because I have that guilty voice talking to me all the time about which things are appropriate to miss and which things I'll feel sad about. But I ask myself Are the kids thriving? But am I going to have regrets? And I don't want to have regrets.

So I constantly have that voice asking me those questions.

ON THE TITLE OF THE BOOK

HOLLEE: *I want to move on to the topic you've all been waiting for, right? The title of the book. So we've gotten some extreme reactions. Some people love it; some people have reservations about* Good Enough Is the New Perfect *[as the title]. So I wanted to get a couple of your reactions. And I'll tell you a funny story. When I was originally talking to one of my good friends, who is an author, about this, I said, "I think we're going to call it* Good Enough Is the New Perfect." *And she said, "Isn't that like* Sucky Is the New Awesome?" *And I think that's the way some people take it. It's not the way I ever thought about it, but I'm going to let you talk about it first because this is about you. Cathy, I know you have some thoughts on it.*

CATHY CALHOUN: *Well, I'm pro the title, just for the record. It's the reason I'm here because I thought, "Wow, that's a great idea." One of my friends tried to introduce me to [Becky and Hollee], and I shun everything because I have too much on my plate. . . . I say no to almost everything. But I found the title so compelling and so liberating. I thought, "Oh my God, that's exactly how I feel."*

You know? It's still perfect for me.... Perfect's still in there. We all strive to be the best we can be, but [I like to] let myself off the hook a little and say, "You know what? You might not be able to check everything off the list or get to every meeting or... have your kid speak three languages and be at every game." In my case, I travel for work. I'm gone one or two nights a week every week since she was [about four] months old. That's a lot of days, a lot of lost time with my child.... But she's doing great. I check in with her. She's safe, she's secure, she knows I love her, she knows I always come back. She's with someone who loves her when I'm gone. She's very independent, and, you know, she's my compass. As long as she's good, I feel good about myself and what I'm doing.

MOLLY MORSE LIMMER: *I was just looking at the title, and I want to take out my pen and cross out "Is the New" and change it to "Can Be."* Good Enough Can Be Perfect. *Because it's what I was saying before—it's not that it's not perfect; it's not that we're giving up anything or doing anything less than we should be, or doing anything less than anybody else does. So I look at the title, and I think to myself [that] somehow it's characterizing working moms as only good enough—and I don't believe that we are. I believe that what we're doing is working very hard to achieve everything we want and not give things up, which is why we've chosen to go for our career dreams while we're also good parents.*

DEBBIE HENRY: *Nobody in this room or any working mom wants to feel that [she's] settling or that [she's] giving [her] kids the short end of the stick, [and] I think that notion is definitely suggested through the title.... It's funny because my mother went back to work when I was two, and I only can remember having a working mom. And anytime I've felt guilt as a working mom or anything, she's always said, "Your kids are thriving. What are you worried about?" And I always say, "But, Mom, there are two issues here." One is: Are my kids thriving? And that's great; that's one issue. The second issue is: Am I going to look back and feel like I've missed out? And that's the issue that I think many of us who have guilt... think about. And that's where I think the choices are... I can't miss this, but somebody else can drive him to that.*

And so that's the tension that I feel about the title—it's in some ways not identifying the good judgment calls that each of us make about where we should be, and where we don't need to be ... and where it really doesn't matter, and what can be delegated out. I don't have ... a care in the world about delegating out the laundry. In fact, I feel like that's a really great way for me to justify what I do so that I don't have to do the laundry. But I do want to be at my kid's first play, and that's kind of where I see the issue.

JEN CANTER: *I'm good enough. Great, perfect. It's not saying, "Good Enough Is the New Happiness." And I take it as: Good enough now is what years ago was Betty Crocker. It was—"I'm going to bake cookies, and I'm going to do everything." I don't [view the title] as offensive in any way. You know what, I'm good enough, and I'm happy, and you might have been perfect, and you're happy.*

MOLLY MORSE LIMMER: *But you're not a perfectionist.*

JEN CANTER: *Right.*

MOLLY MORSE LIMMER: *And those of us who are perfectionists, it's sucky.*

REBECCA MOLLOY: *But I think that people need to look inside themselves and say, "I am who I am, and this makes me happy," whatever that "this" is, and be happy.*

LIBBY WINDSOR: *I feel like I actually do have to regularly make [sacrifices] ... not necessarily with my children and not with my work [but with my personal interests].... I love interior design, and I'd love for my house to look flawless all the time, and it can't. It has to be good enough. And I can't continue to be upset that it's not perfect every night when I walk through the door, as much as I would like for it to be because I would be miserable if I was holding myself to that standard. So I feel like there is an aspect of "hmm, good enough." I wish I knew more of my neighbors. I hardly know any of them. That's my life right now. I don't have time to know my neighbors. That has to be good enough.*

JENNIFER PATE: Good Enough Is the New Perfect *I love. I just think that there is no perfection. I hate the idea of being perfect. I think that we're teaching our children a terrible thing [if we focus so heavily on perfection], so I just want to get that out there.*

ENDNOTES

INTRODUCTION

1. For more insights into socioeconomic groups, we suggest Joan C. Williams and Heather Boushey, "The Three Faces of Work-Family Conflict" (Washington, D.C.: Center for American Progress, 2010).

CHAPTER 1: I QUIT

1. When asked to rate the factors that made it harder to juggle work and motherhood, nearly 67 percent agreed or strongly agreed that they were hampered by a constant "need to be 'the best' at everything." Nearly 54 percent cited financial pressures and nearly 39 percent agreed or strongly agreed that they were "not good at delegating."

2. Donald Winnicott, "Mind and Its Relation to the Psyche-Soma," *British Journal of Medical Psychology* 27 (1954): 201–209.

3. Alice H. Eagly and Linda L. Carli, *Through the Labyrinth: The Truth about How Women Become Leaders* (Boston: Harvard Business School Press, 2007), p. 54.

4. Richard Fry and D'Vera Cohn, "New Economics of Marriage: The Rise of Wives," (Washington, D.C.: Pew Research Center, 2010).

5. Sharon R. Cohany and Emy Sok, "Trends in Labor Force Participation of Married Mothers of Infants," *Monthly Labor Review* 130, no. 2 (U.S. Bureau of Labor Statistics, 2007): 13.

CHAPTER 2: THE INHERITANCE

1. Judith K. Hellerstein and Melinda Sandler Morrill, "Dads and Daughters: The Changing Impact of Fathers on Women's Occupational Choices," *Journal of Human Resources* (forthcoming).

2. "The Next Generation: Today's Professionals, Tomorrow's Leaders," (*Catalyst,* 2001), p. 2.

3. The term the second shift was popularized by sociologist Arlie Hochschild, whose 1989 book by that title examined the after-work housework undertaken by many women in two-career marriages. See Arlie Hochschild, *The Second Shift: Working Parents and the Revolution at Home* (New York: Viking, 1989).

4. Lisa Belkin, "The Opt-Out Revolution," *New York Times* (October 26, 2003): Section 6; Column 1; Magazine Desk, p. 42.

5. Sharon R. Cohany and Emy Sok, "Trends in Labor Force Participation of Married Mothers of Infants," *Monthly Labor Review* 130, no. 2 (U.S. Bureau of Labor Statistics, 2007): 13.

6. Heather Boushey, "Are Women Opting Out? Debunking the Myth" (Center for Economic and Policy Research, 2005), p. 2.

7. Leslie Bennetts, *The Feminine Mistake* (New York: Hyperion, 2007).

8. U.S. Census Bureau, "A Half-Century of Learning: Historical Statistics on Educational Attainment in the United States, 1940 to 2000," Percent of the Population 25 Years and Over with a Bachelor's Degree or Higher by Sex and Age, for the United States: 1940 to 2000, Table 2, 2007.

9. Sharon R. Cohany and Emy Sok, "Trends in Labor Force Participation of Married Mothers of Infants," *Monthly Labor Review* 130, no. 2 (U.S. Bureau of Labor Statistics, 2007): 13.

10. U.S. Census Bureau, "Historical Income Tables—People," Women's Earnings As a Percentage of Men's Earnings by Race and Hispanic Origin, Table P-40, 2009.

11. Barbara H. Wootton, "Gender Differences in Occupational Employment," *Monthly Labor Review* 120, no. 4 (U.S. Bureau of Labor Statistics, 1997): 17.

12. Amara Bachu and Martin O'Connell, "Fertility of American Women," Current Population Reports, U.S. Census Bureau (September 2000): 8.

13. U.S. Census Bureau, "Historical Income Tables—People," Women's Earnings As a Percentage of Men's Earnings by Race and Hispanic Origin, Table P-40, 2009.

14. Barbara H. Wootton, "Gender Differences in Occupational Employment," *Monthly Labor Review* 120, no. 4 (U.S. Bureau of Labor Statistics, 1997): 17.

15. Sharon R. Cohany and Emy Sok, "Trends in Labor Force Participation of Married Mothers of Infants," *Monthly Labor Review* 130, no. 2 (U.S. Bureau of Labor Statistics, 2007): 13.

16. "1995 Catalyst Census Female Board Directors of the Fortune 500," (*Catalyst,* 1995), p. 3; "2002 Catalyst Census of Women Corporate Officers and Top Earners of the Fortune 500," (*Catalyst,* 2002), p. 3.

17. U.S. Census Bureau, "Historical Income Tables—People," Women's Earnings As a Percentage of Men's Earnings by Race and Hispanic Origin, Table P-40, 2009.

18. "2007 Catalyst Census of Women Board Directors of the Fortune 500," (*Catalyst,* 2007), p. 1; "2007 Catalyst Census of Women Corporate Officers and Top Earners of the Fortune 500," (*Catalyst,* 2007), p. 1.

CHAPTER 3: THE NEW MOMMY WARS

1. Friedan described women's growing dissatisfaction with career-less life as "the problem with no name." See Betty Friedan, *The Feminine Mystique* (New York: Norton, 2001), pp. 62–64.

2. Ellen Galinsky, Kerstin Aumann and James T. Bond, *Times Are Changing: Gender and Generation at Work and at Home* (New York: Families and Work Institute, 2008), p. 18.

3. Lisa Belkin, "The Opt-Out Revolution," *New York Times* (October 26, 2003): Section 6; Column 1; Magazine Desk; p. 42.

CHAPTER 4: THE GOOD (ENOUGH) WIFE

1. Gary Becker, *A Treatise on the Family* (Cambridge: Harvard University Press, 1991), p. 30.

2. Adam Isen and Betsey Stevenson, *Women's Education and Family Behavior: Trends in Marriage, Divorce and Fertility* (Cambridge: National Bureau of Economic Research, 2010), p. 3.

3. Suzanne Bianchi, John Robinson and Melissa Milkie, *Changing Rhythms of American Family Life* (New York: Russell Sage Foundation, 2006), p. 115.

4. Sally Clarke, "Advanced Report of Final Divorce Statistics, 1989 and 1990," Monthly Vital Statistics Report 43, no. 9 (National Center for Health Statistics, 1995): 9. The divorce rate hit the same high of 5.3 divorces per 1,000 people in 1979, before dropping to 5.2 in 1980, then back up to 5.3 in 1981. It has fallen consistently since then.

5. U.S. Census Bureau, "Estimated Median Age at First Marriage, by Sex: 1890 to the Present," Current Population Survey Table MS-2, 2009.

6. Benedict Carey and Tara Parker-Pope, "Marriage Stands Up for Itself," *New York Times* (June 28, 2009): 1.

7. U.S. Bureau of Labor Statistics, "Married Parents' Use of Time, 2003–06," American Time Use Survey Table 2, 2008.

8. Ibid., Table 1.

9. Marissa Miley and Ann Mack, "The New Female Consumer: The Rise of the Real Mom," *Advertising Age* (2009): 7.

10. Sampson Blair and Michael Johnson, "Wives' Perceptions of the Fairness of the Division of Household Labor: The Intersection of Housework and Ideology," *Journal of Marriage and the Family* 54, no. 3 (August 1992): 570–581.

11. More tips can be found at www.equallysharedparenting.com.

CHAPTER 5: FINDING THE RIGHT FIT AT WORK

1. For more on "corporate lattice," see Cathleen Benko and Anne Weisberg, *Mass Career Customization: Aligning the Workplace with Today's Nontraditional Workforce* (Cambridge, Mass.: Harvard Business School Press, 2007), p. 3.

2. Cali Williams Yost, "CFOs See Business Impacts of Work/Life Flexibility, But They Can't Execute for Strategic Benefit," *WorldatWork Journal* (2009): 64.

3. Ellen Galinsky, James T. Bond and E. Jeffrey Hill, "When Work Works: A Status Report on Workplace Flexibility," (Families and Work Institute, 2004), p. 2.

4. "The Bottom Line: Connecting Corporate Performance and Gender Diversity," (*Catalyst*, 2004), p. 2.

5. Cathleen Benko and Anne Weisberg, "Introduction to Mass Career Customization," (Deloitte LLC, 2008), pp. 1–13.

6. Joan C. Williams and Heather Boushey, "The Three Faces of Work-Family Conflict," Washington, D.C.: (Center for American Progress, 2010), p. 56.

7. Becky Beaupre Gillespie and Hollee Schwartz Temple, "Work-Life Balance: Mom & Dad, Esquire: More households managing dual law careers," *ABA Journal* no. 95 (May 2009): 30.

CHAPTER 7: I'M THE BOSS OF ME

1. "The Economic Impact of Women-Owned Businesses in the United States," (Center for Women's Business Research, 2009), p. 1.

2. "Lessons from the Trenches: Learning from $1 Million Plus Women Entrepreneurs," (Center for Women's Business Research, 2008), p. 1.

3. Margaret Heffernan, *How She Does It: How Women Entrepreneurs Are Changing the Rules of Business Success* (New York: Viking, 2007), p. 4.

4. Nancy Carter and Christine Silva, "Opportunity or Setback? High Potential Women and Men During Economic Crisis," (*Catalyst,* 2009), pp. 1–3.

5. Robert Fairlie, "Kauffman Index of Entrepreneurial Activity 1996–2008," (Kauffman, 2009), p. 23. The study found that an average of 320 out of 100,000 adults created a new business each month last year even as the recession took hold, up from 300 out of 100,000 adults in 2007.

6. Ibid., p. 8. That pattern is similar to the last downturn, earlier in the first decade of the 2000s, when entrepreneurship levels also rose during the tech bust. Underlying these increases are layoffs and other job reductions, which can push people to launch their own businesses, says Robert Fairlie, the study's author and an economics professor at the University of California–Santa Cruz. Pui-Wing Tam, "The Recession's Effect on Entrepreneurship," *Wall Street Journal Blogs Digital Network* (April 30, 2009), p. 1.

7. Catherine Rampell, "As Layoffs Surge, Women May Pass Men in Job Force," *New York Times* (February 5, 2009): Section A; Column D; Business/Financial Desk, p. 1.

8. U.S. Small Business Administration, Newsline 3, no. 8 (May 2007): 1.

9. Vivek Wadhwa, et al., "The Anatomy of an Entreprenuer: Family Background and Motivation," (Kauffman, 2009), p. 6.

10. Brian Bucks, Arthur Kennickell, Traci Mach and Kevin Moore, "Changes in U.S. Family Finances from 2004 to 2007: Evidence from the Survey of Consumer Finances," (Federal Reserve, 2009), p. 46.

11. Amy Knaup, "Survival and Longevity in the Business Employment Dynamics Data," *Monthly Labor Review* (U.S. Bureau of Labor Statistics, 2005): 51.

12. Francine Blau, Marianne Ferber and Anne Winkler, *The Economics of Women, Men, and Work* 4th ed. (Upper Saddle River: Prentice Hall, 2001), p. 280.

13. Lara Galloway recommends www.themomentrepreneur.com as a starting point.

14. Susan Wright and Elisa Page, "2009 Women and Social Media Study," (BlogHer, iVillage and Compass Partners, 2009), p. 8.

CHAPTER 8: REDEFINING THE SUMMIT IN HIGH-STAKES CAREERS

1. Karine Moe and Dianna Shandy, *Glass Ceilings and 100-Hour Couples* (Athens: University of Georgia Press, 2010), p. 52.

2. "Volume Summary Admitted Applicants by Ethnic and Gender Group," (Law School Admission Council, 2009).

3. "Academic Programs, Enrollment, and Graduates," Survey of Dental Education 1 (American Dental Association, 2009), p. 21; "Enrollment and Degrees Awarded 1963–2008 Academic Years," (American Bar Association, 2008).

4. "Physicians in Primary Care and Sub-Specialties," (American Medical Association, 2000); American Bar Foundation, "Statistics about Employed Lawyers," Household Data Annual Averages Table 11, 2008.

5. "Working Mother & Flex-Time Lawyers Best Law Firms for Women," *Working Mother* (2009); Maria Pasquale and Elizabeth Moore, "Survey of Fortune 500 Women General Counsel," (Minority Corporate Counsel Association, 2009).

6. "Women Representation in U.S. Medical Schools," Women in U.S. Academic Medicine Statistics and Benchmarking Report Figure 1 (Association of American Medical Colleges, 2009).

7. Jennifer Leadley, "Women in U.S. Academic Medicine: Statistics and Benchmarking Report," (Association of American Medical Colleges, 2009), p. 13.

8. Update on Associate Attrition (National Association for Law Placement Foundation, 2008), p. 14.

9. The data shows that the average law school applicant is 22–24 years old. Adding three years for completion of school, the average age of a law school graduate falls within 25 and 27 years, with 26 being the mean age of a law school graduate. "National Applicant Trends," (Law School Admission Council, 2008), p. 5.

10. "Law Firm Diversity Demographics Show Little Change, Despite Economic Downturn," (National Association for Law Placement Foundation, 2009).

11. "Women in Law in the U.S.," (*Catalyst*, 2010), p. 2.

12. "Working Mother & Flex-Time Lawyers Best Law Firms for Women," *Working Mother* (August/September 2009).

13. "Most Lawyers Working Part-time Are Women—Overall Number of Lawyers Working Part-time Remains Small," (National Association for Law Placement Foundation, 2009).

14. Debbie lists these firms by name in her book.

15. "Persons at Work by Occupation, Sex, and Usual Full- or Part-Time Status," Household Data Annual Averages Table 23, 2008.

CHAPTER 9: EVEN THE BEST-LAID PLANS

1. The World Health Organization, "The Global Burden of Disease: 2004," Burden of Disease in DALYs by Cause, Sex, and Income Group in WHO Regions; Estimates for 2004 Table A2, 2008.

2. Ronald Kessler et al., "Lifetime Prevalence and Age-of-Onset Distributions of DSM-IV Disorders in the National Comorbidity Survey Replication," *General Psychiatry* 62, no. 6 (June 2005): 593–602.

CHAPTER 10: REENTRY AND REINVENTION ON THE PATH TO THE NEW PERFECT

1. Carol Fishman Cohen and Vivian Steir Rabin, *Back on the Career Track: A Guide for Stay-At-Home Moms Who Want to Return to Work* (New York: Warner, 2007).

2. Sylvia Ann Hewlett et al., "The Hidden Brain Drain: Off-Ramps and On-Ramps in Women's Careers," (Cambridge, Mass.: Harvard Business Review, 2005), p. 2.

3. Via iRelaunch's Carol Fishman Cohen: Data is from U.S. Bureau of Labor Statistics Current Population Survey Basic Microdata 2006, provided courtesy of Katharine Bradbury, senior economist, Federal Reserve Bank of Boston, Aquent 2004 survey, Center for Work-Life Policy 2004 survey.

CHAPTER 11: MARTINIS ON THE FRONT PORCH

1. Daniel Gilbert, *Stumbling on Happiness* (New York: Knopf, 2006), p. 243.

2. Betsey Stevenson and Justin Wolfers, "The Paradox of Declining Female Happiness," *American Economic Journal:* vol. 1, no. 2 (2009): 190–225.

3. David Brooks, "The Sandra Bullock Trade," *New York Times* (March 30, 2010): Section A; Column 0; p. 25.

4. Pam Belluck, "Strangers May Cheer You Up, Study Says," *New York Times* (December 5, 2008): Section A; Column 0; Foreign Desk; p. 12.

5. Betsey Stevenson and Justin Wolfers, "The Paradox of Declining Female Happiness," *American Economic Journal,* vol. 1, no. 2 (2009): 223.

6. Daniel Gilbert, *Stumbling on Happiness* (New York: Knopf, 2006), p. 243.

INDEX

ACKNOWLEDGMENTS

First, we want to thank the moms who allowed us to tell their stories. Thank you for trusting us, for being vulnerable with us, for coming to New York to share with us, for forcing your husbands to talk to us—and for becoming our friends. This book is your gift to us, and we will be forever grateful that you let us into your lives.

We also want to acknowledge the many moms we interviewed and who completed our New Perfect survey but who do not appear by name—your voices are woven throughout our manuscript and we thank you sincerely for shaping our understanding of modern motherhood.

This book would not have been possible without the dedication of Molly Lyons, our first-choice, stellar agent, and our editor at Harlequin, Sarah Pelz. We've enjoyed working with you both so much, and hope this is the beginning of a long friendship and business collaboration.

Because so many people have helped us in this endeavor, we know we're forgetting someone, but we hope our gratitude shines through nonetheless.

The New Perfect survey and analysis would not have been possible without the steadfast assistance of Dr. Keith Weber of West Virginia University. Superstar librarian and attorney Susan Wolford (who coined the term *Never Enough* on a long car ride) contributed in too many ways to list. Research assistant extraordinaire J. R. Kerns simply rocks. Thank you to Danielle Boyd and Deb Swiney for their help with our early research.

Several friends helped by commenting on drafts of the book at various stages. John Temple and Judy Haverfield Beaupre deserve special recognition for their extensive notes. Special thanks also to the WVU College of Law Faculty, Sheila Simon, Amy Hatch, Tanya Albert Henry and Susie Dodge for sharing their thoughts and suggestions. Thank you to the Hodges Fund for supporting our research.

Thank you to our wonderful friends for introducing us to some of the fabulous moms who appear in the book—we wouldn't have connected with these women without the help of Kara Spak, Julie Penn, Carrie Reed Shufflebarger, Jessica Piecyk, Michelle Krage and Kristin Peace.

Our New York roundtable was made possible by Wade Canter, Jonna Geisel, Tricia Fulks and Megan Bowers.

We received endless support from many of our friends and colleagues. Hollee is particularly grateful to: Jennifer Lipsitz, Andi Weber, Melissa Giggenbach, Hindy Gurevitz, Adrian Kettering, Marjorie Rosmarin, Scott Daffner, Courtney Pritchard, Tiffany Taylor Hastings, Susan and David Hardesty, Joyce McConnell, Anne Lofaso, David Krech, Priscilla Rodd, Deane Kern, Jennifer Mersereau, Matt and Beth Schwartz, Dan and Loranne Temple, Shirley Kohn, Beth Livingston and Elaine Payne.

Becky is deeply grateful to Elsa Johnson for providing daily (and often hilarious) encouragement, being a sounding board for ideas—and for mixing the cocktails when she needed a break from writing. Peter and Anya Beaupre: Thank you for your enthusiasm, ideas and love. Laurie: Thanks for the reminders to go easy on myself. I am also grateful to many other people for talking up the project, sharing their musings on parenthood, covering for me when I needed to write and offering encouragement. This list isn't comprehensive but it includes: Merle Haverfield, Hope Gillespie, Tracey Berkowitz, Henri Cauvin, Alexandra Beaupre, Laura Beaupre, Devon Dudgeon, Pat and Noelle McWard, Mark Zlotkowski, Stephanie Zimmermann, Emily Haite, the Ladies of Seeley Avenue, Meg Ludwig, Juliette Serr, Dayna Moorhead, Heather Moret and Ann Weisbrod. Oh, and Doug Johnson: I really do appreciate the number of times you sat on my porch and said, "You know, Becky, I've been thinking about your book and I have an idea…"

Our blog readers informed us and cheered us on; we love being part of such a supportive community. Thank you to our many friends in the blogosphere, including (but of course not limited to) Laura Weisskopf Bleill, Kelby Carr,

Emily McKhann, Cooper Munroe, Rachel Matthews, Molly McDonough, Alli Worthington, Sara Hawkins, Tami Hackbarth and Jessica Heights.

Becky:

To Mom: Thank you for spending years talking through these issues of work and motherhood with me, for never wavering in your belief, love and support—and for teaching me everything I know about being a mom.

To Dad: For being a role model I could admire, for telling me the truth about Having It All, and for offering your advice, encouragement and love.

To Pete: For always supporting my work choices, for keeping the children fed and the fridge stocked while I worked, and for always saying I love you. I love you more.

To my beautiful daughters, Beth and Katie: You keep me laughing and thinking, and you make me proud every single day.

And, finally, to Hollee: The greatest gift in this project wasn't getting to do work that I loved—it was getting to do that work with an amazing friend. Thank you for your generosity, kindness and humor—and for suggesting that we write a book together in the first place.

Hollee:

To Mom and Dad: Thank you for investing all that you did in me. I hope this makes you proud.

To John: You are the inspiration for everything that I do. Your courage makes me strong. Remember when I was twenty and you told me you could see the woman I was going to be at thirty-five and that made you want to marry me? I'll keep working, every day, to embody that vision. I love you.

To Gideon and Henry: You are my reason for wanting to be my highest self, every day. I am so very proud of both of you. Keep being good to each other and always look for the good in today!

And finally, to Becky: You are the big sister I never had. Thank you for becoming part of my heart.

ABOUT THE AUTHORS

Becky Beaupre Gillespie and Hollee Schwartz Temple are the work/life balance columnists for the *ABA Journal,* the nation's premiere lawyer magazine. Both graduates of Northwestern University's Medill School of Journalism, they first worked together in the early 1990s, when Becky was Hollee's first editor at the *Daily Northwestern.* Like so many of the working mothers they interviewed, Becky and Hollee forged nonlinear career paths, taking detours in their quest to balance work and family. They blog about work/life and parenting issues at TheNewPerfect.com.

Becky is an award-winning journalist who has written for the *Chicago Sun-Times,* the *Detroit News, USA Today* and the *Democrat and Chronicle* of Rochester, New York. Her first experience with balancing motherhood and career happened in 2001, when she called her editor to discuss a story—while en route to the hospital to give birth to her first child. Becky has been happily married for more than twelve years to Pete Gillespie, an employment litigator. They live in Chicago with their two daughters, Beth and Katie, and a variety of pets.

Hollee is a journalist-turned-lawyer-turned-professor at West Virginia University College of Law, where she directs the legal analysis, research and writing program. A graduate of Duke University School of Law, Hollee is a frequent conference speaker—on everything from blogging regulations to email etiquette to work/life choices for the latest generation of parents. Hollee made her best work/life choice in 1998, when she married John Temple, a journalism professor and nonfiction author. The Temples make their home in Morgantown, West Virginia, where they are constantly amused and amazed by their feisty redheaded sons, Gideon and Henry.